AN INTRODUCTION TO THE ANCIENT WORLD

—— ·•· ——

This introductory textbook is unique in covering the history of the ancient Near East, Greece and Rome within the framework of a short narrative history of events. It is designed to offer an easily readable, integrated overview for students of history, classics, archaeology and philosophy whether at college, at undergraduate level or among the wider reading public.

Focusing mainly on the social, political and cultural processes which have influenced later western civilisations, *An Introduction to the Ancient World* considers subjects such as the religions of the ancient Near East, Athenian democracy, the interaction of cultures in the Hellenistic world, the political and administrative system of the Roman republic and empire, gender problems and ancient demography.

Benefits and features:

- Comprehensive: covers 3000 years of ancient history and provides the basis for a typical one-semester course
- Lavishly illustrated: contains 34 maps, 42 line drawings and 96 plates which support and supplement the text
- Clearly and concisely written by two established and respected university teachers with 20 years experience in the subject area, and skilled in training secondary school history teachers
- Well organised: traces the broad outline of political history but also concentrates on particular topics
- User-friendly: includes chapter menus, an extensive bibliography organised by subject area and three appendices

Lukas de Blois is Professor of Ancient History at the University of Nijmegen, the Netherlands, and specialises in Roman and Greek history and ancient historiography.

Robartus van der Spek is Professor of Ancient History at the Free University of Amsterdam and specialises in the history of the ancient Near East and the Hellenistic period.

AN INTRODUCTION TO THE ANCIENT WORLD

L. de Blois and R. J. van der Spek

Translated from the Dutch by Susan Mellor

London and New York

First published 1997
by Routledge
11 New Fetter Lane, London EC4P 4EE

Simultaneously published in the USA and Canada
by Routledge
29 West 35th Street, New York, NY 10001

© 1997 L. de Blois and R. J. van der Spek

Typeset in Stempel Garamond by
Keystroke, Jacaranda Lodge, Wolverhampton
Printed and bound in Great Britain by
Butler and Tanner Ltd, London and Frome

British Library Cataloguing in Publication Data
A catalogue record for this book is available from the British Library

Library of Congress Cataloging in Publication Data
Blois, Lukas de.
[Kennismaking met de oude wereld. English]
An introduction to the ancient world / L. de Blois & R. J. van der Spek
p.   cm.
Includes bibliographical references and index.
1. Civilization, Ancient. I. Spek, R. J. van der. II. Title.
CB311.B5813 1997
930–dc21   96–38099

ISBN 0–415–12773–4 (hbk)
ISBN 0–415–12774–2 (pbk)

CONTENTS

— Contents —

PART II: GREECE

— Contents —

— Contents —

PART III: ROME

— Contents —

— Contents —

PART IV: APPENDICES

ILLUSTRATIONS

MAPS

FIGURES

DIAGRAMS

INTRODUCTION

Ancient history is the history of the cradle of European civilisation. Since the voyages of discovery of the sixteenth century and especially since the colonial imperialism of the nineteenth and twentieth centuries, this civilisation has spread across the whole world; its roots, however, lie in the countries surrounding the Mediterranean, in particular in the cultural centres of the ancient Near East and in those of the ancient Greeks and Romans. It is in those areas that, between 3500 BC and AD 500, many of the distinctive features of modern Western culture originated. Christianity, for example, evolved from Judaism in Palestine and acquired its philosophical accoutrements and organisational structure in the Roman empire; present-day Western philosophy is firmly rooted in Greek schools of thought; many current legal systems are largely based on Roman law; education in the Greek and Latin literary culture is still provided at secondary schools today. Other elements of modern Western culture that originated in the Mediterranean are architecture and the visual arts, literature and also science, which evolved from Greek ways of thinking.

Phenomena of all times and all places first manifested themselves in the Mediterranean in antiquity: this area witnessed the emergence of states and cities and of their governments, the development of decision processes, the origins of expansion and its effects on social relationships and modes of thought, the interaction of different cultures and the birth of world religions.

Our knowledge of ancient history is partly based on what has come down to us through the ages – information that was passed on from generation to generation, from antiquity to the present day. Numerous works of classical historians, poets, orators, philosophers and scientists have been preserved because they were copied over and over again until ultimately the invention of printing made them accessible to a wider public. Of course, quite a few other ancient works have not survived the ravages of time.

Another major source of information on ancient times is the evidence that has been recovered in excavations or has come to light in other ways. Such evidence includes inscriptions (texts engraved in stone or some other durable material), papyri (letters, receipts, poems and other pieces of writing on a type of paper that was made from Egyptian papyrus reed), clay tablets and coins (bearing representations and legends). Papyri have been found almost exclusively in Egypt, where they have been preserved by the dry desert sand. Houses, public buildings, temples, fortifications and other structures and such objects as ornaments, weapons and household goods can also tell us much about the past.

For the history of the ancient Near East in particular we have to rely on evidence of the latter kind, that is, finds recovered for example in excavations. In that area the process of passing down knowledge from one generation to the next came to an end in the first centuries of the Christian era, when the languages and scripts that had been employed for that purpose went out of use. Until the nineteenth century, when large-scale excavations and the deciphering of some ancient written languages opened up a wealth of new information, our knowledge of the ancient Near East was limited to what could be inferred from references in the Bible and in the works of Greek and Roman authors.

But finds have also greatly increased our understanding of Greek and Roman history. Valuable information has been obtained in specialist studies of different categories of finds, such as epigraphy (the study of inscriptions), numismatics (coins), papyrology (manuscripts written on papyri) and archaeology (material remains, architecture, town planning, painting, sculpture, etc.).

History is preceded by prehistory – the period for which we have no written evidence and for knowledge of which we are consequently entirely dependent on material remains. Archaeologists have divided prehistory into three distinct periods on the basis of the different durable materials that were used for the manufacture of objects in those times. These three periods are the Stone Age, the Bronze Age and the Iron Age. The dates of these ages differ from region to region. The span of this chronological system in fact extends into historical times in some parts of the world, for example in the ancient Near East, where the Iron Age started around 1200 BC, some two thousand years after the development of writing. The beginning of historical times also differs from one region to another. The Apennine peninsula, for example, entered history more than two thousand years later than Egypt. The mere fact that writing was introduced in a particular area in a particular period does not always mean that we have a wealth of written evidence for that area and period. Much of the written evidence that has been preserved is poorly legible or provides only limited information, being, say, nothing more than part of a palace's administration of a particular year.

In antiquity itself, information was by no means equally distributed among the different classes and groups of the various societies. There were no newspapers or any other mass media. The lower social classes were dependent on the shreds of information that they picked up in the streets and on village squares, from transients and passers-by, and they were easily impressed by rumours. They were moreover insufficiently educated to be able to critically assess the information that reached them. The notables and the people who travelled to foreign regions, such as merchants and seafarers, were better informed. They maintained relations of guest-friendship with people in other towns and other regions, with whom they also corresponded. Letters and news were exchanged via merchants and other travellers.

Throughout this book, frequent use is made of the terms 'Indo-European' and 'Semitic'. The reason for this is that it is common practice to classify and name ancient peoples on the basis of the languages they spoke. The Semitic languages are

Diagram 1.1   Families of languages

Semitic languages

Old Akkadian

Babylonian ⎫
⎬ = Akkadian
Assyrian   ⎭

Amorite

Aramaic and Chaldean

Canaanite and Phoenician

Hebrew

Arabic

Egyptian
Hamito–Semitic = African family of languages

Ethiopian

Indo-European languages

Sanskrit

Hittite

Aryan or Iranian languages: Median, Persian and Parthian

Greek

Latin and the languages derived from it:
Italian, Spanish, French, Romanian

Slavic languages
Russian, Polish, Serbian, Croatian, Czech, Slovak, Bulgarian

Celtic
languages of Celts, Galatians in Asia Minor, Britons, Celtiberians in Spain; now:
Breton, Welsh, Irish Gaelic

Germanic languages
languages of the Frisians, Franks, Saxons, Batavians, Angles, Goths

Armenian

---

closely related to one another and the same holds for the different branches of the Indo-European family of languages. Hebrew, Aramaic, Akkadian and Arabic are all Semitic languages. The Indo-European languages include Greek, Latin (the language spoken by the Romans), Persian, the Celtic languages and the Germanic languages. The terms 'Semitic' and 'Indo-European' have little to do with race or nation.

To conclude, a few remarks on chronological systems. Nowadays, we are accustomed to a uniform chronological system that is known and used all over the world, but things were different in antiquity. In ancient times, each people had its own chronological system, based on the reigns of kings, the terms of office of high officials or important events. In Athens, for example, time was reckoned on the basis of the terms of office of the archons (the town's chief magistrates) or on the basis of olympiads – the intervals between the Olympic Games, which were held every four years. Events in Athens were said to have taken place in such-and-such an olympiad or during the term of office of this or that archon. The system used in Rome was based on the terms of office of the two consuls (the two chief magistrates in the Roman republic). The same system continued to be used in the imperial age, when the consuls had less power, having become subordinate to the emperor. Another problem is that many events in the third and second millennia BC (not to mention earlier events) can only be dated approximately. The dates of some events in the last fifteen hundred years of ancient history are also uncertain. Where possible, the dates given on the following pages are those obtained in the most recent research.

PART I

THE ANCIENT NEAR EAST

THE ORIGINS OF THE CIVILISATIONS OF EGYPT AND MESOPOTAMIA

On the banks of the rivers Euphrates and Tigris in Mesopotamia (largely what is now Iraq) and the Nile in Egypt emerged civilisations that were to have a profound influence on the history of the eastern half of the Mediterranean. The rise of these civilisations, just before 3000 BC, was characterised by increasing urbanisation, the birth of states and the invention of writing. These civilisations did not appear out of the blue of course; their foundations had been laid over a period that spanned several hundreds of thousands of years. Archaeologists have divided this long period, which is called the Stone Age, into an Old, Middle and New Stone Age on the basis of changes in the stone implements that were produced during that period. In the Old and Middle Stone Ages people lived off what they happened to come across, off the animals they hunted and the plants they gathered. They followed their prey into new areas and were hence constantly on the move. By the end of the Middle Stone Age, man had improved his tools to such an extent that he was able to make more efficient use of the natural resources. That meant that some groups of people could remain in one area for a longer period of time, sheltered from the elements in primitive huts or caves. The next step in man's development was the transition to an entirely new way of life characterised by a greater control of nature: man started to cultivate the cereals which he had until then always gathered as wild plants, and domesticated the animals which he had hunted in the past. This transition took place at different times in different parts in the world, but it is believed that it occurred in the Near East first. The process really got under way around the beginning of the New Stone Age, or Neolithic, as this period is also called. Being of such tremendous importance for the further development of civilisation, this transformation is often referred to as the 'Neolithic revolution', although the whole process actually took thousands of years and the first signs of the fundamental changes that were to take place had already appeared long before the Neolithic.

Two different kinds of agriculture are distinguished, namely rainfall agriculture and irrigation agriculture, 'irrigation' being understood to include both natural and artificial irrigation.

Figure 1.1 Sowing plough. Impression of a cylinder seal (2nd millenium)
Notes: With this instrument ploughing and sowing could be combined. The central figure is pouring seed into a chute, which guides it directly into the furrow.

The best conditions for agriculture based on natural irrigation were to be found in Egypt. Every year, the Nile flooded the land before the sowing season (between July and September). The Egyptians could then sow their crops in the damp soil when the river receded. In Mesopotamia the land was less regularly flooded, the floods moreover occurring only after the sowing season, which meant that the occupants of that region had to practise artificial irrigation. Irrigation agriculture was far more productive than rainfall agriculture, enabling crop yield ratios of about 10 : 1 to 15 : 1. We get a good impression of how high that ratio is when we compare it with later figures for Greece, Italy and medieval Europe, where the average ratio was about 4 : 1 and a good ratio was 7 : 1.

The development of agriculture was of fundamental importance for the further history of mankind. It meant that more people could remain settled in one particular area for a longer period of time and that more people could concentrate their attention on other activities besides food production. People consequently started to specialise in all kinds of crafts and became carpenters, tanners, scribes (at least after the invention of the art of writing, around 3400 BC) and metalworkers (after around 3000 BC, when man discovered how to exploit and smelt copper ore and produce bronze, an alloy of copper and tin).

A civil service and a priesthood emerged (and the associated institutions: the state and the temple). Some of the villages that had originated at the beginning of the Neolithic began to resemble fortified cities; Jericho, for example, had already evolved into a city around 7000 BC. The largest and most influential cities, however, were those that arose on the banks of the major rivers in the fourth millennium BC. It was there, along those rivers, that the largest quantities of food could be produced and the largest numbers of people could live together.

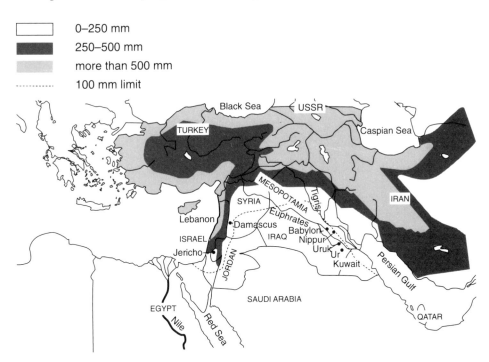

Map 1.1 Rainfall in the Near East

Notes: In the areas with less than 250 mm rainfall no crops can be grown without irrigation. In the areas to the south of the 100-mm limit too little grows to allow stock-keeping.

The core of a Mesopotamian city was the temple, the abode of the state deity, whose needs had to be provided for by the community. Those temples grew into powerful organisations that owned vast estates; they engaged in a wide range of activities, including agriculture, stock breeding and various crafts, for which they employed a large staff. It was the requirements of this temple economy that led to the invention of writing, some time between 3400 and 3200 BC. The Mesopotamian script is known as the 'cuneiform' script – so called after the wedge-shaped appearance of the impressions of which the later characters of that script were composed. The hieroglyphic script of the Egyptians was developed shortly after the cuneiform script.

At first, the cuneiform and hieroglyphic scripts were both purely pictographic (with each word being represented by a picture) or ideographic (with each word being represented by a symbol). Later on, the signs came to stand for sounds (syllables), too. The Egyptian script only rendered consonants, vowels being ignored. Both the Mesopotamian and the Egyptian script remained highly complex forms of writing and were used only by small groups of specially trained professional scribes.

In antiquity, the presence of cities did not lead to contrasts between the urban and rural populations of the kind known to us from later times. In most of the cities the majority of the inhabitants were peasants, who left the city to work on their land every morning and returned in the evening. In the ancient Near East, a far greater and far more important contrast than that between city dwellers and country folk was that between the sedentary and the nomadic way of life. This contrast was closely associated with a major difference in subsistence patterns.

Agriculturalists led a sedentary life; they remained settled in one area because they had to till their land and look after their crops. Herders were nomads; they constantly moved around from one place to another, in search of fresh pastures for their animals. However, there was not always such a clear-cut difference between the two. Primitive agriculturalists sometimes remained in one area for only a short period of time, to then move on again a few years later, when they had exhausted the soil. Some herders moved around within a relatively small area, for example from summer pastures to winter pastures. This seasonal migration is called 'transhumance'. The transhumant nomads liked to remain in the vicinity of the settlements of the agriculturalists, with whom they could then exchange products. Occasionally a group of (semi)nomads would adopt a partly or entirely sedentary way of life and take control of a city. There were also wealthy landowners who owned herds besides land and employed herders to pasture their animals, sometimes at considerable distances from their dwellings.

Throughout the entire history of the ancient Near East the representatives of these two opposed ways of life were constantly flung between feelings of hatred and friendship towards one another – hatred because the sedentary peoples were afraid of being plundered by the (semi)nomads, and friendship because the two groups were dependent on one another for the exchange of products. The contrast between the two different ways of life became a popular theme in the literature of this area. It forms the basis of the Biblical story of the shepherd Abel who was murdered by the agriculturalist Cain.

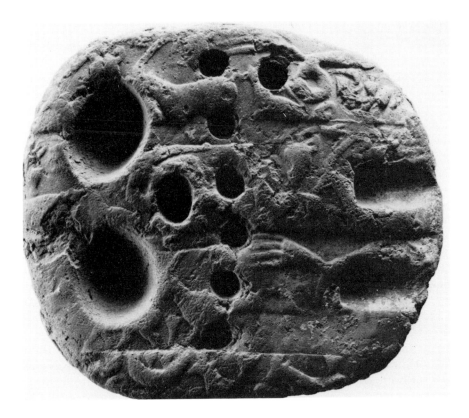

Figure 1.2 Clay tablet from Jebel Aruda, Syria, *c.* 3400–3200 BC

Notes: The tablet shows a number (372?) and impressions made by a cylinder seal. A cylinder seal is made of some hard material in which a design is carved in mirror image. When the seal was rolled over soft clay, the design was impressed in the clay. The impressed clay tablets served to identify the owner (private person, temple, palace) of the objects to which they were attached.

Clay tablets developed from the custom of keeping records of goods (or cattle) by enclosing clay tokens in a sealed clay envelope. The clay envelope had to be broken when the quantities of the goods were to be checked. Later the number of tokens, representing the quantity of goods, was indicated on the outside of the envelope. In a following stage, the tokens were altogether omitted: the envelope became a solid clay tablet indicating a number. Later clay tablets show numbers and marks representing the goods. This is how the first script originated.

At an even later stage, the marks were also used to indicate a sound or a syllable.

The same system of numbers encountered on this tablet, which came to light in an excavation conducted by a team of archaeologists from Leiden (the Netherlands) in Syria, is also known from Mesopotamia and southwest Iran (Elam). This points to the existence of intensive trade contacts that already embraced the whole of the Levant in the fourth millennium BC. This is confirmed by the recurrent motifs that are observable on earthenware all over this region.

Source: Assyriologisch Instituut, Leiden.

The geographical conditions of Egypt and Mesopotamia were very similar in some respects: both areas were dependent on riverwater due to the almost total absence of rain, and both were poor in various important resources, such as metals and timber. In other respects, however, they were totally different.

Conditions for agriculture, for example, were more favourable in Egypt than in Mesopotamia. As already mentioned above, the Nile flooded the land before the sowing season, the Euphrates and Tigris not until later in the year. Whereas the Egyptians could sow their crops in the fertile deposits left behind by the receding river, the Mesopotamians had to go to great efforts to conduct the water to their fields via canals. The water of the Nile was moreover of a better quality; that of the Euphrates and the Tigris contained harmful salts, which became mixed with the groundwater. The groundwater level of the low-lying, flat land was very high and the salts migrated to the surface of the land via capillary cracks in the clay. Protracted irrigation without sufficient drainage could ultimately make the soil unfit for cultivation owing to complete salinisation. That this indeed happened can be inferred from the crops that were cultivated: in southern Mesopotamia the amount of barley cultivated gradually increased, whereas the amount of wheat decreased. The reason for this is that barley is more resistant to salt. Egypt, on the contrary, is believed to have grown more wheat than barley throughout antiquity.

Another important difference between Egypt and Mesopotamia concerns the surrounding areas. In Egypt the transition from arable land to desert sand was so abrupt that it was possible to stand – literally – with one foot in a green field and the other in the dry desert sand. In Mesopotamia the transition from fertile to less fertile land was more gradual. Secondly, being totally surrounded by uninhabitable deserts, Egypt was far less accessible than Mesopotamia, and consequently far more isolated from the outside world. This difference had major political consequences: whereas the history of Egypt is fairly stable and static, with relatively little interference from outside, that of Mesopotamia is characterised by constant invasions of foreign peoples, many of whom assumed control and founded new empires. Nevertheless, a considerable degree of continuity was preserved in Mesopotamia too, as most of the newcomers adapted themselves to the original occupants' cultural traditions.

CHAPTER TWO

THE THIRD MILLENNIUM BC

MEMPHIS, SUMER AND AKKAD

Egypt, the Old Kingdom (2600–2150)

The history of ancient Egypt is divided into periods in two different ways, namely on the basis of 'dynasties' and on the basis of 'kingdoms'. The division based on dynasties was devised by the Egyptian priest Manetho, who wrote a history of Egypt in Greek in the 3rd century BC, in which he divided the chronology of Egypt between thirty dynasties or royal houses. The division into three 'kingdoms' is modern. These kingdoms comprise periods in which Egypt enjoyed great prosperity and political unity. They alternate with 'intermediate periods' of decline and political fragmentation. In the intermediate periods Egypt was not ruled by a single king, but by several local governors who had acquired independence in their own provinces. In those periods several dynasties were consequently in power at the same time – a fact that escaped Manetho, who arranged all the dynasties in successive order.

The three kingdoms are the Old Kingdom (*c.* 2600–2150), the Middle Kingdom (*c.* 2000–*c.* 1800) and the New Kingdom (*c.* 1550–*c.* 1100). The last period distinguished in the history of ancient Egypt is called the Late Period. In that period (from *c.* 750 BC until – in fact – 1922 AD) the country was frequently ruled by foreign dynasties or was incorporated in other powerful empires.

As can be inferred from the above dates, the third millennium comprises the Old Kingdom and a preceding period in which Egypt was united into a single realm, which is known as the 'Early Dynastic period' (*c.* 3000–2600; 1st and 2nd dynasties). It is in this Early Dynastic period that the Egyptian hieroglyphic script was invented. In spite of the fact that Egypt was unified under one ruler in this period, the whole history of this country was to remain characterised by a distinction between Lower Egypt, which comprised the Nile Delta, and Upper Egypt, which embraced the area to the south of the Delta up to the First Cataract (rapid). The king was called the 'Lord of the Double Land', the pharaohs wore double crowns and there was a double administrative system. This duality was in keeping with the Egyptian belief that only things that consisted of two parts were complete.

It was the kings of the Old Kingdom who commissioned the construction of the pyramids, for which the Egyptians are famous all over the world. These monumental tombs testify to the tremendous power of the kings of this period and their strong hold over manpower and material resources. The pyramids were built near Memphis, the capital of ancient Egypt.

The peasants were summoned to work on these ambitious building projects in the periods that the land was flooded. Their readiness to make this great effort is understandable when we consider that the kings were regarded as divine beings. The works of tens of thousands of people, the pyramids are clear testimonies of the great organisational capacity of the early Egyptian state. The largest monuments were built during the 4th dynasty (*c.* 2500); they are all of stone. The younger pyramids, which were built from mudbrick, are smaller.

The Old Kingdom lasted for five centuries. By the end of that period the provincial governors had become so powerful that the pharaoh was no longer able

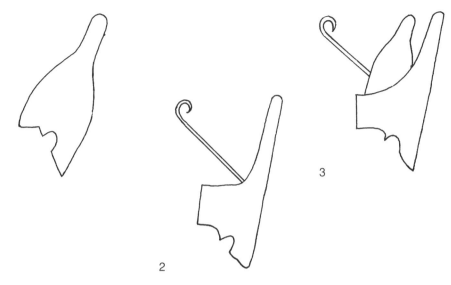

Figure 2.1 The crowns of Egypt
Notes: 1 The white crown of Upper Egypt
2 The red crown of Lower Egypt
3 The double crown

Figure 2.2 The pyramids of Kings Cheops, Chephren and Mycerinus near Giza,
4th dynasty
Notes: The fertile Egyptian land is visible in the foreground. The pyramids in the background
are in the desert. The transition from fertile land to desert sand is still as abrupt as it was in
antiquity.
Source: E.A. Hemelrijk, Haarlem.

to sustain his central authority. The provincial governors had been granted land as a form of 'salary' and this land had been passed on from father to son, along with the office. As a result, the pharaoh had gradually lost his hold on his officials. We now also know that the area flooded by the Nile gradually decreased towards the end of the Old Kingdom. Around the same time, reports of famine started to appear. That is probably the reason why the Egyptians started practising artificial irrigation, in order to be able to make the most efficient use of the scarcer water.

Mesopotamia: Sumer and Akkad

The third millennium also saw the rise of another great civilisation in the Near East, namely that of Mesopotamia. The foundations for this civilisation had been already laid in the fourth millennium, but it was the Sumerians and the Akkadians who brought it to fruition in the third millennium. Of these two peoples the Sumerians were the most important. Exactly when they arrived in Mesopotamia and whether it is they who deserve the credit for the invention of writing and the construction of the first cities in southern Mesopotamia, we do not know. What we do know is that they are the people who made those cities great; they also made extensive use of the art of writing for keeping accounts in their temples and palaces and for composing religious and literary texts. Sculpture, architecture, religious imagery, literary styles and views on kingship, law and society were all developed by the Sumerians. The Sumerians also laid the groundwork for various sciences, including arithmetic, astronomy, botany and medicine. In their schools, the Sumerians learned their complex script by memorising all kinds of texts. Lists of technical terms in numerous different fields have been preserved. The lists of the different professions practised in those days provide a fair amount of insight into the development of specialisation enabled by the major economic improvements brought about by the introduction of irrigation agriculture (see pp. 4–5).

Vestiges of the sexagesimal system of Sumerian arithmetic are still observable in our division of the hour into 60 minutes and of the circle into 360 degrees. The Sumerians passed on their culture from one generation to the next, over many centuries, but also over vast areas, across the whole of the ancient Near East. Their cuneiform script was adopted in regions as far away as southwest Iran (Elam) and even Syria (Ebla), where the Sumerian language was learned and Sumerian texts were studied in schools modelled on those of the Sumerians. That way the cultural history of the entire Levant became infused with the Sumerian civilisation.

And yet the Sumerians never really showed any imperialistic tendencies; they never aspired to gain control over large parts of the Levant. Instead, they continued to live in modest city states. At first, life in those city states revolved entirely around the temple and its high priest or priestess, but later on secular rulers whose duties included leadership in war gradually acquired power and started to operate independently. That led to the emergence of kingship and beside the temple arose a palace, with its own bureaucracy, estates and workshops. Now and then, a king of such a city would capture a few other cities. The Sumerians of later ages regarded kingship as a matter of course, as something that had come down from heaven in the very beginning.

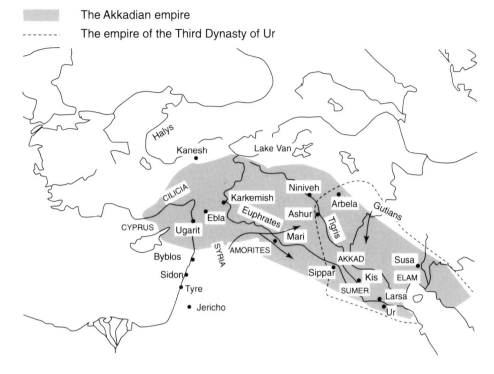

The Akkadian empire

- - - - - - - The empire of the Third Dynasty of Ur

Map 2.1   The ancient Near East in the third millennium BC

For three thousand years the palace and the temple remained the two most powerful organisations in Mesopotamia. Throughout that period those organisations constantly intruded into one another's sphere of influence. Sometimes they would dispute territory or quarrel about the autonomy of the temples; at other times, however, they would be of help to one another. The kings, who were regarded as the representatives of the deities, would for example frequently commission and support the construction of temples.

The Akkadians are so called after Akkad, the city that became the centre of an empire around 2300 BC. This empire, which embraced the whole of Mesopotamia and extended all the way into Asia Minor (see Map 2.1), was founded by King Sargon.

Akkadians were Semites, that is, speakers of a Semitic language. This group of languages nowadays includes Arabic and Hebrew. The 'Akkadians' were already living in Mesopotamia at the beginning of the third millennium (mainly in an area a short distance to the north of the territory occupied by the Sumerians), but it was only when they started using the cuneiform script for their own language, Old Akkadian, that they began to stand out as a distinct group. The Akkadians borrowed much from the Sumerians, including their script, their religious imagery, scientific principles and literary styles. But their culture also contains elements of their own because they continued to worship their own deities (which were however identified with Sumerian gods) and to use their own language. The Akkadians built a large and powerful empire; Sargon's successors even claimed hegemony over the entire world, calling themselves 'King of the Four Quarters of the World'; they also had themselves deified. But they were unable to prevent the local revolts and invasions of tribes from the east that were ultimately to cause the downfall of their empire.

The collapse of the Akkadian empire was followed by the revival of several Sumerian cities, which is referred to as the 'Sumerian renaissance' (c. 2100–2000). The kings of Ur, known as the 'Third Dynasty of Ur', founded another great empire in Mesopotamia. Thanks to the discovery of some 100,000 clay tablets, part of the palace's administration, we are relatively well informed about this empire. These tablets show that the palace had eclipsed the temple and had acquired complete control over the economy.

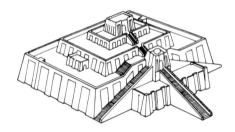

Figure 2.3 The Ziqqurat of Ur, Third Dynasty, *c.* 2100 BC
Notes: Such stepped temple towers were built from the end of the third millennium until into the third century BC. They evolved from the temples on platforms known from late prehistoric times. The temple of Ur was dedicated to the Sumerian moon-god Nanna, who was called Sin in Akkadian.
Source: Reconstruction drawing by L. Wooley (1880–1960).

The empire of Ur was also overthrown by invaders, this time from the west, namely the Amorites. The Amorites, a tribe of nomads who spoke western Semitic languages, were attracted to Mesopotamia by the region's fertile river valleys. They caused much havoc among the occupants of those valleys, whose fields they pillaged. They also cut off the cities' grain supplies. Local officials took advantage of this situation to sever their ties with Ur and established their own independent dynasties.

Epilogue

The third millennium ended with a period of great confusion and stagnation in the two most important cultural centres of the Near East: Egypt and Mesopotamia. Nevertheless, a firm basis had been created on which later generations could continue the work begun by their predecessors. For example, Egyptian painting, relief carving and freestanding sculpture had already acquired their distinctive features, which were to remain essentially unchanged for many centuries.

Although Sumerian died out as a spoken language, it continued to be used as a written language for religious and scholarly purposes, while Akkadian became the spoken language in Mesopotamia and the international language for correspondence and administration; Akkadian started to be used increasingly for literary texts, too. The Sumero-Akkadian culture consequently continued to exert a powerful influence. Traces of that influence are indeed observable throughout the entire history of the Levant right up to the Hellenistic period.

THE SECOND MILLENNIUM BC

THEBES, ASSUR AND BABYLON (*c.* 2000–1600)

Egypt, the Middle Kingdom (*c.* 2000–1800)

Shortly before 2000 BC, a dynasty of provincial governors in Thebes (the 11th) restored unity in Egypt and made Thebes the capital of the new unified realm. The most powerful kings of the Middle Kingdom were those of the twelfth dynasty. They led military campaigns into the Levant without, however, succeeding in gaining permanent control over that area. It is in the reports of those campaigns that we find the earliest mention of the towns of Jerusalem and Shechem. In their campaigns in the south the Egyptians were more successful: there they managed to extend their sway over Nubia (the Sudan) up to the Third Cataract. The kings of the twelfth dynasty are also renowned for their exploits in their home country: they brought the Fayyûm oasis into cultivation and made that area fit to become the centre of their government. During their reigns, pyramids and temples for the dead arose in the Fayyûm. The kings of the twelfth dynasty also put an end to succession problems by choosing one of their sons as their successors and appointing him co-regent during their lives; that son then succeeded his father after the latter's death.

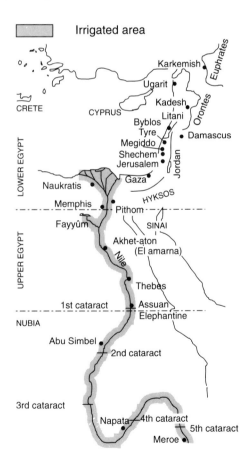

Map 3.1 Ancient Egypt, 3000–525 BC

17

Around 1800 the power of the kings started to decline again, while that of the provincial governors increased. There came an end to the campaigns and fewer building projects were launched. These developments mark the beginning of the 'Second Intermediate period' (c. 1800–1600), the period in which Egypt was for the first time in its history to be ruled by foreigners: the Hyksos. This people, possibly of Amorite origin, settled in the Nile Delta (we recall that something similar had previously happened in Mesopotamia, where a tribe of Amorites had settled). After some time, the Hyksos gained control over the Delta and established their own dynasties. Other local rulers were forced to acknowledge the suzerainty of the Hyksos dynasty.

In Mesopotamia, the early second millennium saw the birth of two nations that were to dominate the history of that region for the following fifteen hundred years, namely Assyria and Babylonia. Oddly enough, much of the credit for these nations' rise to power is due to a foreign people, namely the aforementioned Amorites, who had settled in Mesopotamia around the end of the third millennium (see p. 14). This infiltration of a semi-nomadic people into an area with a highly developed culture, followed by the newcomers' assumption of power in that area, is an example of a phenomenon that took place several times throughout the history of the ancient Near East. The Amorites gained control over Assur, Babylon and Mari (see Map 3.2), but they did not entirely relinquish their nomadic way of life. The titles assumed by some of the Amorite rulers clearly reflect their somewhat hybrid position. They

Old Assyrian Empire (c. 1800)

Old Babylonian Empire (c. 1750)

Old Hittite kingdom

Map 3.2 The Old Assyrian and Old Babylonian empires

would call themselves 'King of the city of X, chief of tribe Y'. The Amorites did not succeed in supplanting the Sumero-Akkadian culture entirely on their own. Sumerian and Akkadian remained the written languages (the latter now comprising two variants: Assyrian and Babylonian) and the cuneiform script continued to be used. After some time, Amorite went out of use as a spoken language too.

The Old Assyrian empire (*c.* 2000–1760)

The city of Assur had already existed in the Early Dynastic period, under the dominion of the empires of Akkad and Ur. It gained independence around 2000 BC. The city's profitable trade, with cities in Asia Minor and elsewhere (see p. 58), brought it to great wealth and prominence. A recession around 1840 BC was followed by a new period of prosperity at the end of the nineteenth century, when the Amorite Shamshi-Adad I seized the throne. He extended his sway over northern Mesopotamia and put his son on the throne in Mari. With Shamshi-Adad I, kingship acquired a more absolute character.

The Old Babylonian empire (*c.* 1800–1600)

In the eighteenth century, Babylon, which had until then been a fairly insignificant city, acquired strong political power, which it was to retain for many centuries. Even in periods of political weakness it continued to exert an influence on Mesopotamian culture. Many of the kings who captured Babylon in later times respected the Babylonians' gods and traditions and acknowledged the city's special status. The foundations of Babylonian culture were laid by the Amorite king Hammurabi (1792–1750), who during his reign conquered almost the whole of Mesopotamia, including Assyria. Hammurabi is most renowned for his code of law (see Fig. 3.1, which is a valuable source of information on the social structure of this period. This law code (discussed in greater detail on pp. 20 and 62) became one of the standard works read at Babylonian schools and as such it had a profound and lasting influence.

The glory of the Old Babylonian empire was short-lived: under Hammurabi's successors the empire already began to crumble, the kings gradually losing their military power and authority. Around 1600 Babylon was even taken by a king of the Hittite kingdom that had emerged in the eastern part of Asia Minor (see Map 3.2 and p. 25), who led a plundering expedition into Mesopotamia. Having sacked Babylon, he returned to his native country. The Old Babylonian empire never recovered from this blow and proved too weak to defend itself against a new wave of invaders, the Kassites from the Iranian mountains. Once again Mesopotamia came under foreign dominion. These newcomers were also to adapt themselves to the original occupants' traditions (see p. 24).

THE 'CONCERT OF POWERS' (*c.* 1600–1200)

The four centuries between 1600 and 1200 were characterised by a more or less stable balance of a group of great powers. They were Egypt (the New Kingdom),

Figure 3.1 The Code of Hammurabi of Babylon, *c.* 1750 BC. Height 2.25 m
Notes: Basalt stele found in Susa, the capital of the Elamite empire. The stele was apparently taken to Susa as war booty by plundering Elamites. Seated on the throne is the sun-god Shamash, who was also the god of justice, because the rays of the sun expose the evil practices that cannot bear the light of day. He is recognisable as the sun-god by the rays at his shoulders. Hammurabi is standing in front of the throne. The text contains a prologue, laws and an epilogue. In the prologue Hammurabi introduces himself as the king whom the gods have appointed to ensure the maintenance of justice. In the epilogue he states that he has made the laws 'to prevent the strong from oppressing the weak and to see that justice is done to widows and orphans'. The stele advises those who have suffered injustice to refer to the code of law. Finally, future kings who do not comply with these laws are threatened with the curse of the gods.
Source: Louvre, Paris.

Mitanni, the Hittite empire, Assyria and Babylonia. This is also the period of the flourishing of what are known as the Minoan civilisation of Crete and the Mycenaean civilisation of the Greek mainland (see pp. 25 and 27). Other important centres of power in this period were the highly developed city states of Syria and Palestine, which had lost nothing of their former glory. They included Byblos, Tyre and Sidon. A little further north was the city of Ugarit, where excavations have brought to light much of great interest, such as Sumerian and Akkadian clay tablets, but also tablets inscribed in a phonetic cuneiform script of thirty signs in the city's own language.

The areas between these states were still traversed by many different nomadic and seminomadic tribes (see Map 3.3).

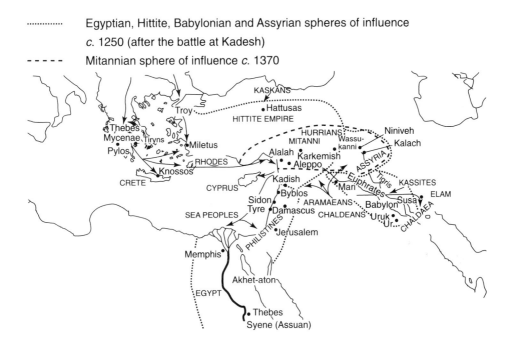

.... Egyptian, Hittite, Babylonian and Assyrian spheres of influence
c. 1250 (after the battle at Kadesh)

- - - - - Mitannian sphere of influence *c.* 1370

Map 3.3 The ancient Near East, 1600–1200 BC

The power of all these states, from the largest to the smallest, was based on a new invention which spread across the entire Near East at a formidable rate around 1600: the war chariot, a fast, two-wheeled vehicle that was drawn by horses. These chariots were owned by a privileged, aristocratic elite that was awarded land in exchange for its services. Without large contingents of chariot warriors it was virtually impossible for a state to safeguard its authority, and many of the small states lost their independence and were reduced to satellite states of the great powers (see Chapter 7).

Egypt, the New Kingdom (*c*. 1550–1100)

Once again it was a dynasty of Theban rulers who restored unity in Egypt. The last king of this dynasty, the seventeenth according to Manetho (see p. 10), shook off the yoke of the last king of the Hyksos dynasty, the fifteenth(!) according to Manetho, and set about evicting the Hyksos. His work was completed by his brother, who is regarded as the founder of the eighteenth dynasty (these historical facts aptly illustrate the defects of Manetho's system).

The eighteenth dynasty (c. 1550–c. 1300 BC) is probably the most famous in the whole of Egyptian history. Its kings, who were referred to by the title of 'pharaoh' (literally: 'great house' = 'palace'), immediately set about building up an empire. Their campaigns took them to the Euphrates in Syria and deep into Nubia. The best-known pharaoh of this dynasty is Thutmose III (c. 1450).

Figure 3.2 Coronation of Queen Hatshepsut by Horus, the falcon-headed sky-god, and Thoth, the ibis-headed scribe of the gods

Notes: Hatshepsut was one of the few female pharaohs. The step-mother and aunt of Thutmose III, she was also his regent because at the time of the untimely death of her husband (and half-brother) Thutmose II, Thutmose III, the son of one of her husband's minor wives, was still under-age. Thutmose III married one of Hatshepsut's daughters, so she was also his mother-in-law. From the beginning of the New Kingdom onwards, Egyptian pretenders to the throne became the legitimate heir by marrying the daughter of the ruling pharaoh's principal wife. This led to many marriages between brothers and (half-)sisters. Hatshepsut, not satisfied to rule as a regent, had herself officially crowned as pharaoh. She made a peaceful expedition to Punt (the east coast of Africa bordering the Red Sea), and brought back a range of exotic plants and animals to Egypt. On Hatshepsut's death, Thutmose assumed control. He totally renounced his former regent, refused to acknowledge her kingship and had her figure chiselled out of all representations, including this wall painting. Thutmose led many military campaigns into Palestine and Syria, beyond the Euphrates and into Nubia in the south.

Source: E.A. Hemelrijk, Haarlem.

Nubia was of particular interest to Egypt because of its gold, the word 'Nubia' meaning 'land of gold'. It was governed by a viceroy (who was referred to as the 'King's son') and stood under fairly direct control of Egypt. Egyptian influence prevailed in Nubia in cultural terms, too. Egyptian temples were erected and Egyptian artistic conventions, religious practices and written culture were adopted. In Palestine and Syria, Egypt exerted less direct control. The kings of the city states in those areas retained their authority, but had to admit Egyptian troops and controllers into their territories. Those regions were only marginally influenced by Egyptian culture. Egyptian cultural influence was in fact largely restricted to coastal cities like Byblos, Tyre and Ugarit, which had already been conducting trade with Egypt for some time.

The most extraordinary pharaoh is without doubt Akhenaton (*c.* 1350). He attempted to transform the Egyptian polytheism into a religion based on the worship of only one god, the sun god Aton. All other cults were suppressed, especially that of the Theban god Amon, whose name was expunged from all records. Akhenaton even transferred the capital from Thebes to a new site, which he called Akhetaton (present-

Figure 3.3 Akhenaton, Nefertiti and their daughters
Notes: The sun disk Aton with the blessing hands is visible in the middle. The rays on the far left and far right bear the symbol of life ('ankh'). Such informal scenes are quite uncommon in Egyptian relief sculpture.
Source: Ägyptisches Museum, Berlin

day El Amarna). During this period of religious reforms changes took place in the nature of Egyptian art, too. The former fairly stereotyped art with its rigid conventions gave way to a freer mode of expression. Figures were given more individual traits and compositions became less formal. The Egyptian convention of portraying faces, hips and legs in profile and eyes and shoulders in frontal view was however retained.

While engrossed in his religious pursuits, Akhenaton however neglected his administrative duties. The city states in Syria and Palestine, which were suffering increasing harassment from nomadic and semi-nomadic tribes, began to take matters into their own hands. Akhenaton sent very few or no troops to assert his authority. His successor, the well-known Tutankhamen, who had a poor constitution and met with an early death, reverted to the old Egyptian traditions and made Memphis the capital of his realm. The eighteenth dynasty came to an end when three generals seized the throne.

Egypt managed to recover its unity once more, in the thirteenth century. That was largely thanks to the efforts of Ramses II (1279–1212) of the nineteenth dynasty, one of Egypt's most ambitious builders. He is the pharaoh who commissioned the construction of the temple at Abu Simbel, which, in the late 1950s, Unesco saved from the rising water of the reservoir at the Assuan Dam.

Babylonia and Assyria

Shortly after the fall of the Old Babylonian empire, around 1600, a tribe of eastern invaders, the Kassites, assumed control in Babylon. They governed Mesopotamia for over four centuries. It is they who introduced the war chariot into Babylonia. The king relied heavily on his followers, to whom he awarded land that was exempt from taxation. The Kassites adjusted themselves to the Babylonian culture, which was essentially the product of the merging of the former Sumerian and Akkadian civilisations. Their temples and their artistic styles were entirely Babylonian in character; Sumerian and Akkadian continued to be used as written languages. That way, continuity was maintained.

The Assyrian empire was weak at first. Its kings were effectively subject to the kings of its northwestern neighbour Mitanni, but they acquired independence when the latter empire was overthrown by the Hittites around 1350. This ushered in a new period in Mesopotamia's history, in which the region was governed by two medium-sized states, Assyria and Babylonia, in a more or less stable balance of power which was to last until the eighth century BC.

Mitanni

Mitanni was a state situated between the upper reaches of the Euphrates and the Tigris. Its occupants were Hurrians (the biblical 'Horites'), who had lived in that area since the third millennium and had over the centuries gradually spread towards Asia Minor and Syria and Palestine. That meant that Hurrians were also to be found outside Mitanni, for example in the Hittite empire. Although Hurrian (which was written in the cuneiform script) was used for official documents in Mitanni and the

Hurrians worshipped their own deities, several Indo-Aryan elements are discernable in Mitannian culture. Some treaties, for example, mention Indian gods and some of the Mitannian kings had Indo-Aryan names.

The Hittite empire

From time immemorial peoples with urban civilisations whose origins are unknown to us had been living in Asia Minor. The language of the people who settled in central Anatolia at the beginning of the second millennium includes distinct Indo-European elements. These people we call the 'Hittites'. Around 1700 BC their kingdom, the Old Hittite kingdom, rose to power, extending its sway over Syria. One of the Hittite kings even penetrated into Babylon around 1600 (see p. 19). However, due to internal power struggles, the Hittite kingdom gradually became weaker and lost its conquered territory. King Suppiluliumas managed to restore Hittite power around 1350 and established what is known as the Hittite new kingdom or empire. He subjected powerful cities in Syria and Asia Minor and settled accounts with his neighbours, the Hurrians in Mitanni, where he installed a puppet on the throne. The Hittites' custom was to conclude peace treaties with the kings they defeated, who were usually allowed to remain on their thrones (what are known as 'vassal-rulers' or 'client-kings'). Large numbers of such treaties have been recovered in excavations in the Hittite capital.

Hittite culture is greatly indebted to Mesopotamian civilization. The Hittites adopted the cuneiform script and used the Akkadian language for certain kinds of texts, such as the aforementioned treaties. These treaties invoke Mesopotamian gods. Several works of Mesopotamian literature, including the Epic of Gilgamesh, were translated into the Hittite language. But other influences are observable, too. Religious texts, for example, were written in ancient non-Hittite languages. Hurrian influences are also evident, especially after the reign of Suppiluliumas. Teshup, the Hurrian god of thunder, even became one of the principal deities of the Hittite empire.

Crete and Mycenae

It was in the second millennium, too, that the cultures of Crete and Mycenae reached their greatest heights, after a development that can be traced back to the third millennium BC. In modern literature the culture of Crete is referred to as the 'Minoan' culture (after the island's legendary King Minos), and that of the Greek mainland as the 'Helladic' culture (after 'Hellas', the Greek word for Greece).

The most important city on Crete was Knossos. Two striking aspects of this city are that it was not fortified and that its wall paintings, in marked contrast with those of the Near East, depicted predominantly peaceful scenes. The frescoes show motifs drawn from local plant and animal life and scenes of open-air religious ceremonies, but no military feats (Fig. 3.4). With its many rooms, the majestic palace of Knossos must have presented an awesome aspect, because the Greeks referred to it as 'King Minos' Labyrinth'.

Figure 3.4 The throne room at the palace at Knossos (partly reconstructed)

This palace was the centre of an economic system comparable with that of the Third Dynasty of Ur or that of the New Kingdom of Egypt. Such an economic system is described in greater detail on page 55. A syllabic script, known as Linear A, was developed for the palace's administration. As this script has not yet been deciphered, we know very little about the people who used it or the language they spoke. The source of Crete's prosperity is less of a mystery to us: the island owed its wealth largely to its flourishing trade. Cretan ships transported goods all over the Mediterranean, calling in at ports in regions including Egypt, Syria and Palestine, the Aegean islands and Greece.

Around 1450 Knossos became the most influential city in political terms too: it conquered the rest of Crete, destroying many palaces in the process. However, its victory was short-lived, for around 1375 an expedition of warriors from Mycenae assumed control over Knossos, and hence over the whole of Crete.

Since about 3000 BC a civilisation had been taking shape on the Greek mainland that was in many respects comparable with that of Crete. It is believed that a people speaking a Greek (i.e. Indo-European) language settled in Greece around 2100 BC. Shortly after 1600 several of their urban centres (Mycenae, Pylos, Tiryns: see Figs 3.5a and 3.5b) developed into flourishing cities. At first these cities were also unfortified, but between 1400 and 1300 their palaces started to be surrounded by imposing defences.

Around this time Mycenaean civilisation acquired an indisputably military element. In their fortified palaces the kings ruled together with an elite of charioteers, who were awarded land in exchange for their services and whose horses were paid for by the state. Although there is no evidence to suggest that any one of the cities ever gained control over the whole of Greece, or even over the Peloponnese, traces of destruction indicate that they waged wars on one another. This military element is almost completely absent from Mycenaean art, which is characterised by abstract designs and floral motifs borrowed from Minoan art. The same impersonal style has also been encountered on the islands in the Aegean, for example on Thera.

Something else that the Greek mainlanders borrowed from their Cretan neighbours besides artistic styles is the latter's script. This they adapted for their own, Greek, language. The resultant script is known as Linear B.

Around 1375 an expedition of Greek mainlanders crossed over to Crete and assumed control of Knossos. They took their script along with them and from then onwards the Greek Linear B was used on Crete (in Knossos), too.

International relations

Thanks to the discovery of an archive of clay tablets at Akhetaton (= El Amarna) in Egypt we are fairly well informed about the international relations of this period. This archive contained several letters that the kings of the great powers wrote to the Egyptian pharaoh, but the majority of the letters were written by the kings of the city states in Palestine and Syria, which were under Egyptian domination. These letters are clay tablets inscribed in the Babylonian cuneiform script. In those days Babylonian was the language of international relations. Besides this archive various other letters have survived from this period.

Figure 3.5a Fortifications at Hattusas, the capital of the Hittite empire
Source: R.J. van der Spek

Figure 3.5b Fortifications at Tiryns, near Mycenae
Notes: Note the remarkable similarity in architecture. Large blocks of stone were fitted together without mortar, like the pieces in a jigsaw puzzle. The arches are false; they do not form a closed span. Greeks of later ages were greatly impressed by the size of the blocks of stone. They used the term 'Cyclopean' to describe such masonry. Cyclops were giants in Greek mythology who had only one eye, above the nose.
Source: R.J. van der Spek.

Another important source of information on international relations are the Hittite treaties that have been preserved in large numbers. Some of these treaties are on unequal terms, between the Hittite king and his vassals, the rulers of the Hittite satellite states (see pp. 25 and 62–4); others, between the kings of the great powers, are on equal terms. It is clear that great pains were taken to ensure that the terms of the latter treaties were reciprocal.

The annals celebrating the king's valiant deeds, which those same kings had inscribed in clay tablets, the walls of temples and other surfaces, constitute a third source of information. Together, these three sources have greatly increased our

Figure 3.6 Ramses II in the battle at Kadesh against the Hittites, 1275 BC
Notes: Ramses II on his war chariot in the battle at Kadesh against the Hittites (1275 BC). The king is the only warrior shown riding his chariot alone, with the reins at his hips. This would have been impossible in practice. All the other chariots are driven by separate charioteers. The illustration emphasises the king's superhuman capacities (cf. p. 49).

understanding of the diplomatic relations of those days. Friendly relations were maintained via the regular exchange of messengers, letters and gifts and through political marriages. Many close alliances were formed for fear of a mutual enemy or because former enemies came to realise that they had nothing to gain by continuing hostilities. During its campaigns of conquest, Egypt, for example, came into conflict with Mitanni, but the two powers made peace with one another around 1400, when the Hittite empire started to pose a serious threat. However, this was to be of no avail to Mitanni, for a few decades later, around 1350, it was wiped off the map by Suppiluliumas. For a long time the Egyptians and the Hittites disputed Syria. Egypt's power over its territories in .the Levant weakened under the reformer pharaoh Akhenaton. Some vassals defected to the Hittite king, others claimed authority as independent rulers (see also p. 24). Pharaoh Ramses II (1279–1212) of the 19th dynasty set about recovering Egypt's lost territory and was quite successful in his campaigns until the Hittites brought him to a halt in the battle at Kadesh (1274). The ensuing status quo resulted in a peace treaty (1259) between Ramses II and Hattusilis III, which has survived in an Egyptian version, carved in the walls of a temple near Thebes, and a Babylonian version, inscribed in a clay tablet that was found in Hattusas.

CHAPTER FOUR

THE FIRST MILLENNIUM BC

DISRUPTION AND RECOVERY (1200–750)

Around 1200 BC the state of equilibrium of the great powers was disturbed. Assyria and Babylonia were confronted with invasions of Aramaic and Chaldean tribes from the steppes and deserts between Palestine and Mesopotamia, which they had great difficulty repelling. The invaders settled in large parts of Syria and southern Mesopotamia, the Chaldeans favouring the area around the Persian Gulf.

The consequences of the attacks of a group of invaders described as the 'Sea Peoples' were far more disastrous. These people, who probably came from the Balkan mountains, pushed their way to the borders of Egypt via Greece and Asia Minor. We refer to them as the 'Sea Peoples' because that is what they are called in an Egyptian source. Directly or indirectly, these peoples were responsible for the downfall of a number of important states: Mycenae (including Crete), the Hittite empire and also the Syrian trading centre Ugarit. None of those states was to regain its former glory. It cost Egypt the greatest difficulty to withstand the attacks of the Sea Peoples in the Nile Delta; in the struggles against these invaders it lost its territories in Syria and Palestine. One of the best-known Sea Peoples are the Philistines, who settled in the southwestern part of the region that was called Palestine after them. The Sea Peoples caused a break in the history of the eastern Mediterranean. What had been powerful states in the centuries before 1200 were wiped off the map or saw their power thoroughly undermined. It was to take the 'civilised' world between a hundred and two hundred years to recover from this blow. By the end of that period, the newcomers had fully adjusted themselves to their new environments and new way of life.

The twelfth century is a great turning-point in history in another respect, too: it also marks the beginning of the Iron Age. Iron had been known throughout the entire second millennium, in particular in Asia Minor, but the products that were made from this metal, such as knives, were then still considered luxury goods. After 1200, however, iron started to be used on a large scale and that is why historians and archaeologists have fixed the transition from the Bronze Age to the Iron Age around 1200 BC.

Egypt, the Third Intermediate period
(c. 1100–715)

As mentioned above, Egypt lost its conquered territories in Syria and Palestine and also those in Nubia. It was not able to preserve unity in its heartland either, as is apparent for example from the fact that Amon's high priest in Thebes managed to set himself up as a semi-independent ruler. Libyans infiltrated the Delta and the Fayyûm region and founded settlements there. Between 950 and 730 Egypt was even ruled by dynasties of Libyan pharaohs.

Egypt did make some attempts to recover its lost territory in Palestine. One of the kings of a Libyan dynasty managed to penetrate into Jerusalem, the capital of the newly emerged kingdom of Judah (c. 935 BC). He robbed the temple, but failed to establish permanent Egyptian authority in Judah.

In what is known as the Late Kingdom (715–332) Egypt was almost constantly ruled by foreign powers and managed to regain its independence for short periods only. The first to take control, around 730, was the Nubian kingdom centred around Napata (see Map 3.1, p. 17), which had broken away from Egypt around 1100, without, however, distancing itself from Egyptian culture (see p. 23). Later on, Egypt was to be incorporated into other powerful empires that emerged in the Levant, namely those of Assyria (between 671 and 655) and Persia (525–404 and 343–332). They will be discussed below.

Syria and the Phoenicians

Small states took advantage of the weakening of the great powers to reassert their independence. Among the states that managed to regain their autonomy in this period are the city states of Syria, in several of which groups of foreigners had settled. Some, for example Karkemish, were ruled by Hittite kings; they are known as neo-Hittite kingdoms.

Other cities passed under Aramaean rule. One of those cities is Damascus, which became the centre of a fairly large territorial Aramaean state, referred to as Aram in the Bible. The original occupants of the ports to the west of the Lebanon Mountains, including Byblos, Tyre and Sidon, were not driven out by foreigners. This region is usually referred to by the Greek term 'Phoenicia'. The Phoenician towns managed to recover from the blows inflicted by the Sea Peoples reasonably quickly and developed into independent city states ruled by a king and a council of elders. It was quite some time before they were forced to acknowledge the supremacy of a great power. Now that they no longer had to compete with Crete and Mycenae they evolved into the most powerful trading cities in the ancient Near East.

The Phoenicians were of paramount importance for Western civilisation: it is they who passed on the culture of the ancient Near East to Europe and it is via them that the Greeks first came into contact with the Near East.

In this period, in which overseas trade by Greeks was still virtually non-existent, the Phoenicians exported Near Eastern products to Greece and other regions in the West.

The influence of the Phoenicians spread across the Mediterranean in a different manner, too – namely in the form of the colonies that the Phoenicians started to found in North Africa, Sicily and southern Spain in the tenth century BC. These colonies, many of which were founded as trading posts, grew into independent cities. The best-known Phoenician colony is Carthage in North Africa, which was founded by colonists from Tyre around 800 BC (the traditional date is 814–13). Carthage was later to become a great autonomous power (see pp. 154 and 178).

The most important Phoenician contribution to civilisation is undoubtedly the invention of the alphabet. The Phoenician alphabet differed from the other writing systems hitherto used in that, instead of a sign for each syllable, it comprised only signs for consonants. With its total of only twenty-two signs, as opposed to the more than 600 signs of the cuneiform script, it was accessible to a much wider public. In Mesopotamia and Egypt the art of writing had been known only to a small group of specially trained scribes. Another great difference with respect to the cuneiform script is that the new alphabet was written on papyrus or leather. Unfortunately, however, both those materials are highly perishable and little written evidence relating to Phoenician history has consequently been preserved. The earliest written texts of the peoples who first adopted the Phoenician script, the Aramaeans and the Israelites, have not survived either.

Israel

The reason why we are nevertheless reasonably well informed about the Israelites is that they conscientiously copied the works of their richly varied literature over and over again to preserve them for future generations. These works, which comprise poetry, histories, laws and wisdom literature, constitute the books of the Old Testament, the basis of the Jewish religion and, together with the New Testament, also that of Christianity (see p. 267). They have survived to this day because these religions, unlike all the others of the ancient Near East, never became extinct. A great problem for historians is that the texts were not written down in the form in which they have been preserved until relatively late, that is, during the Babylonian exile, around 550 BC (see p. 40). Moreover, they are very much coloured by the message they contain: the people of Israel must worship only their own god Yahweh and no other gods; only then will God bless His people, with whom He has concluded a covenant. That was no easy message in a world in which all peoples were accustomed to worshipping many gods.

The earliest history of Israel is particularly difficult for us to reconstruct. The Israelites claim to have descended from Abraham, who left Mesopotamia to live in Canaan (Palestine). There he lived the life of a nomad herder. Famine drove Abraham's grandson Jacob and his twelve sons into Egypt, where the Israelites increased tremendously in number. The pharaoh, however, forced them to work for him; they had to help build two new cities in the Delta: Pitom and Raamses. The book of Exodus tells us how the Israelites escaped from Egypt, led by Moses, and how, after a long journey through the desert, they arrived in Palestine, where they captured cities in which they then settled. Theologians and historians have avidly searched for mention of these events in other sources, but all that they have managed to verify is that Ramses II built Pitom and Raamses and that his successor met with 'the people of Israel' during a raid on Palestine. Archaeological research has likewise failed to produce evidence of a single mass invasion of Palestine. Over the years, scholars have spent rivers of ink hypothesising about the problem of how the people of Israel penetrated into the city states of Canaan and managed to acquire control over many of them. One possibility is that all this took place in a process of gradual infiltration, comparable with that of the establishment of the Amorites in Babylonia and the Hyksos in Egypt. Whatever the case may be, the Israelites faced a precarious future, in which they were to put up many a struggle against the cities of Canaan and later groups of settlers. The Philistines proved particularly formidable opponents, as they had iron weapons whereas the Israelites were still fighting with weapons of bronze. The Israelites lived in fairly disorganised communities scattered across Palestine. In times of war they would sometimes unite under the leadership of 'judges' (cf. the book of that name in the Bible). The fierce battles, in particular that

The kingdoms of Israel and Judah, *c.* 850

The kingdom of David, *c.* 1000

Orontes

Karkar•

• Byblos

PHOENICIANS

Sidon • Damascus

• Tyre

Dan ARAM

• Akko

Megiddo • ← ⌐ ISRAEL

Samaria •

Shechem •

Bethel •

Jordan

• Jericho

Jerusalem

PHILISTINES

• Askelon ←

• Lachis Hebron

• Gaza

• Beersheba MOAB

JUDAH

EDOM

Elath •

Map 4.1 The kingdoms of Israel and Judah, *c.* 850 BC, and the kingdom
of David, *c.* 1000 BC

Figure 4.1 The Assyrian army attacks a town
Notes: Note the diversity of the Assyrian forces: visible are archers, lancers, swordsmen and siege instruments. In one of the siege instruments a figure is reading out a text, probably

against the Philistines, aroused a desire for a king among the Israelites. The first of their kings was Saul. He did not succeed in establishing a dynasty, for after his death David, who had served under the Philistines as well as under Saul, ousted Saul's family and ascended the throne himself (*c.* 1000 BC). David conquered Jerusalem for the Israelites and made that city the capital of his kingdom. He then turned Israel into a fairly powerful territorial state (Map 4.1). This he was able to do because at that time there was no great power in the Near East to challenge Israel's increasing might.

David was succeeded by his son Solomon, who had a temple for the God of Israel built in Jerusalem.

The period of prosperity that followed was to be of only short duration. Even before the end of King Solomon's reign his kingdom began to crumble. After his death, it even broke up into two parts – it had not yet evolved a sufficiently strong sense of unity. For a long time, contrasts had existed between the north and the south. Moreover, many Israelites were not (yet) prepared to pay the costs required for a well-organised kingdom. Solomon's son retained leadership over the southern half of the kingdom only: that became the kingdom of Judah, in whose capital,

in Aramaic because he is holding a piece of papyrus or leather instead of a clay tablet. He is probably proclaiming some propagandistic text or terms of surrender.

Jerusalem, David's descendants remained in control for several centuries. The northern half of the kingdom elected a different king, who founded a new, separate kingdom called Israel. Israel was to have a less stable government. Different dynasties followed one another in rapid succession. The kingdom also had to settle many border conflicts with Aram (Damascus). In the ninth century it acquired a new capital, Samaria.

After the reign of King Solomon, Israel and Judah became politically insignificant states. Both kingdoms were reduced to vassal states of the new power that had arisen in the Levant: Assyria.

THE EMPIRES OF THE LEVANT (750 BC–AD 700)

The neo-Assyrian empire

Assyria held out reasonably well during the difficult times after 1200. The empire continued to be ruled by a king and the army was organised with increasing efficiency in the battles against the Aramaeans. Military innovations (the use of cavalry, the perfecting of siege engines) made the army powerful enough to make raids into distant regions, some as far away as the Mediterranean coast. But it was some time yet before the Assyrians managed to obtain permanent control over large areas.

The first who succeeded in doing so was Tiglath-Pileser III (745–727) and his reign is therefore held to mark the beginning of the neo-Assyrian empire. The Assyrian kings secured the loyalty of more and more vassal rulers and transformed vassal states into provinces, which they put under the authority of Assyrian governors (see pp. 62–4). A case in point is Samaria, the capital of Israel, which Sargon II placed under Assyrian governorship after his predecessor had captured it in 722. The Assyrians' custom when capturing a city was to deport the city's population and replace it by foreigners. This is what happened in Samaria too. Judah managed to retain its status as a vassal state.

The Assyrians are notorious for their deportation policy. They frequently deported large parts of a rebellious population as a means of punishment. Many of the people who were deported from their homelands were forced to help build or expand the capitals of the Assyrian empire, for Assyria, being sparsely populated, was always in great need of specialised craftsmen. Other deportees were incorporated in Assyria's standing army, which the Assyrian kings had formed at the end of the eighth century. The largest numbers of people, allegedly some hundreds of thousands, were deported by Tiglath-Pileser III and his immediate successors. The masses of foreigners, many of whom spoke Aramaic, who were consequently imported into Assyria caused the Assyrian heartland to lose its Assyrian character. The Babylonian-Assyrian language was gradually replaced by Aramaic, which presented the advantage that it was written in a much simpler script, namely an alphabet.

Babylonia also lost its independence. The Assyrians had always more or less spared Babylonia out of respect for its traditions, setting themselves up as protectors of the Babylonian culture against the uncouth Chaldeans, who harassed the Babylonians from their home country along the Persian Gulf. However, when a Chaldean king usurped the Babylonian throne, Tiglath-Pileser intervened and annexed Babylonia (729 BC). Instead of reducing it to a vassal state or a province, he ascended the throne himself, after conducting the traditional Babylonian rituals. The Assyrians' respect for the culture of the Babylonians was based on the ties of language, script, religion and literature and the mercantile relations that had united these two peoples for so many centuries. Ashurbanipal (669–627), the last of the great Assyrian kings, ordered his officials to search for ancient Babylonian texts, which they were to bring to the capital Nineveh where they were to be copied and stored in archives. It is in that city that the best-known version of the Epic of Gilgamesh was found. Other Assyrian kings did not share Ashurbanipal's respect for the Babylonian culture. In 689, after a period of poor relations with the Babylonians, who felt they were not being granted their due privileges, the Assyrians razed Babylon to the ground.

At its greatest expanse, the Assyrian empire also included Egypt (671–655), which it had incorporated after the Egyptians had encouraged the Palestinians to revolt against the Assyrians during the reign of the Nubian dynasty.

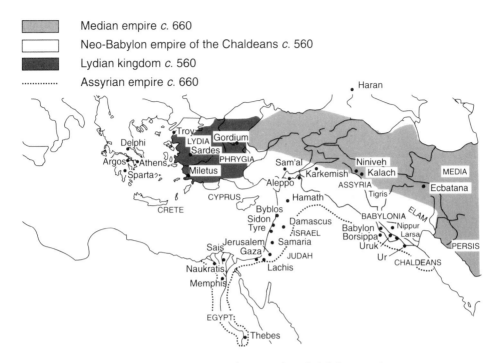

Map 4.2 The Near East in the seventh and eighth centuries BC

The Assyrians were unable to reduce Egypt to a province, but they did succeed in turning several Egyptian provincial governors into Assyrian vassal rulers. One of those rulers, Psamtik I (664–610), threw off the Assyrian yoke around 658. That was the prelude to a new revival of Egyptian influence, which was to last about a century. The new dynasty is called the Saite dynasty (the 26th, 664–525), after the new capital Sais. In their efforts to bring the old Egyptian culture back to life, the Saite kings emulated the former traditions of the Old Kingdom. This period is therefore also referred to as the 'Saite Renaissance'. It was in this period, too, that contacts between Egypt and Greece intensified. Greek mercenaries served in the Egyptian army and Psamtik allowed the Greeks to establish a trading post at Naukratis (see p. 74).

The loss of Egypt heralded Assyria's downfall. The Assyrian kings slowly lost their hold over their vassal states in Palestine, including Judah. Things really started to go wrong after the death of Ashurbanipal (627). The stability of the Assyrian empire was strongly dependent on the king's capacities. Many of the frequent changes of power that followed Ashurbanipal's death gave rise to revolts. The final blow was the result of a combination of factors: three pretenders fighting one another for accession to the throne within Assyria, the outbreak of a revolt in Babylonia and the emergence of a serious foreign threat: the Medes in the East. The new king of Babylon joined forces with the Medes and together they overthrew Assyria. Between 614 and 609 they captured and almost completely destroyed all of Assyria's capitals. On the country's ruins they then laid the foundations for two new

39

empires: the Median empire to the east of the Tigris, with Ecbatana as its capital, and the neo-Babylonian empire, whose capital was Babylon, to the west (see Map 4.2). Egypt temporarily occupied Palestine, only to lose it to the Babylonians shortly after.

The neo-Babylonian empire

The neo-Babylonian empire is often referred to as the 'Chaldean empire'. This term, which was already in use in antiquity, is confusing however. As a result of immigration and deportation Babylonia was in the first millennium inhabited by peoples of different stocks. Besides the original population, there were several Aramaean and Chaldean tribes, which had settled especially in the southern part of the empire, in the marshy area near the Persian Gulf – the 'Sealand', where Shi'ites live today. There were not that many differences between the Babylonians and the Chaldeans. The Chaldeans had been greatly influenced by Babylonian traditions. They had exchanged their nomadic way of life for a sedentary existence, they worshipped Babylonian gods and bore Babylonian names. In the neo-Babylonian empire, official inscriptions, religious texts, letters and contracts were written in cuneiform script. The terms 'Chaldean' and 'Babylonian' increasingly took on the same meaning, especially in the eyes of outsiders, who frequently confused the two. The ruling dynasty is often called 'Chaldean' in Jewish, Greek and Roman sources, but never in contemporary Babylonian cuneiform texts. The Jews, the Greeks and the Romans used the term 'Chaldeans' to refer to Babylonian priests, diviners and astrologers, as if it were a technical term. Meanwhile, however, the gradual replacement of Babylonian by Aramaic (which was closely related to Chaldean) as both the spoken and the written language continued. This process, which had started in the Assyrian era, is difficult for us to follow because most Aramaic texts were written on papyrus or parchment, of which only very little has survived.

The neo-Babylonian empire was actually founded by Nebuchadnezzar II (605–562), who also conquered Syria and Palestine. This king, known to us from the Old Testament, made Judah a vassal state. Later on, when the king of Judah revolted against him, Nebuchadnezzar reduced the kingdom of Judah to a province. According to the tradition established by his predecessors, he then deported its population to Babylonia (what is referred to as 'the Babylonian Exile' in the Bible, 586 BC).

This period was of great importance for the history of the Jews. They were allowed to remain with their families, living in their own communities in Babylonia. It was in this period that they wrote down large parts of their traditions. By continuing to adhere to their own religion, the Jews managed to preserve their identity.

The last Babylonian king, Nabonidus, was an intriguing figure. He was a fervent worshipper of the moon god Sin of Harran and neglected the cult of Marduk, the supreme god of Babylon. He went to live in the Arab desert and left the government of his kingdom to his son, Belshazzar. His behaviour was the cause of great discontent in Babylon, which made that town an easy prey to the new power that emerged in the East: Persia.

Figure 4.2 The Ishtar Gate of Babylon, built by Nebuchadnezzar II (605–562), rebuilt in the Pergamum Museum in Berlin

Notes: The gate and the walls flanking the entrance were built of blue glazed bricks. Marduk, the god of Babylon, was paraded through this gate to the New Year's house, which lay outside the town, on the day of the New Year's Festival (early April) (cf. p. 49).

Source: Staatliche Museen, Berlin.

The Persian empire

The Persian empire evolved from that of the Medes. The Medes and Persians had settled in the Iranian highlands in the ninth century. They spoke closely related 'Aryan' languages, which belonged to the family of Indo-European languages. In the sixth century the Medes extended their sway over a large territory stretching from Iran into Asia Minor (see Map 4.2). We know very little about how their empire was organised, but it is believed that it lacked a powerful centralised administration. Around 560 BC, the Persian Cyrus, a vassal ruler in the Median empire, captured the Median capital Ecbatana and assumed control over the empire, which is from that date onwards called the 'Persian empire'. As the Medes continued to play an important part in that empire it is sometimes also called the empire of the Medes and Persians. The Jews and the Greeks often used the word 'Medes' when referring to Persians.

Cyrus built up an empire of vast proportions. The first of his conquests was Asia Minor, which he took after defeating Lydia (whose capital was Sardis) in the western part of Asia Minor. The Greeks in particular were well acquainted with Lydia, as that kingdom had annexed their cities along the western coast of Asia Minor in the sixth century. The legendary wealth of Lydia's king Croesus was of no avail to him in his battle against Cyrus (547 BC).

Next, Cyrus turned his attention to Babylonia. The Babylonians, who were disappointed with their rulers Nabonidus and Belshazzar, hoped that Cyrus would prove to be a better king and they hence offered little resistance to his campaign of conquest; Cyrus took control of Babylon in 539 BC.

As the Babylonians had hoped, Cyrus indeed showed respect for Babylon and its traditions. He restored the worship of Marduk. In that respect Cyrus behaved in the same way as the majority of the Assyrian kings of the past and his behaviour hence won him great popularity in Babylon. He was also well-loved by the Jews, who were then living in Babylon in exile; they believed that he had been sent to them by God. After he had conquered Babylon, Cyrus allowed the Jews to return to Judah and to rebuild their temple in Jerusalem.

Many Jews made grateful use of this opportunity and in Judah they founded a more or less autonomous temple state ruled by the high priest and a governor, usually a Jew, who was appointed by the Persians. Other Jews remained in Babylon, where they, too, remained faithful to their religious customs. This community survived into the twentieth century.

Cyrus' behaviour towards Babylon and the Jews earned him the reputation of a very mild, tolerant ruler, which he still has today. However, when seen in a wider context, his behaviour was in fact not very different from that of other rulers of the ancient Near East. Like them, he too adapted his approach to the circumstances, treating some subject peoples with clemency, others with severity. Cyrus' final campaign took him to the River Indus in the East, where he was killed in battle. Cambyses, his son, incorporated Egypt into his empire (525) and put an end to the sway of the Saite dynasty (see p. 39).

Darius I (520–485) was the great organiser of that empire. Before he ascended the throne, the empire had consisted of a number of super-provinces or 'satrapies'. One

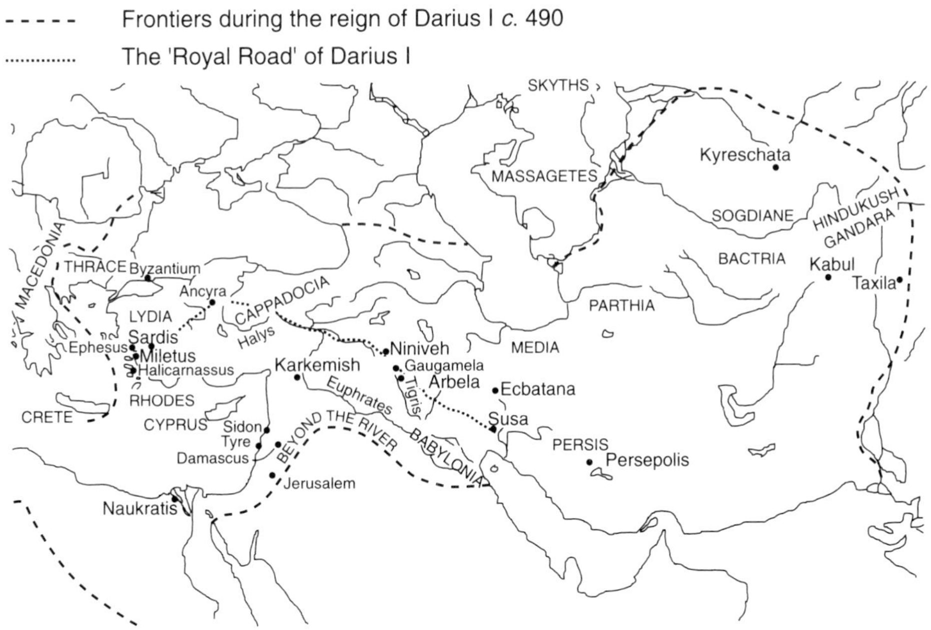

- - - - - Frontiers during the reign of Darius I *c.* 490

.... The 'Royal Road' of Darius I

Map 4.3 The Persian empire, 539–331 BC

of those satrapies was the former neo-Babylonian empire (see Map 4.2). Darius reorganised his empire, creating some twenty smaller satrapies. Each satrapy had to pay a fixed tax. The satrapies were ruled by governors or 'satraps'. In periods of weak central authority, some of those satraps managed to acquire a good deal of power and set themselves up as semi-independent rulers. The kings tried to stop this process by having their satraps' activities checked by secret informers – the 'king's eyes and ears'. The commanders of the satrapy's army contingents were in principle also directly responsible to the king.

Under Darius' successor Xerxes (485–464), a revolt broke out in Babylonia, where Babylonian kings had remained in power for some time. Babylon suffered some damage in the suppression of that revolt, but its temples continued to function.

We will meet Darius and Xerxes again in the part on Greek history, in the discussion of their – failed – attempts to subject Greece. In the fourth century the Persians made a fresh attempt to undermine Greek power, this time via a divide-and-rule policy. Many Greeks crossed over to Persia in that century, most in order to serve in the Persian army as mercenaries.

The Persian empire was essentially a continuation of the former Mesopotamian empires. Its administrative organisation – and its art, too – owed much to Mesopotamian traditions. However, Persian art also betrays influences of the civilisations of other subject peoples and elements borrowed from Greek culture. Like their predecessors, the Persian rulers respected the religious customs of the peoples they subjected. In some respects, however, the Persians adhered to their own customs and traditions. Persis remained the centre of their authority; it is there that

Figure 4.3a Human-headed winged bull, palace of Sargon II at Dur-Sharrukin, *c.* 707 BC
Notes: Such giant bulls were placed at the entrances to Assyrian palaces. These divine beings protected the entrance from evil powers.
Source: British Museum, London.

Figure 4.3b Human-headed winged bull, palace of Xerxes in Persepolis
Note: A clear example of the Persians' imitation of Assyrian art.

they built their new capital Persepolis. They also continued to worship their own, Persian gods. Of profound influence was the Persian prophet Zoroaster, to whom we will return in the chapter on the religions of the Near East. Whether the kings of Persia also ranked among Zoroaster's followers we do not know. For two centuries the Persians ruled over the whole of the ancient Near East. Around 330, however, a new power, this time from the West, made a forceful entry onto the political stage of the Levant and Egypt, namely Macedonia, under the leadership of Alexander the Great.

The Hellenistic kingdoms

Alexander's conquest of the Persian empire brought the ancient Near East, for the first time in its history, under the dominion of a foreign people from a different world, with an advanced civilisation of their own. After Alexander's death, his empire broke up into a number of smaller kingdoms ruled by dynasties founded by his generals. The greater part of the Levant came under the control of the 'Seleucids'. Egypt became the kingdom of the 'Ptolemies'. The area comprising southern Syria and Palestine (including Judah) was a bone of contention between the Seleucid and the Ptolemaic kingdoms (see Map 11.2 on p. 137).

These kingdoms will be discussed later, after we have considered the history of the Greeks up to the reign of Alexander – from which time onwards the history of Greece and that of the Near East are inextricably linked. Two general comments can already be made at this point, however. First of all, in organisational terms, the kingdoms that were formed after Alexander were very much like their predecessors, and secondly, in spite of the fact that the new rulers did not embrace the cultural traditions of the Levant and Egypt as the foreign conquerors of the past had done, the civilisations of those areas nevertheless lived on under the Greek-Macedonian domination.

The Parthian empire

The civilisations of the Levant and Egypt were in fact to outlive the Hellenistic kingdoms. In 129 BC, after a long struggle, Mesopotamia fell to the Iranian Parthians. The Parthian empire lasted until AD 226.

The Sasanian empire

The next empire into which Mesopotamia was to be incorporated is known as the Sasanian empire. Both this and the Parthian empire were greatly influenced by the Iranian traditions of the Persian empire. These empires will be discussed in greater detail on pp. 145 and 274.

The Roman empire

The Romans also appeared on the political scene in the Near East. In 64–63 BC they occupied and annexed Syria, the last remaining part of the Seleucid kingdom. The Egyptian kingdom of the Ptolemies succumbed to the Romans in 30 BC. The written traditions, temple architecture, artistic conventions and cult practices of Egyptian civilisation survived for several centuries under the Roman dominion. We will return to this matter on p. 145. See also pp. 207 and 214.

The Arabs

The Sasanian and Roman empires (after AD 395 the East Roman or Byzantine empire: see p. 289) ruled over the ancient Near East until in the seventh century (see Map 16.1, p. 282), when, after the death of the prophet Muhammad, the Arabs brought about great changes. They conquered an area comprising almost the whole of the Levant and northern Africa. The Islamic religion that they established there has held sway over that area to this very day.

CHAPTER FIVE

RELIGION

Polytheism
Henotheism and monotheism

POLYTHEISM

Most religions of the ancient Near East were polytheistic, which means that many different gods were worshipped. This belief in many gods was associated with the people's world view. They believed that each force of nature represented a divine power. The cosmos had originated when primeval gods had risen from a divine primeval sea. They had given birth to new gods and that process had repeated itself for many generations. These gods were personifications of cosmic phenomena like the sky, air, earth, sun, moon, stars, etc. In Mesopotamia in particular, this cosmos was believed to be unstable. Monstrous forces tried to destroy the gods. It was up to a young, strong god to defeat those forces; for this he was rewarded with supreme power over the other gods and the mortals on earth. This theme is expressed in, for example, the Babylonian creation story featuring Marduk, and in the creation story of the Hurrians revolving around Teshup, the god of thunder. Myths (stories of gods) explaining natural phenomena and the origin of the world are distinctive features of the religions of the ancient Near East.

The annual death and rebirth of the vegetation was also explained in myths. The death of the cereal grain, out of which grew the cornstalk, was associated with the death of a god (Osiris in Egypt), while the vegetation's stagnated growth during the hot, dry period of the year was attributed to the fact that a god spent part of the year in the underworld (Tammuz in Mesopotamia, Aliyan Baal in Phoenicia). The wives or sisters of those gods mourned over their loss and went in search of them (Isis, Ishtar and Anath, respectively).

Every city and – usually – every state had its own supreme god, who was venerated in specific rites. In the Sumerian city of Nippur that god was Enlil, who was also regarded as the governor of the whole world (imperialistic kings therefore strove to conquer Nippur, so that Enlil would grant them control over the world). The supreme god of Babylon was Marduk, the Assyrians venerated Ashsur and the Egyptians worshipped the sun god Re in the period of the Old Kingdom and the Theban god Amon, who was also identified with Re as Amon-Re, during the Middle and Late Kingdoms. The chief god of a city that was made a capital usually also became the state god and the supreme god of the pantheon. That god then stood at the top of a theological system which defined the ties of kinship between the supreme god and the gods of other cities. However, these systems rarely had a fixed order and there were no dogmas determined by any religious or political authority.

Polytheistic religions are flexible and readily accept foreign gods into their pantheons, either as new gods or through identification with existing gods.

At a very early stage already, the gods were represented as anthropomorphic beings, that is, in the form of human beings. They were also endowed with human characteristics. In Egypt the gods were also portrayed as animals or as hybrid creatures, part beast and part man, which greatly astonished other peoples, in particular the Greeks and Romans.

The gods were worshipped to obtain their favour and to ensure that they would maintain world order and the fertility of the land. The worshippers served the gods meals, via offerings, and performed all kinds of rituals during which myths were recited. Worship was a state affair.

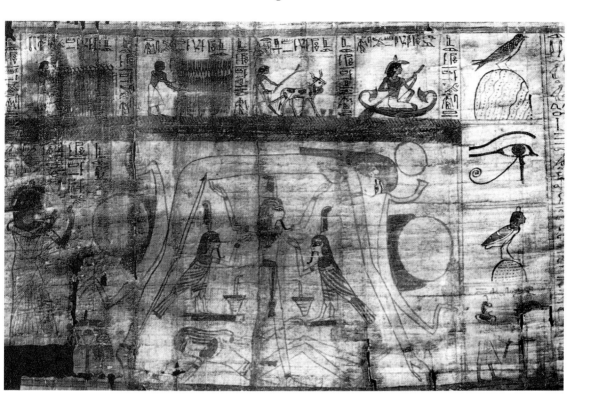

Figure 5.1 The cosmos: papyrus of Paser, twenty-first dynasty, *c.* 1000 BC, showing Egyptian gods
Notes: Nut, the sky-goddess, is shown standing on her hands and feet. Geb, the earth-god,
is reclining beneath her and Shu, the air-god, is supporting (the goddess of) the sky. The birds
next to Shu represent the soul of the deceased or that of the sun-god. The sun is sailing across
the sky in a boat. The top scene shows the deceased's activities in the underworld.
Source: Rijksmuseum van Oudheden, Leiden.

The king played an important part in religious activities. Some kings, like the kings
of Early Dynastic Uruk, Assyria and Egypt, served a double function, as the king and
the high priest. But even the kings who were not themselves high priests regarded
themselves as the supreme god's principal servants; as such they were responsible for
ensuring that the will of the gods was done. Their main task was to win the gods'
favour. To that end they built temples for the gods and took part in all kinds of rituals.
Sumerian texts, for example, mention rituals involving a sacred marriage in which the
king had intercourse with the city god's high priestess to secure the fertility of the
land and a good harvest. The kings of Babylon had to participate in the New Year's
Festival, on which occasion they were temporarily divested of their authority. They
had to avow that they had committed no crimes against the Babylonians and had to
promise that they would respect the Babylonians' privileges. After that, they were
restored to their power for another year. During this festival, which lasted for several
days, the Babylonian epic of creation was recited, to reassert Marduk's triumph over
the powers of chaos.

Figure 5.2 The Egyptian god Osiris, the 'Lord of Eternity'
Notes: In the primeval age Osiris was the king of Egypt. He was killed by Seth. Isis, the sister and wife of Osiris, managed to conceive a son, Horus, by having intercourse with her husband's corpse. Horus avenged his father's death by killing Seth and he then became the king of Egypt. Osiris became the king of the underworld. The pharaoh was the reincarnation of Horus in life and became Osiris when he died.
From the 5th dynasty onwards the king was also believed to be the son of the sun god Re. There are two Horuses in Egyptian religion: the falcon sky-god and the younger Horus, the son of Osiris, who is represented as a child sucking his finger, to indicate his tender age.
Osiris was also compared to a cereal grain, which must die in order to be able to germinate.

In spite of their leading roles in religious affairs, the kings of the Levant were hardly ever considered divine themselves. Only the kings of Akkad, the Third Dynasty of Ur and the Greek-Macedonian Seleucid dynasty had themselves deified. The Hittite kings were believed to become gods after their deaths. In Egypt, on the contrary, the king was regarded as a god. He was believed to be the incarnation of the sky god Horus and the son of the sun god Re. The people looked to him to secure the fertility of their land and for the regular flooding of the Nile. In Egypt, too, religion was a state affair and the king played a leading part in religious rites and in the temple's administration.

Private persons also prayed to the gods, but much less is known about such individual forms of worship. Many private persons had their own patron gods, who mediated on their behalf with other – sometimes more powerful – gods.

Human beings could find out what the gods had in store for them by, for example, studying the stars, the livers of sacrificed animals or the flight of birds. Before venturing on important undertakings, kings would consult priests who specialised in

Figure 5.3 The Phoenician god Baal riding a lion: relief from the ninth century BC
Notes: It was very common to represent gods riding on animals in the Levant. The crown that
Baal is wearing is derived from that of Osiris. The symbols of the moon (crescent) and the
winged sun are visible above the god's head.

these forms of divination. The 'Chaldean' astrologers (see p. 142) acquired great fame
in the Graeco-Roman world.

Egyptians and Mesopotamians held entirely different views on life after death.
The Egyptians believed that life would continue under the same pleasant conditions
as on earth, provided that the body remained intact. They therefore took great
pains to preserve the bodies of the deceased by embalming ('mummifying') them.
To the Mesopotamians, life after death was a bleak prospect: the deceased went to
a dismal area inside the earth, where an unpleasant time awaited them. This we
know from the Epic of Gilgamesh. Gilgamesh, the legendary king of Uruk (c. 2700
BC), set out to seek eternal life, but even he was unable to achieve it. The best he
could do was to achieve fame for himself – as a king – by performing 'immortal'
deeds.

— Chapter Five —

HENOTHEISM AND MONOTHEISM

Polytheism is not the only form of religion. Sometimes people placed all their confidence in one of the gods of a pantheon and regarded all the other gods, whose existence they nevertheless did not doubt, as powerless beings. This form of religion, which is known as henotheism, was to be found in early Israel. Some Assyrian and Egyptian texts also show signs of henotheism. One step further is monotheism. Monotheists worship only one god and deny the existence of other gods; they will generally not tolerate the worship of other gods either.

The world view of a monotheistic religion is consequently very different from that of a polytheistic religion. The cosmos is not believed to be governed by a multitude of divine powers. The sky, earth, sun and moon are not gods; there is only one god, who has created the universe and his creation is material. Monotheism was very rare in antiquity.

A frequently discussed problem is whether the cult established by the Egyptian pharaoh Akhenaton (see p. 23) (c. 1350 BC) was monotheistic. This pharaoh made the sun god Aton his patron god and tried to suppress the cult of the former supreme god Amon. He had all representations and every mention of Amon removed where possible and changed his own name, Amenophis or Amenhotep (meaning 'Amon has mercy') into Akhenaton ('agreeable to Aton'). The other gods he neglected altogether. In some places he even had the word 'gods' expunged.

Aton was represented as the disk of the sun with rays ending in blessing hands – a form of portrayal that differed markedly from the usual – according to which the gods were represented as human beings, animals or a combination of the two. Aton was one aspect of the sun god Re, who was represented as a human being crowned by a solar disk. So the name of Re was still acceptable. Akhenaton accepted the divine status which was attributed to all pharaohs, but he worshipped only Aton. Aton was the creator and benefactor of the world. As we do not know whether Akhenaton actually denied the existence of other gods, it is difficult to say whether his cult was monotheistic or henotheistic.

Akhenaton's views were too revolutionary for most Egyptians, whose traditional world view, based on a multitude of gods, it totally upset. His reforms did not catch on and after his death the Egyptians quickly reverted to their old traditions.

Far more successful was the monotheistic religion professed by the people of Israel, or rather by a small, zealous group of adherents who for many centuries fought stubbornly for the exclusive worship of Yahweh, the God of Israel, while most of their fellow Israelites and most of the kings of Israel and Judah also worshipped other gods besides Yahweh. It was to that same end, to propagate the exclusive belief in one God, that the books of the Old Testament were written (see p. 40). By adhering to this tradition, the Jews who returned from their exile and those who spread across the world in later times managed to preserve their identity, even though (excluding one brief intermittent period) they were to remain deprived of their national autonomy, which they lost at the time of the Babylonian Exile, until 1948.

The Persian religion preached by the sixth-century prophet Zoroaster approached monotheism to some extent. He taught his followers that the world was governed by two principles: Good and Evil. The former was represented by the Persian supreme god Ahura Mazda, the latter by the evil spirit Ahriman. Both were assisted by divine

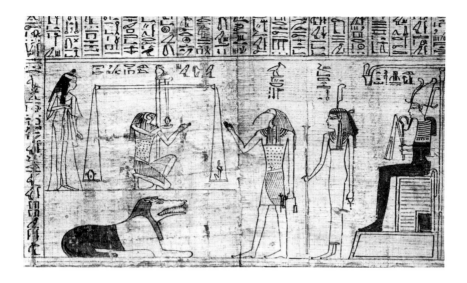

Figure 5.4 The Judgement of the Dead: illustration from the book of the dead of Tahurit, twenty-first dynasty, *c.* 1000 BC

Notes: From right to left: Osiris, the king and supreme judge of the underworld, bearing the insignia of a king; Maat, the goddess of cosmic order, truth and justice, recognisable by the feather on her head; the ibis-headed Thoth, the scribe of the gods and the moon-god, accompanies the deceased into the presence of Osiris; the falcon-headed Horus keeps an eye on the balance's plummet; the dead woman Tahurit. The left pan of the balance, with an urn containing the heart of the deceased, and the right pan, with a figurine representing Maat, must be in balance. If they are out of balance, the deceased will be torn up by the monster at the bottom of the scene and will die a second death: total destruction. This illustration, in which the pans are shown in balance, was intended to magically prevent this. Note the Egyptian custom of portraying human beings with the face, hips and feet in profile and the eyes and shoulders in frontal view.

Sources: Rijksmuseum van Oudheden, Leiden.

helpers ('angels and devils'). Human beings partook of the struggle between the two by following one of them.

Zoroaster's teachings ('Zoroastrianism') were not immediately accepted in Persia; on the contrary, they met with a good deal of opposition. From time immemorial, the Persians had worshipped many other gods besides their supreme god Ahura Mazda, of whom Anahita (the goddess of the waters that bring fertility) and Mithras (the god of light and truth) were the most important. When Zoroastrianism ultimately became the state religion of Persia after all, those lesser gods were degraded to Ahura Mazda's assistants. However, this was not to take place until much later, probably during the Sasanian era (cf. p. 274): here, too, the renunciation of polytheism proved a difficult step. The arrival of Islam in Persia in the seventh century AD soon pushed Zoroastrianism into the background. Nevertheless, several tens of thousands of adherents of this religion are still to be found in Iran today. Among them are also the 'Parsees' of India.

CHAPTER SIX

ECONOMY AND SOCIETY

Agricultural economy, land tenure
'Redistribution economy'
Means of payment
Trade
Social organisation

AGRICULTURAL ECONOMY, LAND TENURE

Throughout the whole history of the ancient Near East, agriculture formed the basis of the economy. Crop cultivation and animal husbandry were the main subsistence activities. Landed property was the principal form of wealth. Merchants, too, eagerly invested their profits in land. In the ancient Near East the temple and the palace were the chief landowners, but at all times there were also private landowners. In Sumer, the principal landowner was originally the temple, which was also the administrative centre of the city in which it stood. At some point however, a separate leader (the king) emerged from the temple administration and established himself in a palace with his own landed property. The palace and the temple were never entirely independent of one another: it was the king who built the temples and the king also participated in important rituals (see p. 49). Sometimes conflicts would arise between the temple and the palace if, for example, the king deprived the temple of some of its possessions or took over the administration of the temple's possessions. In Egypt there were also temple estates and palace estates, but it was often difficult to distinguish between the two because formally all the land belonged to the (divine) king, while the temple was in fact a state enterprise managed by the king. In periods of weak central authority the temples sometimes acquired independence.

'Redistribution economy'

Everywhere in the ancient Near East (including Crete and Mycenae) the economy revolved around the vast palace and temple households. The Near Eastern economy was entirely different from the classical Greek and Roman economy. Egypt had what is known as a redistribution economy, controlled by the palace. Via taxes, the state collected the population's farming surpluses, which it then redistributed in the form of allowances for priests and officials, wages for the builders of the royal tombs, gifts for temples, members of the royal household and the harem, etc. At the very bottom of this system was the Egyptian farmer, who had to support himself with the products of his own plot of land; he could augment his livelihood via barter.

The economy of the Mesopotamian temple and palace domains was based on a similar redistribution system. In early dynastic Sumer the temple was the chief landowner. Part of the land was exploited by the temple's own staff, part was granted to the people employed by the temple and part was leased. The people employed by the temple were paid in food rations, too. Besides farms, the temple domains also included workshops where specialised craftsmen worked. Over the ages, the palace gradually became more important; by the time of the Third Dynasty of Ur the state dominated the entire economy, including that of the temples.

After the collapse of the Third Dynasty of Ur there were more options for private land tenure, but the palace and the temple nevertheless remained the principal landowners until the Parthian period (around the beginning of the Christian era).

Diagram 6.1   Model of a palace economy

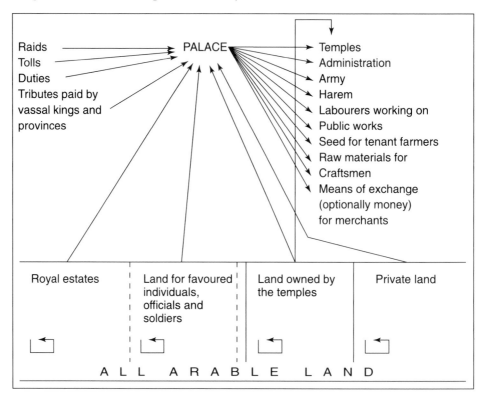

The above diagram gives an impression of how a palace economy functioned. This of course varied from one state to another and from one period to another owing to variations in political conditions. For a start, the relationship between the temple and the palace was always a delicate affair. Sometimes the temple enjoyed a high degree of independence, for example at the beginning of the Early Dynastic period in Sumer; at other times, such as during the reigns of the kings of the Third Dynasty of Ur and in the neo-Babylonian and Persian periods, the temple's activities were entirely controlled by the palace. In Egypt the pharaoh was the high priest and the ultimate authority of all of the temples; the temple was in fact a state enterprise. There were also differences in the ratios of landed property. In Early Dynastic Sumer, for example, the greater part of the land seems to have belonged to the temple; by the time of the reigns of the kings of Akkad and the Third Dynasty of Ur the state had apparently gained control over a larger proportion of the land, whereas a substantial part of the arable land was held in private tenure in the old Babylonian period. We have no exact data on the different ratios. What also varied were the payments made by the palace. Sometimes the palace would grant the people it employed plots of land for their sustenance; at other times it would favour payment in the form of food rations.

In actual fact, the domains of the kings, temples and private persons constituted individual centres of small-scale redistribution economies aiming at autarky.

As for the tolls and duties, they did not always have to be paid: sometimes the king would grant certain temples, officials or private persons (for example, the inhabitants of privileged cities) exemption from taxation.

The clay tablets on which the records of the numerous local offices and depots were kept show that the state concerned itself with all fields of the economy.

Means of payment

In societies without coined money, like those of the ancient Near East, plots of land and food rations were important means of remuneration. High-ranking officials were often granted vast estates for their sustenance. The palace also used land as a means for paying soldiers for military service, for example in the Old Babylonian period. When those soldiers then set out on campaigns, they would lease their land. The land granted to soldiers was not exempt from taxation. A similar system existed in the Assyrian, Persian and Seleucid empires and in pharaonic and Ptolemaic Egypt. After the introduction of the war chariot (*c.* 1600), charioteers were granted extra large plots of land; their horses and chariots were also provided by the state – a custom that was later to be adopted in Mycenaean Greece (see p. 27) and Rome (see p. 158), too.

For traders, the possibility of using fixed means of payment and units of account is of great importance. Pure barter involves many practical drawbacks. Grain, silver, gold, tin and copper have at one time or another all served as means of payment, in fixed units of weight. Units of weight of those materials were also used to express the value of goods. Over the ages, units of particular weights of silver (in Mesopotamia) and copper (in Egypt) gradually evolved into proper means of payment. In the eighth and seventh centuries, the kings of Syria, Assyria and Lydia started to provide lumps of precious metal of a fixed weight with badges. They are regarded as the first coins. They were however exclusively intended for use in social and political spheres (gift exchange). It was not until over a century later that coins acquired a commercial function, first of all in the Greek world. In the Near East, money in coin was introduced only in the Persian era, in particular during the reign of Darius I, when coins started to be used on a limited scale in the western parts of the empire. In those early days a coin's value was still largely dependent on its silver content and its weight.

TRADE

The fact that the economy was based on agriculture does not mean that there was no need for trade. Egypt and Mesopotamia lacked important resources like timber, copper and tin. Excavations have demonstrated the existence of trade contacts spanning long distances, from Asia Minor to Iran, already in pre- and proto-historic times.

However, throughout antiquity, trade was fraught with great dangers, especially trade via land, owing to the poor and slow means of transport and the risk of robbery. Goods intended for trade had to be light, non-perishable and costly if they were to yield profits. Large volumes of goods (such as grain) could only be efficiently transported by ship. It was too expensive to transport goods over distances of more than 50 miles by land because the draught and pack animals (mules) that were used for that purpose were slow and had to be fed, which implied extra costs.

In view of the great risks and investments involved in trade, and as the products that were transported were usually costly, it is not surprising that the majority of the earliest commercial enterprises were commissioned and 'financed' by the wealthiest institutions – the temple and the palace. That does not imply that the merchants were employed by the temple or the palace. We know that in the Old Babylonian empire, merchants managed a treasury jointly with the palace, in which both had deposited silver as opening capital. Thanks to the discovery of an archive of some 18,000 clay tablets at Kanesh in Asia Minor we are also well informed about ancient Assyrian trade. Although the Assyrians had no political power in Kanesh there was a trading quarter populated by Assyrian merchants in that city. The Assyrian government concluded commercial treaties with the rulers of Kanesh. Already, in those early days (c. 1900 BC), customs were in use that were quite similar to modern banking practices. For example, people were already using transferable acknowledgements of debt payable to bearer. Archives of private enterprises that specialised in trade, lease activities, the granting of loans and the exploitation of land have survived from the neo-Babylonian and Persian eras. The Phoenician cities maintained trade contacts with countries in other parts of the Mediterranean and they consequently also played an important part in spreading knowledge of the cultures of the ancient Near East to those countries.

SOCIAL ORGANISATION

All the societies of the ancient Near East were stratified, that is, a distinction was made between different groups of people on the basis of birth, wealth and status. Almost everywhere the king was at the top of the social hierarchy. Under the king were groups of high- and lower-ranking officials who enjoyed the emoluments associated with their offices. In some periods, only the members of a social elite were admitted to the administrative posts, but in times when the king enjoyed powerful authority, persons who were not members of that elite were sometimes also appointed to those posts.

The ordinary population consisted of groups that differed from one another in terms of wealth or in the kinds of work they did. From the earliest written sources we know that families and private persons owned tradeable land and that in those early days there was already a considerable range of widely varying professions. It is not so easy to classify the population on the basis of social position. What complicates the picture is that one person could simultaneously own private land, exploit a plot of land that the palace had granted him as a fief in exchange for military service, and additionally lease land from a private person. Whether a person owned land or leased it from another tells us little about that person's status.

Finally, there was also a distinction between free men and slaves. Freedom was a relative concept in the ancient Near East, because everyone was essentially a slave to

Diagram 6.2 Labour force

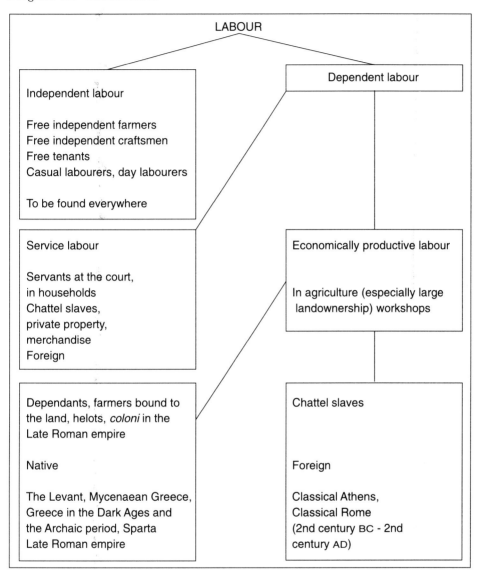

the king. However, there was also a group of people who can be termed slaves proper. That group can be further subdivided on the basis of the different kinds of slavery that existed in those days. The kind of slaves who were treated as merchandise enjoyed the least freedom. That category consisted of people who had been made slaves after being taken captive in wars or in raids. They were consequently usually foreigners.

Some people were reduced to slavery by debts. A debtor who was unable to pay his debts became his creditor's property for a certain period of time or for the rest of his life. Those slaves usually enjoyed more rights and their position was legally defined. Hammurabi's famous law code (*c.* 1750 BC) restricted the term of debt slavery to three years, the laws of the Israelites to a maximum of six years. However, not everyone abided by those laws (cf. slavery in Greece, p. 90, and in Rome, p. 167). Some parents sold their children as slaves, especially to the temples. That was one way in which poor people could ensure a livelihood for their children.

Slaves were used for all kinds of tasks, varying from estate management to work in the mines. Many performed household duties. At no point in the history of the ancient Near East did slavery however assume the importance it was later to have in classical Greece and Rome.

The prisoners of war who were not killed were often forced to work in the temples or palaces. Their status could then vary from that of a household slave to that of a kind of tenant farmer or craftsman, who was granted land and/or food rations for his sustenance. Landowners, temples and palaces preferably employed free tenants to till their land. Even if they had slaves, they would often grant them lease contracts for the tilling of their land. Large domains sometimes included entire villages. Their occupants were not slaves – they were not tradeable merchandise – but they were not free to do as they pleased either. From Assyrian and Seleucid sources we know that any people living on a plot of land that was sold to a new owner were included in the sale agreement. Small-time landowners tilled their land themselves or with the help of their families; they couldn't afford slaves.

From Hammurabi's law code we know that not everyone was equal before the law. Punishments varied from severe to quite light, depending on whether the offence in question had been committed against a court official, a common subject or a slave.

GOVERNMENT

KINGSHIP

Throughout almost the entire history of the ancient Near East, kingship was the normal form of government. Peoples who were not ruled by kings were considered barbaric. According to Mesopotamian tradition, kingship, like other expressions of human civilisation, had come down to earth from heaven.

The main functions of the king were those of military commander, supreme judicial authority and high priest. Most kings accompanied their armies to the battle-field in person. Some scholars maintain that kingship came into being with the appointment of the first military commander. The king also administered justice, either in person or via judges who pronounced legal decisions on his behalf. Many codes of law set up by Near Eastern kings have survived. The best known is that of Hammurabi, but we also have codes of law from Ur (*c.* 2100 BC), Assyria and the Hittite empire. The laws of Israel laid down in the Old Testament are different in that they were not formulated by kings, but by priests.

Most of these law codes are casuistically formulated: an introductory clause starting with 'when' describes a case (*casus*), an offence, while the main clause stipulates the punishment. From this we can infer that these codes of law are actually written reports of legal decisions – a form of case law. The Roman legal system also included this form of law.

The king's function in religious practices has already been discussed in Chapter 5, on religion.

Most kings had absolute power, but in some periods the king had to consider the opinions of councils of elders and/or free citizens. This is believed to have been the case in Early Dynastic Sumer, in Assyria before the Amorite *coup d'etat* in 1800, in the old Hittite kingdom and in some Phoenician cities. A typical phenomenon is that the checks to the king's authority decreased as his kingdom expanded. This same phenomenon is also observable in the history of the expansion of the Roman empire.

THE ADMINISTRATIVE MACHINERY

In administrative matters the king was assisted by officials, who were usually paid in land for their services. That land frequently became hereditary property – a development that implied a serious threat to the king as it gave his officials the means and opportunity to act on their own authority (e.g. as happened at the end of the Old Kingdom in Egypt). Assyrian kings successfully minimised the risk of this taking place by rigorously dismissing high officials and reclaiming their land and by appointing many eunuchs as their officials.

The administration of a large empire, that is, a state including vast foreign territories over which it has acquired supremacy, involved special problems. A distinction can be made between an empire's heartland and its peripheries – the regions brought under the heartland's sway. In the ancient Near East the latter regions were usually governed as either vassal states or provinces. When a state was made a vassal state its king was allowed to remain in power, provided that he promised to give allegiance to the king who had defeated him, renounce foreign

Figure 7.1 Part of the black obelisk of Shalmaneser III, king of Assyria 869–824 BC
Notes: King Jehu of Israel lies prostrate at the feet of Shalmaneser and offers him tribute. The cuneiform text reads: 'Tribute of Jehu (Ia-u-a), the son of Omri (Hu-um-ri-i)'.

Omri founded a dynasty in Israel, but Jehu did not belong to that dynasty. The expression literally means 'Jehu of Omri-country'. Countries were often described in this manner. The relief clearly reflects the relation between the king, represented as a large figure, and a vassal ruler, shown as a smaller figure.
Source: British Museum, London.

politics and pay tribute. The kings of the Hittite empire transformed many subject states into vassal states (see p. 25) and so did the kings of Mitanni, Egypt (its possessions in Syria and Palestine) and those of the neo-Assyrian empire. However, if a vassal ruler rose against the king or failed to pay the due tributes or if a newly appointed vassal ruler proved disloyal, the king would reduce that ruler's territory to a province and place it under the authority of a governor whom he himself appointed.

The practice of reducing vassal states to provinces became increasingly common after the reign of the Assyrian king Tiglath-Pileser III (745–727) and was continued in the neo-Babylonian, Persian and Hellenistic eras. It had however been applied much earlier already: the kings of the empires of Akkad (c. 2300 BC) and Ur (c. 2100) had already appointed officials to act as governors of the regions they conquered. Well-organised empires, such as the neo-Assyrian and Persian empires, appointed stationary or itinerant inspectors who were to keep a close watch on the governor's activities and report anything out of the ordinary to the central authority.

Sometimes provinces would come to form such integral parts of the empire that the distinction between the heartland and the peripheral districts became blurred. This could happen, for example, when provinces were treated in the same manner as the heartland, and a uniform culture embracing the whole of the empire was created. The history of the Roman empire presents excellent examples of such a development (see pp. 236ff and 277). In the Near East this development was greatly encouraged by the mass deportations that generally took place whenever a state was transformed into a province. It was usually the top layers of a society and the craftsmen who were deported on those occasions. They were granted land in the heartland or in the newly annexed provinces. Some were enrolled in the army; they were then granted land in exchange for their services. The deportees were relatively loyal towards their new ruler, out of gratitude for their newly acquired position and because of the vulnerability of that position – for the original population viewed the arrival of these newcomers with disfavour. Some deportees were less fortunate. They were set to work on major building projects in the capitals or were presented to temples or private persons as slaves. The neo-Assyrian king Tiglath-Pileser III and his immediate successors are particularly notorious for their mass deportations.

The later Assyrian kings made less use of this policy; the numbers of people who were deported from their homelands also gradually decreased. However, deportation continued to be used as a means of oppression until the Hellenistic era. In the neo-Babylonian, Persian, Seleucid and Parthian eras, the deportees managed to retain their identity for quite some time. Some communities even had their own governments; there were for example self-governing communities of Egyptians, Syrians, Phrygians, Lydians and, in particular, Jews. From time to time groups of exiles were allowed to return to their home countries. The best documented example is the return of the Jews from their exile during the Persian era.

One of the main motivations for expansion was undoubtedly the lure of riches in the form of booty and tributes. Lists of spoils taken in raids and tributes make up large parts of the royal inscriptions, especially those of the Assyrian kings. Exemption from taxation was a great privilege. In the Assyrian empire, only the ceremonial capital near Assur and sometimes a few highly respected other cities in the empire, such as Babylon, were granted this privilege. In the Persian empire the heartland, Persis, was exempt from taxation. Some important trading centres, such as the Phoenician cities, were allowed a fairly high degree of autonomy because the large imperialistic states realised that it was in their own interest, too, that those cities continued to thrive. In the first place, they would benefit from those cities' wealth via the taxes they imposed, and secondly, goods that were of importance to them, too, were imported via those cities. When the Phoenician cities were incorporated in the Persian empire they became important bases for the Persian fleet. In the Seleucid era, too, exceptions were made for certain cities, in particular Greek cities (see pp. 136ff.). A king who violated the – often time-honoured – privileges of such cities was bound to meet with difficulties. The practice of granting the heartland exemption from direct taxation where possible remained customary throughout the whole history of the ancient world. It was also applied in Athens (p. 103) and Rome (p. 186).

THE ARMY

Wars evolved from minor skirmishes concerning territorial issues and raids aimed at securing means of support into organised expeditions with the objective of permanent occupation of the invaded territory. The size of the army increased accordingly.

For a long time war was a seasonal affair. The ordinary, peasant population was called up to fight in a war but had to be back home in time to harvest their crops. Over the ages, the army gradually evolved into an institution. Of great importance with respect to this development was the introduction, around the end of the Late Bronze Age (1600–1200), of the custom of awarding soldiers land and supporting an elite of charioteers. From the end of the eighth century, the Assyrians had a standing army that enabled them to engage in warfare all the year round, although they continued to levy troops from the farming population on a seasonal basis, too.

In the Persian era, more and more use started to be made of mercenaries besides native soldiers. Large empires were unable to levy sufficient troops from their own population and so the subject peoples had to supply contingents to reinforce the army.

A final noteworthy phenomenon is that already, in these early days, military innovations such as the war chariot spread fast, and were quickly adopted in all the regions where they were introduced.

PART II

GREECE

CHAPTER EIGHT

THE DARK AGES,
1200–800 BC

The fall of Mycenaean civilisation (*c.* 1200, see p. 32) had far-reaching consequences. The strictly organised palace economy collapsed completely and was never to re-emerge. The Linear B script that had been used for the palaces' administration passed into oblivion; the Greeks of later centuries used a totally different form of writing. Linear B was rediscovered only at the end of the nineteenth century, when tablets inscribed with the script came to light in excavations. The meaning of the tablets was, however, to remain a mystery for several more years, awaiting the deciphering of the script in 1952. The Mycenaean cities that had enjoyed such wealth and luxury in the centuries preceding the fall were destroyed, never to be rebuilt. Many of their occupants fled to the west coast of Asia Minor. This movement of people is also known as the 'Ionian migration'. The Greeks who settled in Ionia were later to contribute greatly to the revival of Greek culture. The population of Greece itself shrank drastically and its once so splendid material culture became severely impoverished. The beginning of Greece's dark ages is also the time of the invasion of the Dorians, who settled in the Peloponnese, on Crete and in the southwest of Asia Minor.

We are poorly informed about the social structure in the dark ages. Most of what we do know has been inferred from archaeological evidence and the 'Iliad' and the 'Odyssey', the great epic works that are attributed to the poet Homer (*c.* 750 BC). The 'Iliad' describes an episode from the war that a group of Greek kings (among whom was Agamemnon of Mycenae) waged against the city of Troy – or Ilion, as it was also known – in northwest Asia Minor. The 'Odyssey' tells the story of the adventures of Odysseus, the king of the island of Ithaca, on his journey home after the destruction of Troy. These epics are based on ancient tales that were recited by bards at the courts of kings and noblemen. The Trojan War was assumed to have taken place at the height of Mycenae's wealth and power, but the society described by Homer bears very little resemblance to the society known to us from the Linear B tablets; it is, instead, substantially a reflection of the world in Homer's own time and preceding centuries. In Homeric society a king was not a leader in a palace economy associated with an extensive city life, but a wealthy landowner who was the *primus inter pares*, the first among equals, in times of war. His peers were the heads of large agricultural households. All military power rested with these nobles, because they could afford to arm themselves. They would ride out to battlefields on horseback, to then descend to fight their opponents in individual duels. The rest of the population had virtually no part whatsoever in military affairs. The values of this aristocracy had a profound influence on Greek mentality. The nobles were expected to protect their households, and therefore they had to show themselves to be strong, able-bodied men. The competitive element inherent in this ideology also found expression in games. Well known, for example, are the Olympic Games which were organised for the first time in 776 BC.

CHAPTER NINE

THE ARCHAIC PERIOD, 800–500 BC

INTRODUCTION

The eighth century BC saw the first of a series of important changes which marked out a new course in the history of the civilisation of Greece. What was to follow was not a revival of the former Mycenaean culture but the emergence of an entirely new culture, with a character all of its own. The individual character of this culture does not imply that Greece was at this time an isolated area, cut off from contacts with the outside world. The Archaic period in Greece coincides with the era of the great empires of the Levant with their age-old cultures – the neo-Assyrian, neo-Babylonian and Persian empires, all of which lay fairly close to Greece. It was in the Archaic period, too, that the Greek trading post Naukratis was established in Egypt (*c.* 650 BC) and that the Greeks in Asia Minor came into contact with Lydia and Phrygia. In this same period even the Greek cities in Asia Minor were to come under Persian control, when Cyrus conquered that area in 547 BC (see p. 42). Sea-borne trade was in these days in the hands of the Phoenicians, who traded their goods in Greece, too. Seen against this background, it is not surprising that Greek religion, art, science and material culture betray various Eastern influences.

As mentioned above, the Archaic period was a time of great changes – cultural changes, but also demographic, economic, social and military changes. These changes, which were all closely related, and influenced one another, were ultimately to bring about the peculiarly Greek constitutions of the succeeding, Classical period.

DEMOGRAPHIC AND ECONOMIC CHANGES

Archaeological research has shown that the Greek population increased explosively in the eighth century. This meant that more mouths had to be fed and that necessitated great changes in farming practices. Farmers started to concentrate more on crop cultivation, at the expense of stock-keeping for which too much land was required. Waste land was brought under cultivation and the range of crops was expanded.

Some Greeks took to the sea, hoping to make a living through piracy or trade. It is noteworthy in this context is that whereas in Homer's works (*c.* 750) seafaring traders are still all Phoenicians, the slightly younger poet Hesiod (*c.* 700) already mentions overseas trade contacts maintained by Greeks (such as his own father).

A third consequence of the growth in population was the development of cities, as a result of the fusion of expanding villages. These cities were ideal outlets for the landowners' increased agricultural produce. It was via these cities, too, that the luxury goods from the Near East which were coveted by the wealthy elite were imported into Greece. Many noblemen consequently took up residence in the cities.

The polis

The eighth century is also the century of the birth of the polis. A *polis* was a community with its own political organisation; the word 'political' is in fact derived from *polis*. The term *polis* is usually translated as 'city state'. A typical *polis* comprised a relatively small territory with an administrative centre, usually urban, which contained the chief sanctuary and a meeting place, the *agora*, where the magistrates and the people assembled when decisions were to be taken. Later on the *agora* came to serve as a marketplace, too. The town usually contained a fortified hill (*acropolis*), on which the occupants could take refuge in times of danger.

The *polis* was governed by officials with specific responsibilities, such as military leadership, jurisdiction or the supervision of religious practices, who were appointed in some kind of election. This does not mean that all the *poleis* had the same form of government. What they did have in common was that only very few were ruled by kings (Sparta was one of the few *poleis* where kingship was not abolished). In most *poleis* the noble landowners monopolised the political offices. We refer to them as 'noble' because they claimed their privileges by reason of birth; such a constitution is called an aristocracy (see Diagram 9.1, p. 91). The strong emphasis on high birth was probably connected with the increased importance of land tenure. In the ancient world, ownership of land was often justified by family claims to ancestral land. In Greece this had led to an outlook revolving around an *oikos* (household, comprising parents, children, grandchildren and sometimes also dependent farmers and slaves), which preferably belonged to an important *genos* (clan, lineage) that could boast descent from a famous ancestor.

The *polis* was of supreme importance to its occupants, who gradually became true *polis* citizens (Greek: *politai*). The status of *polis* citizen came to be more important than that of the member of a clan.

A principal concern of all *poleis* was 'freedom and autonomy' – the freedom from domination by a great power or by a different *polis*, which implied autonomy, that is, the possibility of making one's own laws.

The Greeks regarded life in a *polis* as the most ideal and most humane form of existence. The idea of being incorporated in a large empire was intolerable to them and they did everything within their power to prevent the risk of that ever happening. Their efforts were successful until 338 BC. When the Greeks were ultimately forced to succumb to the superior powers of the Macedonians and the Romans (see pp. 110 and 183), they tried to preserve their autonomy in local affairs where possible.

The *polis* was not the dominant political unit in the whole of Greece. In less-developed areas, tribal structures prevailed in the form of so-called *ethne* (plural of *ethnos*, which literally means 'nation'): groups of small communities that joined forces in special circumstances, in particular in military operations. Sometimes cities were formed within these *ethne*, which later developed into *poleis*. Ancient Greece never achieved political union. The Greeks did however feel united by their common language (even though it included various dialects, such as Doric in Sparta and the southwest of Asia Minor, and Ionic in Athens and the western part of Asia Minor), by their worship of the same gods and by their communal traditions, such as the Olympic Games which were organised at Olympia in honour of Zeus, the supreme god of the Greek pantheon.

The Greek world showed a marked resemblance to Phoenicia, whose towns were also independent, autonomous city states and whose occupants likewise shared a common language and religion. The Greeks in fact borrowed much from the Phoenicians, including their alphabet and many of their artistic motifs. They may well have got the idea of living together in *poleis* from the Phoenicians also. Something else in which the Phoenicians showed the Greeks the way was colonisation. The settlements that the Phoenicians founded in the western Mediterranean (see p. 33) served as good examples to the Greeks in their search for a solution to their demographic problem.

Colonisation

In an economy as primitive as that of Greece the measures mentioned above were not effective enough to generate sufficient food for the country's growing population, and Greece hence became 'over-populated'. Many people responded to the increased population pressure by going in search of a new world. That marked the beginning of the Greeks' well-known colonising movement. The very fact of the foundation of the Greek colonies presupposes a certain amount of experience in trade and shipping and knowledge of the geography of the Mediterranean. It is therefore believed that the first of the Greeks' overseas settlements – Al Mina in Syria, Cumae in southern Italy, Naukratis in Egypt – were established for commercial reasons. The main stimulus to the colonising movement was, however, hunger for land. The majority of the colonists settled as farmers in the fertile areas along the shores of the Black Sea, in Sicily and southern Italy (see Map 9.1a). The latter two areas in fact attracted so many Greek settlers that they were collectively known as *Magna Graecia* ('Greater Greece') in antiquity. Large, flourishing Greek cities arose in those areas, some of which are still important towns today, preserving the relics of their glorious past. Impressive remains of Greek architecture can be admired for example in Syracuse, Naples, Taranto and Paestum (Poseidonia; see Map 9.1b).

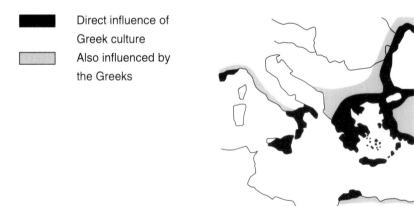

Direct influence of Greek culture

Also influenced by the Greeks

Map 9.1a Influence of Greek culture in the Archaic and Classical periods, *c.* 600–330 BC
Note: During the Greek colonising movement Greeks spread over large parts of the Mediterranean and many peoples came into contact with Greek civilisation.

- •   Greek mother cities
- ·   Greek colonies
- ★   Phoenician mother cities
- ☆   Phoenician colonies
- □   Carthaginian colonies

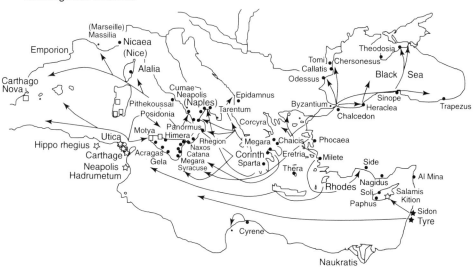

Map 9.1b   Greek and Phoenician colonisation

The term 'colonisation' is actually misleading. A Greek colony (*apoikia*) was not a foreign territory governed by the city that founded the colony, but a new, independent *polis*, which was bound to its mother city only by moral and religious ties. It is hence not surprising that the Greek colonists, in their search for suitable locations for these independent *poleis*, steered clear of areas containing well-organised states, such as the Levant, Egypt and Etruscan Italy (see p. 152). The settlements that the Greeks did establish in the latter areas, such as Naukratis in Egypt and Al Mina in Syria, were not independent *poleis*.

Although most colonies were not founded for commercial reasons, they did encourage trade. Trade was very important for the Greeks as it enabled them to obtain grain, which was in short supply in Greece, from areas where it grew in great abundance. Corinth imported most of her grain from her colonies in Sicily while Athens, which founded only very few colonies, obtained her grain mainly from the regions surrounding the Black Sea. Once food could be imported from overseas, the impulse to further colonisation slackened. The Greeks' quest for new land came to an end almost completely around 550 BC, when their colonisation campaigns met with increasing opposition from the Persians, Carthaginians and Etruscans.

The waste land that was brought under cultivation in Greece was used to grow new crops, such as olive trees. Sealed in earthenware vessels, the products of these crops (olive oil) could be exported. And indeed, we note a considerable increase in pottery production in this period. Trade greatly boosted industry in the cities: ships had to be built and earthenware vessels had to be produced to enable the transport of the new products. The young *poleis* also vied with each other in building bigger and bigger temples. All this activity implied a good deal of extra work for those not involved in agriculture. It did not, however, lead to a contrast between an urban and a rural population. Most city-dwellers were farmers whose land lay outside the town. They left the town every morning to till their fields or they had a member of their families, a slave or a tenant, do the work for them. Throughout the whole history of the ancient world there were only very few cities that, because of the majority of their inhabitants were not engaged in agriculture, were dependent on imports from regions with surplus grain. This was the case only in extremely large cities such as Athens in the fifth century, Alexandria in Egypt and Antioch in Syria in the Hellenistic period (see pp. 111, 130, 136) and Rome around the beginning of the Christian era.

SOCIAL CHANGES

The economic and demographic developments described above had social consequences too. In the first place, they led to the emergence of a group of *nouveaux riches* – people who had managed to make a fortune in one way or another. Some had grown rich through trade; they often invested their profits in land. Others had had the foresight to start growing new crops in the relatively infertile soil of their land. These crops were more profitable than barley or other cereals per unit of land.

For the old-fashioned small farmers struggling to remain self-sufficient, however, things became increasingly difficult. Their family property had to be split up amongst their children with every new generation, and as the population expanded the lots became smaller and smaller until they were ultimately too small to support a farmer and his family. The small farmers were, moreover, unable to switch over to the new crops: olive trees do not bear fruit for the first few years after they have been planted and the farmers did not have the necessary resources to tide themselves over the years without income. Nor did they have any surplus land on which they could have grown other crops besides cereals. Many small farmers had to take out loans as they did not produce sufficient surplus grain to sow their next crop. But as their crops didn't become any bigger and they nevertheless had to repay their loans, most of them were reduced to debt-bondage, having secured their loans on their person as was customary in those days.

Military changes

In the 'dark ages' only the noble elite had engaged in warfare (see p. 70). This changed in the Archaic period, when the *nouveaux riches* and middling farmers could also afford to equip themselves with armour. That armour comprised a helmet, a breast plate, greaves, a spear and a shield. The latter, which was in this period attached to the (left) arm at two points, at the hand and at the elbow, was of particular importance. The soldiers were called 'hoplites' after *hoplon*, the Greek word for this shield. Most of these hoplites did not possess a horse, but that was no disadvantage in a battle, as the horsemen always descended from their horses to fight. The hoplites did not fight in single combat as the nobles had done, but in a body in close array known as a *phalanx*. The hoplites had to ensure that the ranks remained closed so that the unprotected right sides of their bodies were covered by their neighbours' shields. This called for a strong sense of solidarity. See Figure 10.5a.

Wars in the Archaic period were nothing more than small-scale border conflicts. As the main objective was usually plunder, they were over after one or two clashes. Sometimes there were long periods without any actual fighting in wars between *poleis*.

CULTURAL CHANGES

It was in the Archaic period, too, that the foundations for Greece's great cultural achievements were laid. Greek painting, architecture and sculpture, the literary genres, religious imagery and cult practices and, last but not least, Greek philosophy all have their roots in the Archaic period. It is in these cultural achievements that Greece's indebtedness to the Near East is particularly evident.

The alphabet

A first major cultural asset that originated in the Near East is the alphabet, which the Greeks borrowed from the Phoenicians in the tenth century BC (see p. 33ff). The Greeks introduced an important innovation however: they adapted this alphabet, which consisted exclusively of consonants, for their own language by using some of the existing characters for vowels and adding a number of new characters. The resultant alphabet proved extremely efficient. After only a few minor modifications it was adopted by the Etruscans and later also the Romans, who ultimately passed it down to us. Today, that same alphabet is still being used for writing in numerous different languages all over the world. For what purpose the alphabet was introduced into Greece is not entirely certain. It may well be that the Phoenicians were the people with whom the Greeks first came into contact when they ventured overseas in search of trade, and that the alphabet was introduced for business purposes.

Literature

Whatever the reason for the introduction of the alphabet may have been, the oldest pieces of Greek writing known to us are literary texts. These texts were, however, not intended to be read by a wide public; they were written down so that they could be memorised and recited. That is why the oldest texts are all in verse, whether they are epics, like the works of Homer (*c.* 750 BC) and Hesiod (*c.* 700 BC), political pamphlets, such as those of Solon (see p. 89), or the works of the earliest philosophers (see p. 85).

Homer was of tremendous importance to the Greeks. His epics, the 'Iliad' and the 'Odyssey' (see also p. 70), were regarded as a kind of Bible. The study of those epics was a compulsory part of Greek education until well into the Hellenistic age. The world that is described in these works is that of the nobility in the dark ages.

Homer's representation of the competitive mentality of the nobles and his portrayals of the gods as superior anthropomorphic beings with the same mentality as the aristocracy had a profound influence on Greek thought and religion.

Thanks to Hesiod we know something about the lower classes of early Greek society. His epos 'Works and Days' presents a picture of contemporary farming practices and describes the harshness of a farming existence. In this work we also learn about the injustice that the farmers suffered at the hands of the nobles, whose bribery and extortion Hesiod criticises. In his 'Theogony' Hesiod systematised the legends about the gods of the Greek pantheon (see below, p. 85, for a further discussion).

Greek literature after Homer is characterised by a trend towards greater individualism. Whereas we know nothing whatsoever about the man who wrote the 'Iliad' and the 'Odyssey', the later author Hesiod already tells us something about his personal circumstances. But it was not until after about 700 that Greek poetry began to strike a truly personal note, with short lyrical poems conveying the poet's deepest feelings. That is also when the first Greek love lyrics were written. Other poems express views on society, varying from criticism of the aristocratic way of life to fear of the aristocracy losing its power.

The visual arts

Our knowledge of Greek painting is almost entirely restricted to vase painting. The Mycenaean form of pottery decoration disappeared within a very short time in the dark ages. The ninth century saw the birth of a new style of vase painting in Athens, characterised by zigzags and swastikas, to which stylised human figures were later added (see Figure 9.1a). The mythical creatures and plants of the style that began to take shape in Corinth around 725 BC betray affinities with the art of the East. Yellow is the predominant colour of this style, which is known as the Orientalising style (see Figure 9.1d). In the sixth century Athenian vase painters started to decorate their vases with figures painted in black silhouette. This 'black-figure' style was later superseded by the 'red-figure' style. The Attic vases depicting scenes from Greek mythology and everyday life were distributed over a very wide area. Thousands of these vases can still be admired in museums today (see Figures 9.1b and 9.1c).

The poses of the free-standing statues that have survived from the Archaic period suggest that the earliest Greek sculpture owed much to the sculpture of Egypt (see Figures 9.2a and 9.2b). However, it did not take the Greeks long to shake off these influences and develop an entirely original style of their own.

Architecture

Greek architecture also acquired many of its distinctive features in the Archaic period. The most impressive buildings were the temples, which, being the dwellings of the gods (and of their statues), were modelled on the dwellings of mortals. The most conspicuous aspect of their plans is the lavish use of Doric, Ionic and – from the fourth century onwards – Corinthian columns (see Figures 9.3a–9.3c). The best preserved Greek temples are to be found in southern Italy and Sicily (Fig. 10.13, p. 128).

Figure 9.1a Drinking beaker in the Geometric style, found in the 'Kerameikos', Athens' cemetery: eighth century BC
Source: Allard Pierson Museum, Amsterdam.

Figure 9.1b (below) Panathenaic amphora, *c.* 510 BC. Black-figure style
Notes: The scene represents a running contest. Filled with olive oil, this amphora was one of the prizes that could be won at the Panathenaic Games.
Source: Allard Pierson Museum, Amsterdam.

Figure 9.1c Oil flask from Athens, *c.* 465 BC. Red-figure style
Source: Allard Pierson Museum, Amsterdam.

Figure 9.1d Corinthian oil flask, *c.* 615 BC. Orientalising style
Notes: Note the sphinx. Winged mythical creatures, part man and part beast, were common motifs all over the ancient Near East. A well-known example is the large sphinx near the pyramids of Giza in Egypt. The sphinx was also represented in Phoenicia. See also the winged bull colossi of Assyria and Persia shown on p. 44.
Source: Allard Pierson Museum, Amsterdam.

Religion

Greek religion had much in common with ancient Near Eastern religion (cf. p. 48). In the first place it was a polytheistic religion. The gods, especially after Homer had described them in his epics, were seen as anthropomorphic beings; there was no official dogma; rites played an important part in establishing a good relationship with the gods; each city (*polis*) had its own patron god or – very often – goddess, whose temple stood on the *acropolis*, where the *polis*' religious ceremonies took place. The Greeks' views on death and the after-life showed close similarities with the Mesopotamian notion of a shadowy, sombre underworld, where more or less the same dire fate awaited all the souls of the deceased. Of a somewhat different nature was the Orphic movement in Greek religion. This mystery religion was based on the assumption that the body and

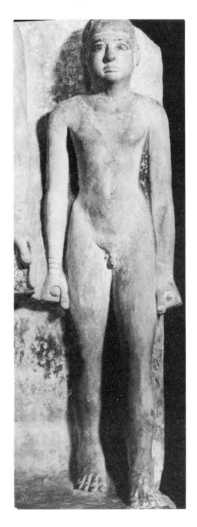

Figure 9.2a Egyptian sculpture of a nude male: Old Kingdom, 5th dynasty, *c.* 2400 BC.
From a private grave at Saqqara

Notes: Greek Archaic sculpture was clearly modelled on Egyptian examples. But whereas Egyptian sculpture remained virtually unchanged from the Old Kingdom until the Late Period, Greek sculpture underwent important developments, towards a more realistic representation of stances. See p. 119 for the sculpture of the Classical period and p. 139 for that of the Hellenistic era.

Source: Rijksmuseum van Oudheden, Leiden.

the soul were separate entities. The soul was believed to be imprisoned within the body, from which it could free itself after death, via reincarnation, asceticism and purification rites. This principle of the disunion of body and soul – and the resultant depreciation of the body – had a profound influence on the philosophers Pythagoras and Plato, and eventually became an important doctrine in Christianity, too.

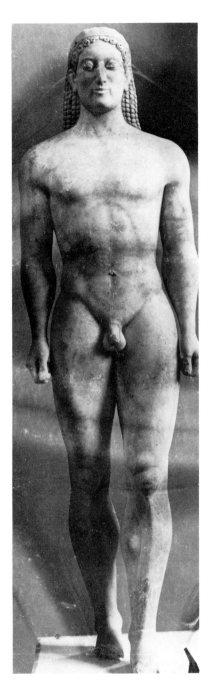

Figure 9.2b Archaic sculpture of a young man (*kouros*): probably sixth century BC, *c.* 530
Source: Athens National Museum.

The belief in a blissful life after death, at least for the initiates of the secret religious rites, held a central place in the mystic cult of the corn goddess Demeter at Eleusis (Demeter means 'mother earth'; she was already worshipped in the Mycenaean period). This cult celebrated the release of Persephone, Demeter's daughter, from Hades (the underworld), where she was imprisoned for one third of the year. Her rebirth symbolised the sprouting of the ear of corn from the dying corn grain.

A similar belief was associated with the death of Osiris in Egypt (see p. 50). A different natural phenomenon, the death of nature during the dry season, was symbolised in the cult of Adonis, a god of Phoenician origin (see p. 48). 'Adon', meaning 'Lord', was the term used by the Phoenicians to address their god Baal.

The Greek pantheon, whose gods featured in Greek myths and in sculpture and were worshipped in the official *polis* religion in the major temples, was essentially Homer's creation. Homer had represented the pantheon as a sublimated aristocratic society. His gods were formidable, beautiful, strong, immortal men and women with both the good and the bad qualities of mortals. In the Trojan war they assisted heroes in both camps. The best-known gods were, first of all, the supreme god Zeus, the god of thunder, who resided on Mount Olympus in northern Greece together with the other gods. His main sanctuary was at Olympia in the Peloponnese, where the Olympic Games were held in his honour every four years. His wife was Hera, the patroness of marriage. Zeus had a daughter Athena, the goddess of war and the arts and crafts, who was worshipped in Athens in particular. Apollo was the god of light and reason. Dionysus was the passionate god of wine, intoxication and the wild forces in nature. Sometimes the gods had sexual intercourse with mortals. Heracles (Roman Hercules) was born out of such a union between Zeus

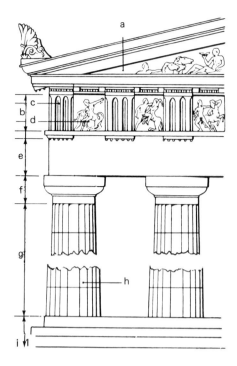

Figure 9.3a Doric order
Notes: a. tympanum; b. frieze; c. triglyphs; d. metope; e. architrave; f. capital. The differences between the three orders are most apparent in the capital; g. column; h. fluting; i. stylobate; j. volute; k. base; l. acanthus scrolls.

The Doric order originated in Greece, probably in the seventh century BC. A well-preserved Doric temple is to be found at Paestum in southern Italy. The Parthenon in Athens (fifth century) is another example of a Doric structure. The Ionic order was developed in Ionia (Asia Minor) and the Aegean islands, but was also used in Greece, for example for the little temple of Athena Nike on the acropolis in Athens. The Corinthian order is a little younger (end of the fifth century).

Greek architecture was widely imitated by the Romans. It had a profound influence on European and American architecture of later centuries, in particular that of the Renaissance (sixteenth century) and that of Classicism (end of the eighteenth century) and neo-Classicism (end of the nineteenth century).

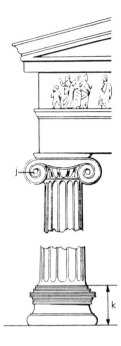

Figure 9.3b Ionic order

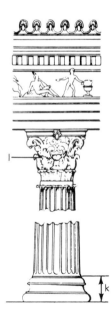

Figure 9.3c Corinthian order

and a mortal. He was venerated for his strength and his courageous Twelve Labours.

Our knowledge of the legends on the origins of the Greek gods we owe to Hesiod's 'Theogony', which has notable analogies in Mesopotamian, Phoenician and Hurrian-Hittite succession models. The legends of these models explain how the supreme god – Marduk, Baal and Teshup, respectively (Zeus in the Greek pantheon) – acquired his supremacy in struggles with the primordial deities (see p. 48). As no such genealogy is to be found in Homer it is most likely that Hesiod got the idea of recounting the history of the deities from Eastern examples, with which he may have become acquainted in the Greek settlement of Al Mina in Syria.

There were however also marked differences between the religious world of the Greeks and that of the ancient Near East. In the first place, the Greek temples never played such a central part in economic, cultural and administrative affairs as, for example, did the Sumerian temples. Nor did the Greek temples have large estates or a priesthood with the power to manipulate politics. The Greek myths that have come down to us did not originate in the temples either. Homer and Hesiod were laymen, who gave their personal interpretations of the gods on their own authority, although they do claim to have been inspired by the 'Muses', the daughters of Apollo who presided over the arts and literature.

Philosophy

Natural philosophy and physical science arose in the seventh century BC in Ionia in Asia Minor (at the periphery of the Eastern world) and in the Greek colonies in the west (southern Italy and Sicily). Some original minds in those areas no longer accepted the explanations for physical phenomena given in the myths (see p. 48). Instead, they tried to fathom the nature of the primal substance from which everything had evolved and to analyse processes in the natural world via logical reasoning. Very little of what these early philosophers committed to writing has come down to us. We would probably find their ideas rather naive today. They are, however, important in that they represent the first steps towards a new, rational way of analysing and explaining natural phenomena, which was to become the basis of Western scientific thought.

These thinkers did not repudiate the deities of their religion, but simply placed their findings alongside the traditional religious beliefs or tried to combine their ideas with the ancient myths. This approach brought the philosopher Xenophanes (sixth century) to a monotheistic, logically reasoned theology. Xenophanes believed that the gods of the myths were only helpers and different embodiments of the one supreme god. He criticised Homer's accounts of the gods' deeds, which he considered quite ribald. This view was to find increasing support among later Greeks and Romans, especially among the elite. It was only in the fifth century that a few philosophers approached a theology that denied the existence of the gods of the Greek pantheon. Anaxagoras (c. 500 – c. 428) and Democritus (c. 460 – c. 370) believed that everything ultimately consisted of indivisible parts, which Democritus called 'atoms'. Anaxagoras maintained that the movement of those parts was controlled by a divine spirit, the mover of the cosmos, but whether Democritus shared that opinion we do not know. Anaxagoras, then, came quite close to a mechanical, materialistic conception of the universe.

The most renowned philosopher in the Greek West was Pythagoras. He was born on the island of Samos, but emigrated to Croton in southern Italy around 531. He believed that the cosmos was logically composed of seven spheres according to certain numerical ratios; the lowest sphere was that of the earth. Knowledge of numbers and measures (mathematics) was the key to understanding the cosmos and nature. Pythagoras' belief that the human soul, which he saw as a separate entity, was imprisoned in a body at birth and moved on to another body after death, was inspired by Orphism.

Pythagoras was not only interested in studying order in nature; he also aspired to create order in the Greek cities in southern Italy. His followers, the Pythagoreans, developed a political philosophy which they attempted to implement in practice. Some Greek cities in southern Italy, such as Tarentum (present-day Taranto) in the fourth century BC, were indeed ruled by Pythagoreans for some time. They believed that the business of government was best left to wise, philosophically trained experts. The well-known Athenian philosopher Plato (see p. 122) counted several Pythagoreans among his friends.

POLITICAL CHANGES

The economic, social and military changes brought about political changes, too. The Archaic period saw the rise of new forms of government and of what was to become one of the most important legacies of the ancient world: Greek political thought.

The gradual crumbling of the economic and military basis on which the power of the nobility was founded ultimately led to the fall of the aristocracy in most *poleis*. This process started with demands for:

1 written legislation that would put an end to the aristocracy's arbitrary rule;
2 admission to the offices (this was demanded by the non-aristocratic wealthy citizens; they were in a position to make this demand because they had military power as hoplites);
3 cancellation of debts, abolition of debt-bondage and redistribution of land (demanded by the impoverished farmers and debt bondsmen).

Tyranny

Almost everywhere in Greece the fall of the aristocracy went hand in hand with the appearance of tyranny. The Greeks borrowed the word *tyrannos* from one of the languages of Asia Minor. It was originally used for an autocrat who had seized absolute control to which he was not officially entitled. A king could also become a 'tyrant', by assuming powers that transcended those of a *primus-inter-pares* king. This happened for example in Argos. The Greek tyrants were almost all members of aristocratic families who had come into conflict with other nobles. A case in point is Cypselus (c. 657–625), who, with the support of members of the lower ranks of the aristocracy and poorer citizens, took over control in Corinth, which had hitherto been ruled by a single noble family. Originally, 'tyranny' was a fairly neutral term. But as the new ruler was unable to justify his exceptional position of power his despotism soon became unpopular and consequently cruel. 'Tyrannical' then acquired a pejorative meaning. Very few city states were ruled by tyrants for longer than two generations. Their form of government was then replaced by an oligarchy or a democracy.

Sparta

In Sparta the hoplites put an end to the rule of the aristocracy. Sparta had already evolved into a hoplite state *par excellence* in the seventh century. Nevertheless, Sparta, which – unlike other Greek states – had two co-regent kings, did not institute a tyranny but maintained hereditary kingship. To be able to understand this we must first consider the unique composition of the population of the Spartan *polis*. Sparta was dominated by a group of Dorians who had subjected the city's native population during the dark ages. Of these Dorians, who were referred to by the Homeric term 'Lacedaemonians', the occupants of Sparta, or Spartiates, enjoyed full civil rights, whereas the occupants of the cities around Sparta, the *perioikoi*, had only local autonomy in their cities. The subject population had no rights whatsoever; they were called *helots*. The helots belonged to the state and are therefore also referred to as 'state slaves'. Their land had been split up and assigned to individual Spartiates, for whom they had to till that land. The Spartiates themselves did not work, but spent their entire lives in military training.

Like Athens, Sparta founded hardly any colonies. Instead, she stilled her hunger for land by conquering Messenia in two wars, between 700 and 600 BC. The Spartiates reduced the inhabitants of Messenia, who were also Dorians, to helots. This however meant that they then faced the difficult task of having to control a group of people who outnumbered them. This, and the constant threat of the fairly powerful Dorian neighbour state of Argos, with which the Spartiates were frequently at war over the hegemony of the Peloponnese, induced them to devote their full attention to military training. Spartan boys were taken from their mothers at the tender age of seven. From then onwards they were raised by the state. They were rigorously trained in the endurance of hardship and were turned into tough, strong men. When they reached manhood they joined a mess, whose members ate, trained, slept and fought together. Each Spartiate had to pay a contribution to his mess. The Spartiates were hence entirely dependent on a powerful militia for the preservation of their privileged position. As the aristocracy had not been very successful in the wars against Messenia and Argos, the hoplites had been able to get their own way in Sparta at a very early stage.

Sparta's reforms are attributed to the law-giver Lycurgus, a man about whom nothing is known with any certainty. Nowadays it is usually assumed that he introduced his political reforms after 700 BC. After Lycurgus, the Spartiates were referred to as *homoioi*, or 'equals'. This equality referred to their equal position in the hoplite *phalanx* and to their equal vote in the *apella*, the assembly to which only they had access. They may also have been assigned equal lots of land with groups of helots in Messenia. But in other respects the Spartiates were not entirely equal. For example, in addition to their land in Messenia they also owned private lots of land, and those lots differed in size. What also led to inequality was that some Spartiates neglected their farms by failing to keep their helots under strict control. Others, on the contrary, made a fortune from bribes, taxes and booty obtained abroad. Another popular way of becoming rich was by marrying an heiress of a well-to-do Spartan family that had produced no sons. These wealthy Spartiates forced up the contributions to the messes until the poorer ones could no longer afford to pay them. They were then reduced to the status of second-class citizens.

Sparta's public assembly never evolved into a truly democratic body. The real power was in the hands of the *gerousia*, a council of thirty men of at least sixty years of age who were chosen for life by the assembly. The readiness with which the assembly accepted the *gerousia*'s supremacy is understandable in a state in which military discipline was more highly esteemed than a critical mind. Sparta's two kings were also members of the *gerousia*; for them the age requirement of course did not apply. To return to the question of why kingship was retained in Sparta: as the two co-regent kings, who belonged to different royal families, balanced one another, there was never any risk of the kingship becoming very powerful. The kings' sole task was to command the army in wartime. In later times an additional magistracy was created alongside the monarchy. This was held by five *ephors* (overseers), who were chosen annually by the *apella*. They were responsible for the city's day-to-day administration. The creation of this additional magistracy probably helped to prevent calls for further democratic reforms because the ephors, who were supposed to represent the citizens' interests, counterbalanced the kings.

In the ancient world the Spartan constitution was highly esteemed for being a 'mixed constitution', comprising a monarchy (two kings), an oligarchy (the *gerousia*) and a democracy (the *apella* and the ephors). The strict Spartan lifestyle, which appeared to be the key to the city's success, was also greatly admired. In the sixth and the early fifth centuries BC Sparta was indisputably the most powerful city state in Greece.

Sparta was anxious to corroborate her hegemony in the Peloponnese but did not like the idea of doing so by conquering more cities and then having to control even more helots. In the sixth century she solved this problem by creating the Peloponnesian League, in which she united most city states in the Peloponnese, including Corinth, under her leadership. Argos did not join this league. Outside Greece, Sparta established relations with Lydia and Egypt, which were then both in conflict with Persia (see p. 42). With this act Sparta showed herself to be hostile towards tyranny, for Persia's custom was to rule over conquered Greek city states by placing local pro-Persian tyrants in control. The Greek cities in Asia Minor (Ionia) were governed by such tyrants.

Many contemporary and later admirers praised Sparta as an exemplary state, in spite of the fact that the city could boast virtually no cultural achievements whatsoever, as she had devoted all her attention to military training and had avoided contacts with the outside world. Indeed, Sparta always remained more of a village than a city, and present-day tourists will find very little to remind them of the city's glorious past, as Sparta did not commission any imposing buildings – at least, not in classical times.

Athens

Athens underwent a unique development that culminated in the famous Athenian democracy. It is this democracy that made Athens the bearer of Greek culture *par excellence*. Athens, in contrast to Sparta, was for some time ruled by tyrants, but this city's tyranny differed somewhat from that of other city states.

Athens had remained inhabited after the fall of Mycenaean civilisation and was not affected by the Dorian invasion. The development of the geometric pottery style around 900 marked the beginning of a period of great prosperity and cultural achievement. By *c.* 850 trade contacts had been established with Al Mina in Syria. Around 730, however, Athens' progress came to a temporary standstill while other city states, such as Corinth, began to flourish. The explosive growth of her population did not induce Athens to found colonies. Apparently Attica was large enough to accommodate the greater part of the increased population. Some peasant families must however have met with difficulties when the family property became too small to be divided amongst the next generation.

Athens was ruled by an aristocracy. Kingship had been abolished fairly smoothly some time during the dark ages and the king had been replaced by three, later nine, *archons*, who exercised the former king's functions of army commander, high priest and supreme judge. Only the members of the old-established aristocratic families (*eupatridae* – families with noble fathers) were eligible for these functions. After their one year's term of office they became members of the council of nobles, the Areopagus or 'Council of the Hill of Ares', so called after the place where they held their assemblies. The Areopagus had considerable effective political power.

However, in Athens too, the position of the aristocracy was undermined by the economic, social and military changes outlined above. Around 630 BC, one Cylon tried to make himself tyrant, but his attempt was unsuccessful because the aristocracy could then still rely on sufficient support. Some ten years later, however, the aristocrats' unrestrained power suffered its first blow when Draco codified the prevailing customary law. He put an end to blood feuds. But as his law code did not entail any true reforms the feelings of discontent remained. These conditions were conducive to tyranny, but in 594 Athens averted that danger for some time by granting an *archon*, Solon, special powers to settle the conflicts between the nobility and the rest of the population. Solon had to find solutions for the dissatisfaction of two groups. The first comprised the wealthy citizens who demanded a share in the political power from which they had hitherto been excluded because they did not belong to the nobility. The second group consisted of the peasants who had fallen into debt and now demanded the cancellation of their debts and a redistribution of land. Solon belonged to a noble family of moderate means. He had spent some years of his life earning his own living by engaging in overseas trade. Around 600 he had participated in the conquest of the island of Salamis from the neighbouring city of Megara. Because of all this he was highly respected by all classes.

Solon's first step was to divide the Athenian citizens into four property classes. The first two classes comprised the wealthiest nobles and the nobles one level below them plus the *nouveaux riches*. The third class consisted of the common peasants, the *zeugitai*. The *thetes*, who had very little or no property, constituted the fourth class.

It should be borne in mind that this classification applied to Athenian citizens only. Apart from Athenian citizens, Athens' population also included *metics*, or resident aliens, many of whom had lived in Athens for several generations already. They were free, but did not enjoy civil rights. There were also slaves in Athens.

In Solon's system the two highest classes had access to the office of *archon*. The three highest classes were allowed to serve on a newly created Council of Four Hundred (whose establishment was a blow to the Council of the Areopagus). All four were admitted to the general assemblies (it was not all that common for people without landed property to be admitted to assemblies in Greece). Solon, then, replaced birth by wealth as the criterion for political influence.

Although reduced, the aristocracy's power was not yet broken. Most of the rich were still nobles. The associations of the *oikos* and the *genos*, which were united in kinship groups ('phratries'), remained intact and retained their prestige at a local level. These associations still had a function in jurisdiction too.

For the impoverished farmers and debt slaves Solon proclaimed the *seisachtheia*, the 'shaking off of burdens': he cancelled all their debts, freed debt slaves, bought back Athenians who had been sold as slaves abroad and forbade Athenian citizens to offer their own person as security in obtaining loans. There were in those days also Athenian citizens who were known as *hektemoroi* – 'sixth parters'. They had to give one-sixth of the produce of their land to a nobleman. We do not know the origin of this obligation. Some believe it was some form of payment of debts, while others regard it as payment for protection by the nobleman. Whatever the case may be, Solon also abolished the status of the *hektemoroi*.

Solon's measures had far-reaching consequences. From then onwards, Athenians could no longer become slaves to other Athenians. However, that did not mean the end of slavery, for Athenian landowners and proprietors of craft centres simply purchased foreign slaves whenever they needed more labour. Athenians – like many other Greeks – regarded wage labour as a form of slavery. There was in their eyes only a marginal difference between selling one's labour and selling one's person. And as they made every effort to avoid having to do such demeaning work themselves, a major part of the need for labour had to be met by slaves.

Solon also took measures to secure sufficient food supplies. He forbade the export of grain and encouraged farmers to grow olive trees, whose products could be exported. It was indeed under Solon that the associated industry of pottery production started to flourish in Athens (black-figure painting: see p. 79).

Another of Solon's reforms involved the replacement of Draco's law code by a new code and the establishment of the *heliaia*, the people's (jury) court. Every year, a list was drawn up of six thousand citizens, from among whom a certain number of jurors (often five hundred and one) would then be chosen by lot to pass judgement in a particular case.

There is one important demand which Solon did not satisfy, namely that for a redistribution of land, which he considered too radical. In conceding to cancel all debts, Solon was actually tackling the problems' symptoms instead of their causes. For some farmers his measures were satisfactory (*hektemoroi* were not necessarily small farmers), but they did not solve the problems of farmers with insufficient land. As those farmers and their families were now moreover forbidden to secure loans on

Diagram 9.1 Different forms of government

Monarchy
'Sole rule'. The rule of a single, usually hereditary, king with a legitimate claim to power.

Tyranny
'The rule of a tyrant'. A tyrant is an autocratic ruler who has seized control without having a legitimate claim to that control.

Aristocracy
'Rule of the best' (Greek: *aristoi*). The 'best' are usually understood to be the members of noble families. In an aristocracy birth is hence the criterion for power.

Oligarchy
'Rule of a few' (Greek: *oligoi*). The rule of a small group of – mostly rich – politicians, who do not necessarily have to be of noble birth.

Timocracy
Forms of government in which *property* criteria are the qualifications for access to the administrative offices.

Democracy
Rule of the *demos* – the (male) population with citizen rights. In a democracy the public assembly has decisive power.

---

their person, it had become virtually impossible for them to borrow money. Many of them no longer managed to make ends meet and moved to the city of Athens.

Peisistratus, a scion of a noble family of modest means, took advantage of the discontent among the poor in Athens and the small farmers in Attica. With their support, he seized power and made himself tyrant.

Peisistratus remained in control for only one year (561) after this first attempt, but in 546 he made a more successful bid to power. Having built up considerable resources by exploiting gold mines in Thrace he was able to hire a good bodyguard, with which he defeated the aristocrats and their supporters. Peisistratus could apparently not rely on sufficient hoplite support and had to take his recourse to the lower classes and mercenaries. He did not abolish Solon's constitution, but he did make sure that things went the way he wanted them to. He reduced the power of the aristocracy even further by instituting a system of travelling judges, which meant that the common people were no longer exclusively at the mercy of noblemen in local disputes. He even showed the population that the aristocrats were not as omnipotent as they seemed by banning many nobles and confiscating their property; that property he used to help small farmers switch to cultivating more profitable crops, in particular, olives. He also embellished the city of Athens. He promoted national religious festivals, the *Panathenaea*, in honour of Athena, Athens' patron goddess, and the *Dionysia*, in honour of Dionysus. His aim in all this was to strengthen the bonds between the population and their *polis* at the expense of local ties and aristocratic traditions.

Whether Peisistratus organised land distributions we do not know. It is not very likely that he did, because the contemporary authors, who all descended from noble families, would not have remained silent about such a burning issue, for the land owned by the elite would have been at stake. But even if he did not distribute land, Peisistratus did improve conditions for the common people. The commissions for the construction of new temples and the increased industrial activity provided the necessary employment. The small farmers in Attica benefited greatly from his relief measures. It was thanks to Solon and Peisistratus that the majority of the Athenian citizens were able to support themselves as small farmers in the Classical period.

After his death (528), Peisistratus was succeeded by his sons, Hippias and Hipparchus. As elsewhere, the tyranny did not outlast this second generation. In 514 Hipparchus was killed by Harmodius and Aristogeiton following a private feud. Although this murder was actually of little consequence, the murderers were celebrated as heroes - 'tyrannicides' - in literature and sculpture.

In 510 the aristocrats collectively put an end to the tyranny with the support of Sparta, which shared their hostility towards tyrants (see p. 88). Hippias fled to the Persian empire.

As was customary after the abolition of a tyranny, a struggle then broke out between rival members of the aristocracy. In 508 Cleisthenes, a member of the Alcmaeonid family, emerged triumphant from this struggle. He owed his success to the fact that he had allied himself with the common citizen people, the *demos*. The consequence of this was that he had to grant the *demos* a share in political power, to which end he had to curtail the aristocracy's power even further. This made Cleisthenes the founder of the famous Athenian democracy.

Cleisthenes divided the territory of the Athenian *polis* (that is, Attica) into ten *phyles* or districts. Each of these *phyles* consisted of three *trittyes* (a coastal *trittys*, an inland *trittys* and an urban *trittys*). The smallest unit was the *deme*, a village or parish, of which there were more than one hundred (see Map 9.2).

This division became the foundation of the Athenian polity. Fifty men from each *phyle* were granted seats in the Council of Five Hundred (*Boule*). A list of candidates was set up for each *phyle*, from among whom the fifty were chosen by lot. In Athens, drawing lots was considered the most democratic procedure, for elections involved the risks of demagogy or of popular leaders becoming too powerful. The members of the Council of Five Hundred were appointed for one year. It was not permitted to sit on the Council more than twice, and not in consecutive years. This meant that many Athenian citizens had an opportunity to become members of the Council and gain political experience. The Council was responsible for day-to-day administration and for preparing the agenda and decisions for the public assembly. The latter however had the right of amendment and the right to accept strongly deviating proposals or to reject a proposal altogether. The public assembly voted by call and took the final decisions. All this made Athens a 'demo-cracy': the people, the *demos*, took decisions of policy (that is, the male citizens – women, metics and slaves had no share in the decision process).

Cleisthenes' system meant a blow to the aristocrats, who still enjoyed considerable power on a local level. The boundaries dividing the *phyles*, *trittyes* and *demes* cut right

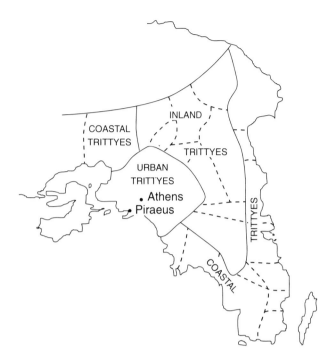

Map 9.2 Cleisthenes' division of Attica into *trittyes*
Notes: Each *phyle* comprised an urban, a coastal and an inland *trittys*, So each *phyle* consisted
of three *trittyes*. Some historians have taken the fact that the *trittyes* were all situated along the
main roads to the centre of Athens to imply that they were created specifically to facilitate the
mobilisation of citizens: the recruits from the individual *trittyes* would have been able to
quickly make their way to Athens when an army was to be formed.

across the noble families' spheres of influence. The *deme* was moreover a small-
scale democracy, with its own chosen administrators, council and public assembly.
All the inhabitants of the *deme* were equal and they all had ample opportunity to
gain administrative experience on a local level. Nevertheless, the nobles still had
considerable prestige and often managed to get themselves appointed to the important
offices. But they too had to abide by the rules of the democracy. Moreover, until 461,
the Council of the Areopagus still exercised some control over local administration,
although we do not know exactly how much power it had. As this council consisted
of ex-archons, there were still many aristocrats among its members. The *archons* were
still the highest magistrates and they were still chosen from the highest two property
classes of Solon's class system, which had not been abolished. Although the *nouveaux
riches* now also qualified for the archonship it was usually members of the old
aristocratic families who were appointed to this office. The archonship lost much of
its former esteem in 487 BC, when it was decided to appoint archons by drawing lots.
The prestige of the office of *strategos*, or general, on the other hand increased, because
the ten generals, who commanded the army and the fleet, continued to be elected
from among the most suitable candidates. They could be re-elected any number of

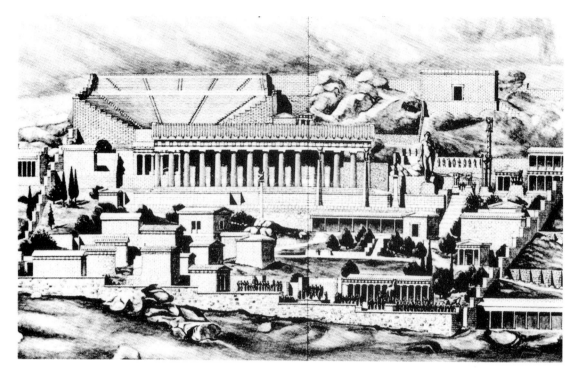

Figure 9.4 The sanctuary of the god Apollo at Delphi

Notes: This temple was a sanctuary for all the Greeks. The Delphic oracle of the god Apollo was very famous. If a Greek was anxious to find out whether an undertaking would be successful, he would visit this temple, ask the god a question and present a gift (or make a vow). The priests then brought a prophetess into a state of ecstasy and listened carefully to her utterings. They believed that the god would convey his answer via her pronouncements. They translated the god's answer into poetic – usually ambiguous – formulas, which they passed on to the person seeking advice. Greek cities would often consult the Delphic oracle on the eve of important enterprises, for example before founding a colony or before introducing political reforms. The priests of Delphi consequently had considerable political influence in the Greek world and even in adjacent areas, for example in Asia Minor.

Source: Artist's impression of the temple, Delphi museum.

times after their one year's term of office. The generals were to acquire considerable political power after 487 (see p. 115).

The last measure that Cleisthenes is believed to have introduced is 'ostracism'. Once a year, the public assembly was asked whether there was any need for an ostracism. If there was, those present at the next meeting had to write the name of a person they considered a threat to the state on a potsherd. The person whose name occurred on most sherds was then banned for ten years. However, he retained possession of his property. Several politicians fell victim to this practice in the fifth century. Some managed to regain their prominent position after returning from their exile, but for most it meant the end of their careers.

THE CLASSICAL PERIOD

— Chapter Ten —

THE PERSIAN WARS

A round the middle of the sixth century BC the expanding Persian empire reached the western coast of Asia Minor. In 547 the Persian king Cyrus the Great (560–530) conquered Lydia and, in so doing, gained control over the Greek cities on the western coast of Asia Minor, which the Lydians had captured shortly before then (see p. 42). In most of these cities the Persians selected local aristocrats who were favourably disposed towards them and appointed them as tyrants. They were to govern the cities under the supervision of the Persian satraps (see p. 43).

In 499 BC the Greeks of Asia Minor tried to depose their tyrants and break away from the Persians. But their attempts were unsuccessful: in 495–494 the Persians squashed their revolt in a series of battles on land and at sea. Shortly after, in 490, the Persian king Darius I (520–485) set out on an expedition to punish Athens, which had sent a small fleet to assist the rebels. The Persians sailed across the Mediterranean and landed at Marathon in Attica (Map 10.1), where they were defeated by the Athenian hoplites under the command of Miltiades. This battle won Athens fame throughout the entire Greek world. In spite of her fifty-year-old hostility towards Persia and her reputation as the strongest military power in Greece, Sparta did not take part in the Ionian revolt or in the battles of 490.

Ten years later, in 480, Darius' successor, Xerxes, resumed the hostilities. In the belief that the only way of securing his control over the west of Asia Minor was by subjugating the free Greeks of the Greek mainland, he set out to Greece with a large army and a fleet. The army marched along the coast so that it could be provisioned by the fleet sailing alongside it (see Map 10.1). Most Greek states had in the meantime united in a league which was led by Sparta, but in which Athens also had much influence. Around 483 Athens had followed the *strategos* Themistocles' advice and had created a large navy. In that year, a fresh rich vein of silver had been discovered in the mining area of Laurium in southern Attica (see Map 10.3). The profits of this silver were not divided among the citizens as some Athenians had wished, but were spent on building warships of a new, fast and more manoeuvrable type known as *triremes* (Fig. 10.1). Some Athenians, especially among the higher classes, failed to see the need for a strong navy. In their opinion, the battle at Marathon had shown that an army of hoplites was all that was required to defeat the Persians. What they were probably afraid of was that the poorest citizens (the *thetes*), who would row the ships, would acquire more military importance and hence a dominant position in the Athenian democracy. Themistocles did not share this opinion. He believed that a powerful navy was vital for Athens, in particular in view of the city's heavy reliance on the import of grain (see p. 103): only with a powerful navy would Athens be able to repel the Persians and secure her trade routes against Greek rivals at sea.

In 480, at the pass of Thermopylae (see Map 10.1), the Greeks made an unsuccessful attempt to stop the Persians advancing by land and sea. The Spartan king Leonidas sacrificed himself and three hundred of his men to cover the retreat of the Greek army and navy. The Athenians evacuated their city and took their cattle along with them to the island of Salamis opposite Athens. Xerxes then destroyed the abandoned city, but his navy was defeated by the Athenians and their allies in the bay of Salamis. One year later (479) the Greeks, under the leadership of the Spartans, defeated the Persian

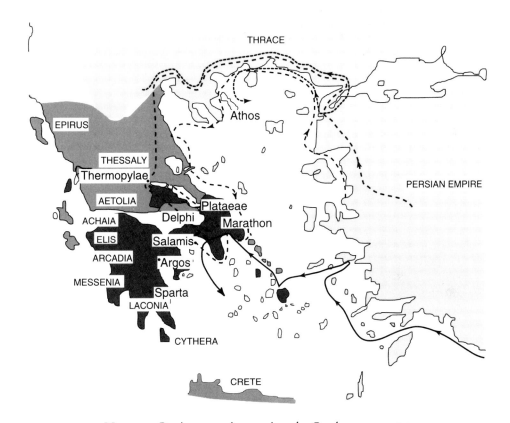

Map 10.1 Persian campaigns against the Greeks, 492–479 BC

Notes: The army that the Persians composed for their expedition of 480 was very large by contemporary standards (approx. 80,000 men according to a reliable estimate). As Greece was relatively poor in resources, some of the provisions for this large army had to be supplied by sea. That is why the Persian fleet sailed alongside the army. When the Persian fleet was defeated off Salamis (480), the Persian army, which stayed behind in Greece, had to be reduced in size. That made it easier for the Greeks to defeat the Persian land forces, too.

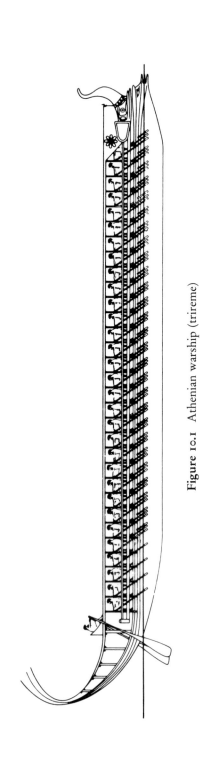

Figure 10.1 Athenian warship (trireme)

Notes: The ship's most dangerous weapon was its ram (right). Such a ship was usually manned by 100 to 150 or even more rowers, 10 to 20 marines (hoplites) and a few seamen (steersman, captain, sailors).

The Athenian fleets sometimes included transport ships bearing soldiers, weapons and horses, which enabled them to sail to their destination and then fight the enemy both on land and at sea.

army, too, at Plataea. The fighting then shifted to the west coast of Asia Minor, where the Athenian fleet liberated the Greek cities from the Persians – a fact which the latter refused to acknowledge until 449, when the hostilities came to an end. The battles against the Persian army and navy were to appeal to Greek imagination for many centuries. In Europe they later came to represent the triumph of the free Greek states over Asia, thanks to which Greek culture, the source of Western civilisation, had been saved from suffocation by Eastern despotism.

SPARTA AND ATHENS AFTER 479 BC

After 479 Sparta left the command of the battle against the Persians to Athens. The Spartans had no fleet to speak of and the theatre of war, the west coast of Asia Minor, lay overseas. The Spartans moreover didn't like the idea of having large forces fighting battles far away from home for long periods of time because they were constantly fearful lest the helots should rise against them. A helot revolt did indeed break out in Messenia in 464 BC, after a severe earthquake, and it took the Spartans almost four years – and a great deal of effort – to suppress it. In 462/1 Sparta desperately appealed to Athens for help, but when the Athenian general Cimon, who sympathised with Sparta, arrived with his troops he was sent back home again. The Athenians responded to this rebuff by waging war on Sparta and her allies from 461 until 446. For twelve years (461–449) both Persia and Sparta were Athens' enemies. Sparta, however, had by this time entered a period of stagnation. The class of Spartiate full citizens had dwindled as a consequence of a fall in birthrate and the degradation of impoverished Spartiates to second-class citizens (see p. 88). The privileged Spartiates had come to represent an even smaller minority amongst the other Spartans, the *perioikoi* and the helots.

THE DELIAN LEAGUE (477–404 BC)

In 477 Athens founded her own league against Persia: the Delian League. Most Greek islands, the Greeks on the west coast of Asia Minor and some other Greek cities joined this league. Only a few large islands supplied ships and soldiers; most member states contributed money to the league's treasury (kept on the island of Delos), which largely financed the league's fleet and army. In the fifth century the league became an instrument of Athens' power politics, especially after 460, when Pericles gained control of the city. Although the Delian League had originally been founded for a specific purpose – the battle against the Persians – it was not dissolved in 449, when the hostilities against the Persians came to an end. The league's territory (Map 10.2) had in fact become Athenian territory. Allies who wished to secede from the League were forced to remain members and to continue to pay the tributes. Athens started to interfere in her allies' internal affairs; she meddled in their legal and financial matters and brought friendly democratic governments to power in several member states. The Athenians also established a network of colonies (*cleruchies*) at various strategic points (usually islands) in the league territory. These colonies were not new, independent city states as the colonies of the Archaic period had been, but were regarded as additions to the Athenian *polis*; the colonists kept their Athenian citizenship. In actual fact, these colonies were Athens' military bases. This form of colonisation led to an increase in the number of Athenian hoplites. Most of the colonists were citizens without property (*thetes*), for whom this was a way of obtaining land and rising to a higher property class, that is, that of the *zeugitai*. This was to Athens' benefit for it was the *zeugitai* who provided the lion's share of both the heavy infantry and the naval forces. The *thetes* who became *zeugitai* could no longer be used as rowers, but that was no problem for Athens, because the city could recruit plenty of rowers and sailors from among volunteers from the league member states. Most of those volunteers were lured by the pay and the prospect of booty, though some may have wished to join the navy for idealistic reasons, for many of the poor citizens of the member states of the Delian League were great admirers of the Athenian democracy. Almost all of the states that wanted to resign from the League and deserted Athens were led by oligarchic regimes. In the course of the fifth century a polarity emerged in Greece: Greeks in favour of a democracy supported Athens while those with an oligarchic disposition (usually the rich) sympathised with Sparta.

The Athenian empire and her allies

Sparta and her allies

Neutral states

Map 10.2 Greece on the eve of the Peleponnesian War

Athenian leaders in the fifth century

In the fifth century Athens was led by a number of admirable statesmen who knew how to address the public assembly and who were also competent army and fleet commanders: Themistocles (*c.* 490–470), Cimon (*c.* 470–461) and Pericles (460–429). They were all members of the aristocratic elite but their loyalty was with the democracy. The Athenian citizens elected them generals time and time again. Themistocles and Pericles realised that their objective, which was for Athens to acquire hegemony over the whole of Greece, would ultimately bring them into conflict with Sparta. They therefore built long walls around Athens and her port Piraeus (see Fig. 10.2). The idea was that the Athenians would then be able to import everything they needed via the sea, while Sparta's land forces idly besieged the city, because the Athenian fleet still retained the supremacy over the seas surrounding Greece that it had acquired in the Persian wars. The policies of Themistocles and Pericles were characterised by expansionism in external affairs and a trend towards democracy in internal affairs (see pp. 115–16). The more conservative Cimon wanted to avoid conflicts with Sparta, but he lost his popularity and was ostracised when a war broke out between Athens and Sparta in 461 (p. 99).

Athens' aim in that war was to extend her influence over central Greece and the Peloponnesian coast opposite Attica. At the same time, the Athenians supported the Egyptians' revolt against Persia (*c.* 455). All this proved too much: in 454 Athens suffered a crushing defeat in Egypt and in 446 the city found herself forced to conclude a compromise peace agreement with Sparta and abandon her ambition to extend her sway over central Greece. By this time the Greeks had already made peace with the Persians (in 449).

After their failure in Egypt (454) the Athenians, allegedly out of fear of a Persian expedition to Delos, transferred the league treasury from Delos to Athens and assumed control over the league's financial affairs.

The years between 446 and 431 marked a summit in Athens' history in terms of the growth of her power, her prosperity and her cultural achievements. This greatly alarmed Sparta, which had managed to recover somewhat from the blows inflicted on her and was still the unrivalled supreme power in the Peloponnese. Other Greek states also viewed Athens' success with growing anxiety. They began to look to Sparta to defend the autonomy of the Greek city states against Athens' imperialistic tendencies. Most Greek city states that were not members of the Delian League were moreover ruled by aristocratic or oligarchic leaders, who dreaded the spread of democracy.

Athens' state income

Athens' power politics and her magnificent achievements in the visual arts, architecture and literature rested on a sound financial basis. The city had a regular income consisting of her allies' tributes, which were paid into the League treasury, but of which Athens was the main beneficiary, the profits of the exploitation of the silver mines at Laurium and the tolls and harbour dues that were levied at Piraeus. On top of this there were the head taxes and market dues paid by the foreigners

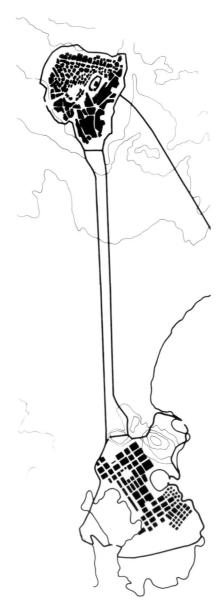

Figure 10.2 The 'long walls' between Athens and Piraeus
Notes: As can be seen in this figure, Piraeus was a newly built city, with a regular layout, whereas Athens was an 'organically' grown city.
Source: H. Rottier, *Stedelijke Structuren*, p. 50, Coutinho, Muiderberg.

who worked in Athens and Piraeus (the *metics*). Those taxes and the harbour dues brought in large sums of money, because after the Persian wars Athens had become the most important market and commercial centre in Greece. Large numbers of Ionians and other Greeks had settled in Athens as merchants and craftsmen. Athens had in fact inherited the trade and industry of the Ionian cities that had suffered such hard blows in the Ionian revolt and the Persian wars.

Athenian citizens were not required to pay direct taxes on a regular basis. Taxation was imposed only incidentally, in times of financial emergency. Wealthy citizens were occasionally expected to equip a warship or to finance a building project or a theatrical performance. These financial services to the state were called *liturgies*. In the fifth century Athens also derived revenues from the gold mines in Thrace (see Map 10.2). Thrace also yielded the timber for Athens' ships.

Another – indirect – source of financial benefit was Athens' powerful political position. Thanks to her large navy, Athens could virtually monopolise the trade with the cereal-producing areas in southern Russia, and could consequently keep grain prices low within the city. Athens managed to retain this advantageous position until the end of the fourth century BC, when the decay of the city's power spelled the beginning of hard times for Athens' poor.

THE GREAT PELOPONNESIAN WAR (431–404 BC)

After a short period of peace (446–431), a new war broke out between Athens and Sparta in 431, when Athens came into conflict with Sparta's maritime allies Corinth and Megara. This war was far more intensive than the previous one (461–446). The Greek historian Thucydides, who described this conflict, was even of the opinion that the Peloponnesian War (431–404) was the fiercest war ever fought in Greek history. The Athenians and the Spartans both rallied their allies behind them. Most of the Greek states that had hitherto remained neutral now took sides with Sparta (see Map 10.2). In the past, wars between Greek city states had been minor skirmishes and plunderings, with only one or two pitched battles, after which peace had been made. In the Peloponnesian War, however, the entire Greek world, from Ionia in the east to Sicily in the west, was engaged in constant fighting involving large land and naval forces.

Pericles entered the war well prepared. He had created a treasury of 6000 talents (see Appendix 2, p. 301) and had developed a long-term strategy. His aim was to launch a series of brief attacks on Sparta from the sea and to entice the Spartans into a vain attempt to besiege Athens and Piraeus, which would use up all their resources and exhaust their men. To that end he concentrated the population of Attica within the long walls surrounding those cities. Pericles had no faith in pitched battles on land because Sparta still had the best hoplites in the whole of Greece and, as she had so many allies, her troops would moreover vastly outnumber those of Athens. Sparta's weakness was her war fund: the city could not afford to finance a protracted war. Athens suffered several major setbacks during the war. Her leader Pericles died in 429 and between 429 and 427 a severe plague killed about one-third of the city's population. Moreover, Athens did not adhere strictly

Figure 10.3 Pericles (*c.* 495–429) wearing the helmet of a heavily armed soldier (hoplite)
Source: Rome, Museo Capitolino.

to Pericles' plans and launched several risky expeditions after all. Nonetheless, in spite of all this, the city held its own in the first stage of the war (431–421). In 421 Athens concluded a peace treaty on reasonable terms. Athens' enemies had not succeeded in breaking the city's power.

However, due to a combination of factors, Athens lost the second stage of the war (413–404). One of these factors was the loss of the best part of the city's army and navy in a reckless and totally vain attempt to gain control of Sicily. Between 415 and 413 Syracuse, which was at that time the most densely populated Greek city after Athens, defeated the Athenians with the help of Sparta.

The aristocratic demagogue Alcibiades had persuaded Athens' assembly to embark on this enterprise, but he himself defected to Sparta when grave scandals in his private life made it impossible for him to remain in Athens. He advised the Spartans to establish a permanent military base in Attica, to help Syracuse and to open up relations with Persia. Sparta followed his advice and in 413 the war flared up again, opening the second phase of the Peloponnesian War. The Spartans occupied fort Decelea in Attica (see Map 10.3), from where they obstructed agriculture all over Attica and prevented access to the silver mines at Laurium. Thousands of slaves escaped and Athens was cut off from major food supplies and sources of income.

Map 10.3 Attica at the time of the Peleponnesian War, 431–404 BC

Notes: Sparta's allies are underlined.
Laurium: silver mines.
Decelea: the fortress that the Spartans occupied in 413 at Alcibiades' advice. From there they could cut off access to the mines of Laurium, obstruct all agricultural activities in Attica and keep a close watch on Athens. x = fortifications or battlefields

Persia sided with Sparta and gave the Spartans the means they needed to build up a strong fleet. This induced many of Athens' allies to defect to Sparta. At first, the Athenians managed to win some battles at sea under the leadership of Alcibiades, who had returned to Athens again after private conflicts with Spartan rulers and Persian satraps. In 405 however, the Athenian fleet was decisively defeated by the Spartan Lysander off Aigospotamoi in the Dardanelles (see Map 10.2). In 404, lack of food forced Athens to surrender.

Athens had suffered severe losses. It is believed that the number of adult male citizens in Athens decreased from about thirty-five thousand to about twenty-one thousand between 432 and 400. The Delian League was dissolved, the long walls were pulled down and a pro-Spartan oligarchic government was installed in Athens, which began a reign of terror. That government was not to last long though, for after only one year it was overthrown and a democratic regime was restored. The Spartans resigned themselves to this shift in power.

Figure 10.4 Pallas Athena, the patron deity of the city of Athens
Notes: Roman copy of a Classical Greek sculpture. Athena was the goddess of science and the arts and crafts, but also of warfare, which is why she is here represented with a helmet and a spear.
Source: Rome, Musei Vaticani.

THE YEARS BETWEEN 404 AND 336 BC

In the years after 404 no Greek state was powerful enough to unite the whole of Greece under its leadership. Between 404 and 338 coalition wars kept flaring up between Sparta, which still led the Peloponnesian League, Thebes, which was

Figure 10.5a A hoplite

Figure 10.5b A lightly armed Greek soldier

steadily acquiring considerable power and led a league of city states in Boeotia (see Map 10.4), and Athens, which had managed to recover surprisingly rapidly from the devastating defeat she had suffered in 404. Athens had not lost all her maritime power, and was still the most important market town, the most densely populated city and the leading cultural centre in Greece.

Sparta found herself faced with an increasing shortage of Spartiates. It is believed that by 371 Sparta counted no more than about two thousand Spartiates, as opposed to at least twenty thousand adult male helots – and that is a low estimate of the number of helots.

The Persians had meanwhile started to stir up dissension between the Greek *poleis* and leagues to prevent the risk of them uniting and then turning on Persia – something which they greatly feared because they had begun to lag behind the Greeks in military tactics and experience. The Persians' interference in Greece can be split into two phases: in the first half of the fifth century they launched attacks on the Greeks, but between 413 and 340 they reverted to divide-and-conquer tactics and tried to play the Greek states off against one another by constantly subsidising different states. The following example illustrates their strategy. In what is known as the Corinthian War (395–386), the Persians first supported Athens and some of Sparta's defected allies (Corinth, Thebes) because Sparta had prevented the Persians from reasserting their authority over the west coast of Asia Minor after 404. Around 394, the Persians granted Athens financial support to restore her fleet and rebuild the long walls but, when Athens consequently threatened to become too powerful, the Persians helped Sparta instead.

In 386 the Persian king, acting as an arbitrator, dictated the terms of the peace between Sparta and Athens. Athens' rebuilding programme was checked; Sparta was to remain the most powerful state in Greece and the Persians were to regain control over the Greek cities along the west coast of Asia Minor.

Athens and her allies of the Second Athenian League
Thebes and her allies
Sparta and her allies
The Chalkidian League
Macedonia (also called 'Macedon')

Map 10.4 Greece *c.* 360 BC, just before the rise of Macedonia

The Second Athenian League (377–355)

But Sparta's hegemony was soon to be challenged again. In 377, while Thebes was also acquiring considerable military power, Athens established the Second Athenian League, in which she united her anti-Spartan allies. This league was dominated less by Athens than the first league had been. The allies were not required to pay tributes to the federal treasury, they retained their autonomy in internal affairs and they had a say in the League's foreign politics in the League's own assembly. This League was to have a short life. When, after 362, Athens began to show imperialistic tendencies and started to plant colonies of Athenian citizens (cleruchies) in the League territory, her chief allies revolted (357–355) and the League collapsed.

Social and military changes

A new development in all these wars was the increasing use that was made of mercenaries, of whom there was no lack anywhere in Greece. In the Peloponnese in particular, many impoverished peasants became the victims of the concentration of land in the hands of the wealthy. There was little that could be done to stop this process in the oligarchic states in that region, for the wealthy landowners were also the rulers of the states and only citizens above a certain property qualification had political power; the mass of poor citizens didn't have full citizen rights in those states. Moreover, it may well be that the peaceful conditions that Sparta had been maintaining in the Peloponnese since about 546 BC had led to over-population.

The year 371 marked a turning point in the coalition wars between Thebes, Sparta, Athens and their allies. In that year the Theban Epaminondas, a genius in military tactics, destroyed the Spartan army at Leuctra (see Map 10.4). He then marched on to the Peloponnese, where he freed the helots in Messenia (but not those in Laconia) and dissolved the Peloponnesian League. Sparta lost over half of her citizens with full citizen rights, her League, which had been her main weapon for almost two centuries, and one of her principal sources of helots. The city was reduced to a second-class power of no more than regional importance. This led to a chain reaction of interstate wars and revolutions in the Peloponnese. The poor citizens demanded land reforms, cancellations of debts and less oligarchic governments. The revolutions gradually spread to central Greece, leaving a flow of exiles and destitute drifters in their wake. For many of those people the only chance of earning a living was by hiring themselves out as mercenaries. This led to a massive outpouring of thousands of Greeks, who crossed the Aegean Sea to enlist in the Persian army.

Thebes and Athens were unable to fill the vacuum left by Sparta. Thebes' power had depended too heavily on the skills of one outstanding statesman and general, Epaminondas. When, in 362, he was killed at Mantineia, in the battle against the Spartans and the Athenians who had sided with Sparta out of fear for Thebes' rising power, Thebes soon lost her commanding position.

The rise of Macedonia

After 360 it was Macedonia that benefited from the discord between the Greek states. Until then, Macedonia had always been a backwater, where the social and economic conditions of Homeric times (p. 70) still prevailed. The land was governed by a king, who was the highest ranking member of a landed aristocracy. The nobles ruled over the subordinate, dependent farmers on their estates in a paternalistic manner. The farmers provided the infantry, the aristocrats themselves constituted the cavalry.

Philip II (359–336): the end of the Classical period in Greek history

The Macedonian king Philip II (359–336) modernised his army after the Theban model and took possession of the Thracian gold mines, which had been exploited by Athens in the fifth century (see p. 103). Philip was a great admirer of Greek culture and his aim was to use his army and his newly acquired gold to extend his sway over the whole of Greece. In a series of skilfully planned military campaigns and diplomatic manoeuvres he managed to turn the dissension in Greece to his own advantage. Between 342 and 338 the Athenians and the Thebans attempted to stop him, but he defeated their armies in 338 BC, in the decisive battle at Chaeronea (see Map 10.4). Philip tried to set up a form of government that would be acceptable to the Greeks and, in 337, all the Greek states with the exception of Sparta accepted his proposal to create a new league together with Macedonia. This was the 'League of Corinth'. The member states did not have to pay tributes. Under the terms of the agreement they were to enjoy full freedom and autonomy in their internal affairs and there were to be no more interstate wars or revolutions. Philip's intention was probably to lead the League in an attack on Persia and to conquer Asia Minor, but before he was able to set about realising his plans he was killed in 336, following a private quarrel.

Historians have all along seen the year 338 as a major turning-point in Greek history, marking the end of the era of the free, autonomous city states. The contemporary Greeks, however, did not all see things that way: opinions regarding Greece's future differed, even among the Athenians, Philip's greatest enemies. For example, the well-known Athenian orator and politician Demosthenes (384–322 BC), who

Figure 10.6 Demosthenes (384–322 BC)
Notes: Having risen to power as a legal orator in Athens, Demosthenes became one of Athens' leading politicians around 356. His speeches have remained renowned into our times, in particular the speeches in which he expressed his anxiety about the rise of Philip II and urged the Athenians to defend their freedom, autonomy and power.
Source: Rome, Museo Capitolino.

fiercely opposed Philip, wanted Athens to remain entirely independent and to retain all her power. The orator and publicist Isocrates (436–338), on the other hand, saw the unification of all the Greeks under a powerful leader as an effective answer to the endless succession of revolutions and wars between states. In his opinion, the conquest of Asia Minor, followed by a large-scale establishment of Greek colonies in that region, would solve many problems in Greece. He therefore urged the Greek states to join forces in an attack on Persia. In actual fact, the Greeks had already started migrating to Asia. Thousands of Greek mercenaries were enlisting in the Persian army and trade with the East was also intensifying. This trade was conducted via the Greek cities on the west coast of Asia Minor, which had passed under Persian control again in 386. These phenomena foreshadowed what was to follow in the next stage in Greece's history, the Hellenistic era (p. 136).

THE ATHENIAN POPULATION IN THE FIFTH AND FOURTH CENTURIES BC

In the fifth century BC Athens became the economic and cultural centre of Greece and the most densely populated city in the Greek world. It is believed that by about 432 the city counted some thirty-five thousand adult male citizens, between twenty thousand and thirty thousand or even more adult male slaves and between ten thousand and fifteen thousand adult male metics (free non-Athenians who lived and worked in Athens and Piraeus). Many Greeks, especially from Ionia, which was threatened by Persia, and from Athens' allied cities, took up permanent residence in Athens and Piraeus. Moreover, vast numbers of slaves were imported into Attica. These slaves had widely differing backgrounds. Some were captives and deportees from hostile regions, such as the Persian part of Asia Minor. Others were offered for sale by slave traders: punished offenders, abandoned children who had been raised by slave traders and victims of piracy, banditry and war in different parts of the surrounding world.

The metics

The metics enjoyed personal freedom, but had no Athenian citizen rights. They had no vote in the assembly and were not allowed to take a matter to court themselves, at least not in the fifth century (in the fourth century they were granted this right). The metics had to pay fixed direct taxes (see pp. 101–3) and were liable to service in the Athenian army. They were not usually allowed to possess land in Attica; only very rarely was a metic granted the right to own land, as a reward for services rendered to the city state. Most metics were craftsmen, sailors or day labourers, but some were wealthy doctors, bankers, merchants or architects, who participated actively in Athens' economic and cultural life.

The slaves

In Athens, slaves worked alongside free citizens and non-citizens in agriculture and transport, housekeeping and skilled trades. Large concentrations of slaves were to be

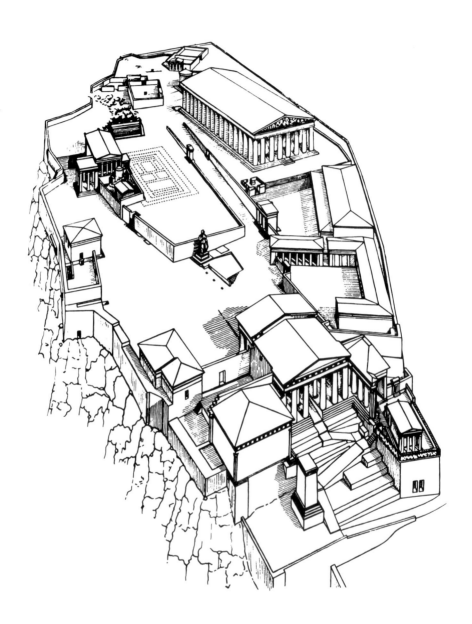

Figure 10.7 The Athenian Acropolis, the city's religious centre
Notes: At the bottom of the picture are the porches of the Propylaea, which provided access
to the Parthenon (the temple of Athena; upper right) and the Erechtheum (the sanctuary where
sacred relics from the time of the city's foundation were kept; upper left).

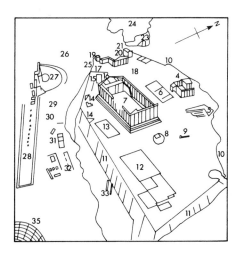

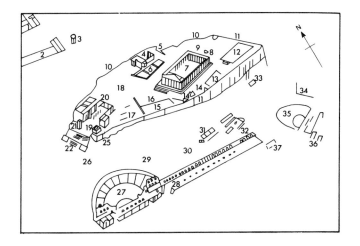

1. Hadrian's library; 2. Roman *agora*; 3. the Tower of the Winds; 4. the Erechtheum; 5. Mycenaean stairway; 6. old temple of Athena?; 7. the Parthenon; 8. the temple of Rome and Augustus; 9. the site of the *temenos* of Zeus Polieus; 10. Themistocles' wall; 11. Cimon's wall; 12. Acropolis museum; 13. Pheidias' workshop?; 14. foundation trenches of retaining walls predating the construction of the Parthenon; 15. Chalkotheke; 16. *temenos* of Athena Ergane; 17. *temenos* of Artemis Brauronia; 18. place where the statue of Athena Promachos stood; 19. temple of Athena Nike; 20. the Propylaea; 21. base that supported the statue of Agrippa; 22. Beule gate, third century AD; 23. cave of the Furies; 24. Areopagus; 25. site of the Aigeion; 26. place where the statue of Aphrodite Pandemos stood; 27. Odeum of Herodes Atticus; 28. Stoa of Eumenes (or Roman?); 29. site of the *temenos* of Aphrodite; 30. site of the *temenos* of Themis; 31. old Asklepieion; 32. later Asklepieion; 33. Thrasyllus monument and Corinthian columns; 34. Odeum of Pericles; 35. theatre of Dionysus; 36. temples of Dionysus; 37. monument commemorating Nicias.

Source: H. Rottier, *Stedelijke Structuren*, Coutinho, Muiderberg, 1980, p. 40.

found in important workshops and trading centres, in dockyards and in the mines of Laurium, where some ten thousand slaves are thought to have worked around 432. When slaves bought their freedom or others bought it for them, or when they were released from slavery, they acquired a status that resembled that of the metics. In some cases they were forced to continue to perform the tasks they had carried out as slaves. A free man or woman could purchase the freedom of a slave he or she wished to marry. Some slaves were bought free by usurers, who would then force the freed slave to repay them, sometimes at high interest rates. Sometimes a master would grant a well-educated slave permission to earn the money needed to purchase his freedom by carrying out extra, paid tasks for others besides the work his master required him to do. The slaves of Attica were less given to revolt than the helots of Sparta. Coming as they did from all corners of the world, they could hardly communicate with one another. Moreover, the status of the different kinds of slaves in Attica differed and so did the way in which they were treated by their masters. Domestic slaves, such as private teachers and secretaries, and the slaves who managed shops and farms were better off than many poor, freeborn citizens, while the slaves of small farmers and craftsmen were regarded almost as members of their master's family. For the slaves who worked in the quarries and the mines, however, conditions were far from rosy.

The helots of Laconia and Messenia, who lived together in villages, constituted homogeneous national groups; they were all ruthlessly oppressed. The Laconian helots are believed to have descended from the pre-Dorian population of that region (see p. 70).

The presence of so many metics and slaves meant that Athens could mobilise a large proportion of her civilian population for years on end in times of war; the metics and slaves could then take over the tasks of the mobilised men and life at home could continue as usual. Even in times of peace, Athens kept a standing fleet of up to sixty warships. Each ship was manned with a crew of at least one hundred and twenty, of whom about twenty were marines and sailors; the others were rowers (thetes and volunteers from elsewhere). Unlike the Romans in the late republic and the imperial age (see p. 237), the Athenians were not generous with their citizen rights and privileges, which included the ownership of land within the *polis*.

Women in Athens and Sparta

Athenian society was a male society. Women had no share in decision-making and enjoyed at best a secondary form of citizen rights, via their fathers, husbands or brothers. They were not allowed to appear in court themselves and their property was managed by their husbands, their fathers, a brother or some other male member of their families. In Athens, married women lived indoors, where they performed their daily tasks. Those tasks were in fact quite plentiful, for in those days many products were still made at home and a large part of the children's education and most medical care were provided at home. Athenian married women were not supposed to go out unchaperoned. The marriageable age for a female was 14 to 15. For men it varied more; most men married when they were between 20 and 35.

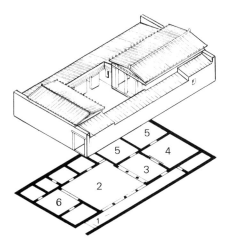

Figure 10.8 A Greek private house
Notes: 1. entrance; 2. *aule* (inner court); 3. front porch; 4. *megaron* (a hall reserved for men);
5. bedrooms; 6. *exedra* (an open alcove); other rooms: living rooms and rooms for servants.
Only wealthy Greeks owned houses like this.
Source: J.H. Croon and A.R.A. van Aken, *De antieke beschaving in hoofdlijnen*, Elsevier,
Amsterdam, 1981, p. 191.

There was one group of women in Athens who were less restricted in their movements: the *hetairai*, who were something of a cross between a courtesan and a female companion. Some of those women were well educated and cultivated; they were often to be found in the company of the Athenian statesmen.

In most other Greek cities the position of women will have been very much like that in Athens, except in Sparta, where the wives of the Spartiates lived a different existence. As the male members of the families lived in messes and spent most of their time in military training, their wives were allowed to move about freely and had a very attenuated family life. Spartan women received good athletic training, just like the men. The idea was that they would then give birth to better warriors.

FURTHER DEVELOPMENT OF THE ATHENIAN DEMOCRACY

In the fifth century BC the Athenian democracy was further expanded. In 487 Themistocles' proposal for a new system for selecting archons was accepted: the criterion that the archons were to belong to the two highest property classes (see p. 93) was retained, only now they were to be chosen by lot. From this point onwards the office of archon was frequently held by citizens who, besides their wealth, had nothing on which to pride themselves. The archons consequently came to lose much of their influence in administrative affairs to the generals, for they (and also the treasurers) were still elected by the public assembly for their outstanding talents. Almost all the Athenian rulers of the fifth century were generals, who were elected over and over again, until they died (Pericles in 429) or fell into disgrace and were ostracised (Themistocles in 470, Cimon in 461; see pp. 99–100).

The Council of the Areopagus in 462/1

In 462/1 the power of the Council of the Areopagus, the most conservative bastion in Athens, was drastically curtailed. After the conservative general Cimon had marched his hoplite forces to the Peloponnese to help Sparta in her struggle against the helots (see p. 99), the democratic rulers Ephialtes and Pericles saw to it that the Areopagus lost all its political power. From then onwards this council served only as a court of law for capital crimes. The supervision and control of legislation and the magistrates were transferred to the Council of Five Hundred, the assembly and the popular law courts. To facilitate this control, the magistrates were required to give account of their actions at the end of their term of office. This shift in power spelled Cimon's downfall and the defeat of the conservatives, who wished to spare Sparta and found the democracy too radical.

Pericles

Pericles was the most influential politician in Athens after 460. Under his leadership Athens introduced a system of state pay for state service that enabled poor citizens to play a part in decision-making and administrative matters. In the second half of the fifth century, citizens were granted a small allowance (about half a day's wages) for sitting on the Council of Five Hundred and on the juries of the law courts. From 399 onwards those who attended the public assemblies were also paid for their time. On religious and national feastdays the citizens were paid lump sums. As all this implied considerable extra expenses, Athens stiffened the qualifications for citizenship: from Pericles' time onwards only those Athenians whose father and mother were both Athenians were granted full citizen rights.

During Pericles' time and the following century the public assembly, the body that took the decisions in the Athenian democracy (p. 92), convened at least forty times a year. The site where these meetings were held, Mount Pnyx in the centre of Athens, had room for about six thousand persons at the most. The citizens who had farms in Attica probably didn't attend the meetings that often. It is generally assumed that the public assembly was dominated by inhabitants of Athens itself, who could afford to miss a day's work on a regular basis. The allowances that were handed out from 399 onwards seem to have done little to change this situation.

The democracy and the fleet

The effect of the introduction of the system of state pay for state service and the shifts in political power in 462/1 was that the group of citizens who attended the assemblies – and the poor citizens one step below them – acquired more influence in jurisdiction, decision-making and the executive. At the same time, the poorer citizens were also acquiring more military importance, for it was they who provided most of the sailors and rowers for the war fleet. On one occasion, in 411, the Athenian fleet saved the democracy. That year, a group of oligarchs took advantage of the sense of despair that had pervaded Athens since the disaster on Sicily and the resumption of the Peloponnesian War (see p. 104). Large parts of Athens' population blamed the democratic government for the blows that the city had suffered and a moderate oligarchic government was instituted. However, in the end the fleet, which was stationed off Samos, threatened to sail to Athens to restore the democracy by force. Daunted by this threat, the Athenian rulers then reverted to the democratic system of before 411.

Old and new politicians

Until 429, all of Athens' rulers were still members of the aristocracy. The nobles were at a great advantage in terms of property (and the income they derived from it in the form of revenues and interest), spare time, educational background and experience. Moreover, the fact that they belonged to the old, respected families appealed to the voters, even in the democratic system. They were supported by citizens from all ranks of society, whose loyalty they secured by granting them services, different forms of patronage or charity. The poor were dependent on the wealthy for charity, the small shopkeepers for their patronage. The aristocrats were also supported by their political friends among the higher classes and by influential financiers. Their splendour and their liturgies (p. 103) greatly impressed the masses.

However, in the last decades of the fifth century and in the fourth century Athens was from time to time led by politicians of a different stamp. After Pericles' death, there were no leaders who were good generals and admirals and who were at the same time capable of managing financial affairs and manipulating the public assembly. The leading Athenian politicians after 429 were either good military men, good public speakers or good financiers, but these qualities were never combined in a single ruler. Because of their different backgrounds and different attitudes, these politicians frequently came into conflict with one another. Most were still members of the aristocratic families, but some were entrepreneurs, such as Cleon, a manufacturer of leather goods and a gifted orator, who moulded Athens' assembly to his will between 429 and 422. A radical democrat, he was very much against concluding a compromise peace treaty with Sparta. Contemporary authors, who were usually aristocrats themselves or associated themselves with the aristocracy, used the derogatory term *demagogues* to describe this type of non-aristocratic politician. Lacking the aristocracy's traditional means of power, these politicians had to exploit their debating skills to persuade the people at large to accept their viewpoints.

The stability of the Athenian democracy

The stability of the Athenian democracy in the Classical period caused much amazement among both contemporary and later observers. But in actual fact there was not that much cause for wonder. By the Classical period the democratic regime had firmly taken root among the Athenian population. It had already proven tremendously successful before 431. The control of the assembly and the popular law courts over the officials with executive powers was well arranged; under normal conditions, officials with oligarchic inclinations had no chance of changing the constitution.

The shared history of warfare and the privileges which distinguished the Athenians from their allies, the metics and the slaves had created strong feelings of solidarity among the Athenian citizens of all classes. These bonds were moreover strengthened by the Athenians' great pride in their city's outstanding literary and artistic achievements. Written speeches that have come down to us from this period praise Athens' military and cultural fame as if it were the merit of the *polis* as a whole, of the collective Athenian *demos*.

Some modern historians relate the stability of the Athenian democracy to Athens' imperialistic tendencies. This imperialism offered the nobles great opportunities for winning fame and yielded substantial material benefits for many social groups. The thetes could earn money and obtain booty by joining the navy, poor peasants were granted land in Athens' colonies, and hundreds of educated Athenians acquired good positions in administration, jurisdiction and banking in the league territory – at least in the fifth century. Athens' powerful position in the trade to the Black Sea moreover ensured cheap grain (see p. 103). These material advantages may explain why the poor citizens never persuaded the assembly to distribute the property and land of the aristocracy and why they left intact the wide gulf that separated them from the wealthy Athenians. In the Athenian democracy there was no equality in terms of property or income, only equality before the law, in the application of the law and in most political rights of the adult male citizens.

The adherents of the above theory maintain that it was because of these conditions, and the fact that they could continue to hold the highest offices, that the rich accepted the democracy and were prepared to make themselves useful to the entire *demos* through their administrative activities and liturgies.

Criticism of the Athenian democracy

But not everybody admired the Athenian democracy. From the mid-fifth century onwards, oligarchically minded authors criticised the democracy for giving the poor the opportunity to tyrannise the wealthy and sensible citizens and for granting the ignorant masses far too much power. In the fourth century the criticism intensified. Many nobles held the democracy responsible for the blows that Athens had suffered since 431; they claimed that the assembly, under the influence of demagogues, had pursued a whimsical zigzag course that had ultimately led to Athens' defeat. They saw how in their own times differences of opinion between generals, financiers and orators were resulting in confused and inconsistent policies. Moreover, it was the rich and the nobles who had to pay the head taxes that were regularly imposed to cover the many deficits that occurred after 413 and 404, when Athens lost her tribute reserve, and the damage caused in the war in Attica (see p. 104) had to be repaired on top of the city's usual expenses. On various occasions in the fourth century, Athens sent a fleet out on an expedition without giving it sufficient money, forcing the crew to resort to piracy.

Figure 10.9 Relief from a funerary monument
Notes: This relief gives a good impression of the high level of achievement reached by sculptors in Classical Athens.
Source: Marburg photographic archive; Rome, Museo delle Terme.

ATHENS AS THE CENTRE OF GREEK CULTURE IN THE CLASSICAL PERIOD

Later generations of Greeks and Renaissance Europe saw the period between 480 and 338 as the Classical era, the heyday of Greek civilisation. In those hundred and fifty years, Athens was the unrivalled centre of Greek culture and the school of Greece. The city acted as a magnet for the most talented artists and scholars from all over the Greek world, in particular from Ionia, which had been the centre of Greek civilisation in the Archaic period and was now threatened by the Persians. In Athens, everyone was free to say, write or produce whatever they liked, providing that certain religious taboos were respected: no one could deny the existence of the gods or insult one of Athens' state gods with impunity.

Another important reason why so many artists flocked to Athens was that Athens was a relatively wealthy city. Both the state and private persons granted artists commissions and spent large sums of money on major religious festivals (liturgies).

The presence of so many talented, creative Greeks from all corners of the world fostered fruitful exchanges before a wide public, which saw and heard so much that it was able to make critical judgements. A remarkably large proportion of the Athenian population could read to some extent.

This favourable combination of factors (talent, money, freedom and an interested, critical public) created an ideal environment for major achievements in the fields of architecture, the visual arts, literature and philosophy. During Pericles' reign, Athens was lavishly embellished – partly with the money of the Delian League – with temples, statues and colonnades, and important literary genres were developed.

Attic drama

Attic drama (tragedy and comedy) is believed to have evolved from the traditional alternate singing of a choir and its leader during the processions which formed part of the celebrations held in honour of Dionysus, the god of wine, intoxication, ecstasy and the wild forces in nature. The Athenian tyrants of the second half of the sixth century had promoted the cult of Dionysus because it was not connected with any of the old aristocratic clans (see p. 91). Like the Panathenaea, the major celebrations of Athens' town goddess Athena, this cult belonged to the *polis* as a whole. The democratic government that succeeded the tyrants was also favourably disposed towards such cults.

Most tragedies focused on the relations between mortals and the gods - for example on conflicts between man-made laws and divine ordinance, or between man's aspirations and his destiny as ordained by the gods. These and other subjects were usually derived from the same ancient legends and myths which had previously inspired the epic poets of the Archaic period (see p. 77).

A comedy was a political cabaret, presented in the form of a play. The choir played parts in both tragedies and comedies. Its singing was accompanied by music and dancing. The performances (liturgies), which were held in open-air theatres, were financed by wealthy citizens and metics. Contests were held during the Dionysian celebrations, in which plays written by different poets competed for a prize, awarded

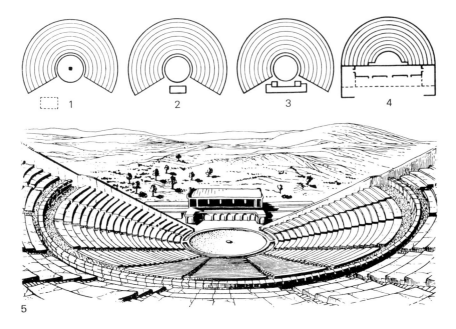

Figure 10.10 Schematic representation of the development of the theatre
Notes: 1. *orchestra* surrounded by the seats for the audience; 2. the area intended for the audience (*theatron*) was separated from the *orchestra*; a *skene* (= stage) was added behind the *orchestra* to serve as a background; 3. the *skene* (which began to play an increasingly important part as a stagehouse for the dramatic action) was raised and made deeper; 5. the theatre at Epidaurus presents a good example of this phase in the development of the theatre. 4. the Roman theatre: the area reserved for the audience (*cavea*) was semicircular, the actors' stage extending over almost the entire width of the diameter.

One of the best preserved ancient Greek theatres is that at Epidaurus. Every year this theatre, which can seat 14,000 persons, attracts flocks of visitors from all over the world who come to see the ancient tragedies brought back to life at the Epidavros festival.

by a jury. Around the end of the fifth century, repeat performances started to be organised of the most popular plays. That marked the birth of Attic drama, which rapidly spread across the whole Greek world.

Philosophy

In Classical Athens, philosophers did not focus on nature alone; man and his intellectual capacities, his behaviour and his state and society all became objects of philosophical speculation.

The sophists

In the second half of the fifth century and in the early fourth century, itinerant teachers started to give paid lessons in rhetoric. Eloquence in speech and writing was a great advantage in the democratic organs, in the law courts and at all kinds of celebrations and other public events. The teachers of rhetoric were called sophists. Athens became one of the most important centres of their activities. There, the teachers found a wealthy public for whom eloquence was of the greatest importance. The sophists' lessons gave rich young men who could afford to pay for this form of education an extra advantage over others.

Besides providing lessons in rhetoric, the sophists also reflected on such matters as state and society, language and standards of human behaviour. To these fields they tried to apply the rational, logical way of thinking of natural philosophy. Some sophists can be said to have been pioneers in grammar and linguistics. Radical sophists maintained that laws and rules were mere man-made conventions and agreements; they were not to be seen as absolute or divine.

Rhetorical education

In the fourth century BC, a special system was developed for rhetorical education. This system gradually spread over the whole Greek world. Between the age of eight and twelve, the children of the elite were taught how to read, write and figure in their own homes or at their teachers' homes. In the next three years of their lives they learned all about the authors of Classical Greek literature, after which a rhetorician trained them in the art of oratory. Rhetoricians taught their pupils in schools; they did not travel around like the sophists. The best-known rhetorician of fourth-century Athens is Isocrates, whom we have already come across above (see p. 111).

These forms of education cost money and hence were not accessible to the poor. The Greek upper classes who had received a grounding in rhetoric developed a cultured, elitist, spoken and written language. This language, and their cultural background, distinguished them from the poor and from parvenus who had money, but had not enjoyed a good education.

In the fourth century, rhetoric had an increasing influence on all kinds of prose writing and even on drama. At the same time, literature acquired a certain bourgeois element. Whereas fifth-century authors had derived many of their themes from heroic epics, which were steeped in the standards and values of the old aristocracy, authors in the fourth century started to focus on issues like education, standards of human behaviour and other aspects of bourgeois ethics. All this was taking place around the time that the aristocracy's political influence was declining. As we have already seen above, in the Athenian democracy the nobles gradually lost their monopoly of power to talented orators and military and financial experts who were no longer all members of the aristocracy.

Socrates and Plato

The sophists' chief opponents were the Athenians Socrates (469–399) and his most gifted pupil Plato (429–347). Socrates was of the opinion that laws were rooted in absolute moral standards, which he attempted to discover by asking people for the definitions and exact meanings of concepts like wisdom, piety, courage, etc. Ironically, the Athenians, who were suspicious of all his questioning, regarded him

Figure 10.11 Scene showing a Greek school, represented on a vase
Source: H. Blanck, *Einfürung in das Privatleben der Griechen und Römer*,
Darmstadt, 1976, p. 91.

as the worst sophist. In 399 a popular law court condemned him to drink poison
because, it was felt, he was 'corrupting the young'. Socrates did not write down
anything himself, but we do know something about his ideas from the works of
his pupils Plato and Xenophon, an Athenian aristocrat who is best known for his
historical writing and his military achievements.

Plato tried to solve Socrates' problem. He believed that all things on earth were
imperfect approximations to prototypes and forms that existed in a higher sphere,
the sphere of *ideai* (unfortunately this term is often erroneously translated as 'ideas').
For example, all tables on earth were embodiments of the idea table in that higher
sphere and could for that reason be called tables. Plato believed that the human
soul existed before birth, when it had knowledge of the *ideai*. At birth, the soul was
incarcerated in a mortal body and it lost most of its knowledge of the *ideai*. Only by

Figure 10.12 Socrates (469–399)

Notes: The son of a sculptor or a mason, Socrates was originally a middle-class craftsman. On several occasions he fought as a hoplite in the Athenian army. He appears to have died a poor man. As a young man he was interested in natural philosophy, but later he focused more on ethics and the definition of concepts. Unlike some sophists, he believed that laws had absolute power. He took an active part in the political life in his city. In 406 he presided over the assembly which, in a rowdy meeting, condemned various admirals to death. Although they had that year won a major sea battle against the Spartans (near the Arginusae islands), those admirals had failed to save the many Athenians who had fallen overboard in a rising storm.

Source: Rome, Museo Capitolino.

thoroughly studying every aspect of reality, starting with a foundation course in mathematics, could man slowly regain his soul's former knowledge and experience. For Plato, the highest form was the form of the good, which is sometimes synonymous with god. Plato's ideal state was a sober agricultural *polis* with a limited, fixed number of citizens who were grouped into three classes: governing philosophers, guardians and workers. The philosophers had to undergo a thorough training to learn as much as possible about the *ideai* and acquire expertise in administration and jurisdiction. Such men would then have both the most appropriate moral background and the required skills to provide the best form of government conceivable. As the guardians' task was to defend the state, they had to be trained in military tactics and morale. The workers had to provide for the material needs of the two higher classes and produce whatever the community required; they were to have no political power. It was best if the philosophers had no private property and no families. There would then be no risk of them being tempted to further their private interests at the state's expense. The positions of the two higher classes were not to be hereditary: each generation would have to select the most suitable candidates for the offices of philosopher and guardian.

In 367 and 361 the Syracusan tyrant Dionysius II (367–357) invited Plato to visit him in Sicily. But he was disappointed with Plato's advice and sent the philosopher home again on both occasions.

Around 390 Plato founded the Academy, a school in which he discussed his theories with pupils and other interested parties. This school was to remain a centre of Platonic philosophy until AD 529. Plato's followers were later also referred to as academics.

Aristotle (384–322)

Plato's most brilliant pupil was Aristotle. He did not believe in Plato's world of *ideai*, but thought that all things on earth could be logically grouped into species and categories by analysing their inherent properties and qualities. Aristotle was a universal scholar. He wrote about formal logic (i.e. the art of reasoning in a logical and coherent manner), nature, the supernatural, poetry, prose, ethics and political science. Aristotle's political ideal was a state in which virtue and competence in all aspects of human activity would be the standards of government and citizen life: a higher form of 'aristo(= the best)cracy'.

For the particular situation of his own time, he found a *polis* with a mixed constitution (combining monarchic, aristocratic and democratic elements) the most desirable. This constitution was to be acceptable to the population at large and was to steer a middle course between the unhealthy extremes of tyranny and the arbitrary rule of the masses. In Aristotle's opinion the presence of a powerful middle group was important for a state's stability. The assembly was to convene only rarely and was to allow itself to be led and advised by a group of trained experts. If there could be no mixed constitution, then a democracy was more preferable than a tyranny or an oligarchy. Aristotle maintained that all citizens were capable of participating in administrative matters. The sum of the expertise of all individuals was important for good government. A democracy could make use of the expertise of all the citizens, which was better than the collective expertise of a small group or the expertise of a single leader, as in an oligarchy or a tyranny.

Aristotle also established a school: the Lyceum. In those days the words 'Academy' and 'Lyceum' referred to buildings or locations in Athens.

Historical writing

Herodotus (c. 485–425)

The fifth century BC also saw the birth of historical writing. The 'father of history' was Herodotus. Although he was born in Halicarnassus, in the southwesternmost corner of Asia Minor, he spent a large part of his life in Athens. He wrote about the Persian wars and the events that led up to them and about the customs, traditions and histories of many different peoples and states in Asia and Greece. Instead of recounting legends, he tried to write down accurate accounts, based on interviews and critically assessed information. His work actually evolved out of the Ionian tradition of geography and ethnology: already in the Archaic period Ionian merchants had shown a keen interest in learning more about the lands and the peoples they visited on their travels.

Thucydides (c. 460–400)

The Greek historian who is most admired today is the Athenian Thucydides. In his 'History of the Peloponnesian War' he made a great effort to chronicle the events as accurately and objectively as possible. Whereas Herodotus had taken a wide view of contemporary and past events, Thucydides narrowed the scope of history to the fields of politics and warfare. He was the first to make a fundamental distinction between cause and occasion, for example in his analysis of the outbreak of the Peloponnesian War. He also tried to explain backgrounds and underlying motives in speeches, which he put into the mouths of his protagonists. Thucydides concentrated on the history of his own time. Other Greek historians were later to follow his example.

Rhetorical historical writing

After Thucydides, historical writing came to feel the influence of rhetorical education (p. 122). From the fourth century BC until the end of antiquity, the historical works that were written in both Greek and Roman cultural circles were phrased in the language that the elite learned at the schools of rhetoric. This was a language full of all kinds of stylistic motifs, dramatic effects and moralising clichés, which was also used for show speeches and other forms of rhetorical prose. Good historians, however, used this language to describe events as they had actually happened. They did not revert to writing florid, inaccurate folk tales and heroic legends, which, nonetheless, continued to exist alongside historical works throughout the whole of antiquity. Important events were immortalised in both historical works phrased in affected rhetorical prose, which were read by a small literate circle of political experts, and in fantastic folk tales.

THE GREEKS IN THE WESTERN MEDITERRANEAN

The city states that the Greeks had founded along the coasts of southern Italy, Sicily and southern Gaul (see Maps 9.1a and 9.1b, pp. 74 and 75) in the colonisation period (750–550) had risen to great prosperity. The remains of imposing temples and other buildings that can still be admired along those coasts today bear witness to the material wealth of these cities in the sixth and fifth centuries BC. This wealth was largely the consequence of the fertile soils and the favourable locations of the sites that the colonists had selected for their settlements. Thanks to the good transport possibilities of those sites, the surplus agricultural produce could be easily exported. In the course of the sixth century, the Greeks' colonisation in the west came to an end. The trading city Carthage, which was a colony itself founded by the Phoenician city of Tyre around 800, rose to power and kept the Greeks out of northern Africa, southern Spain, Sardinia and the western point of Sicily. The Etruscans, then the best organised and most highly developed people in Italy, held a powerful position in central Italy, the Po valley and Campania. Together with the Carthaginians they frustrated the Greeks' attempts to found colonies on Corsica around 540.

The tension intensified around the beginning of the fifth century. In 480 (the year of Salamis) the Carthaginians attempted to gain control over all Sicily, but the Syracusan tyrant Gelon (485–478) routed them at Himera. He then turned Syracuse into the most powerful Greek polis in the west, and the most densely populated Greek city after Athens, by transferring parts of the populations of Greek cities all over Sicily to Syracuse. His brother Hieron I, who succeeded him, destroyed the Etruscan navy in 474 in the great naval battle off Cumae (a Greek city near Naples). That marked the beginning of the gradual decline of the power of the Etruscans, who were from then onwards no longer a threat to the Greek city states. However, a new danger was emerging in southern Italy in the form of the tribes living in the hinterlands of the Greek cities, who opposed the Greeks with increasing success in the course of the fifth and the fourth centuries.

Around the middle of the fifth century, Sicily was the seat of constant battles between Syracuse and the native tribes in the interior of Sicily. Between 415 and 413 Athens attempted to gain hegemony over Sicily (see p. 104). A few years later, in 409, the first of what was to be an endless series of wars broke out. The contenders were the Sicilian Greeks, led by Syracuse, and the Carthaginians. These wars were to continue, with the odd breathing space, until in the third century BC and were not to end until Rome conquered the whole of Sicily (241 BC, see p. 178).

The constant wars had important consequences for the internal relations within the Greek cities. Syracuse, for example, was ruled by a democratic government for only a very short period, from 466 until 405. For almost the whole of the rest of the Classical period that city was governed by tyrants. Time and time again successful generals managed to seize control and make themselves tyrants. They relied on the support of their mercenaries and the poor citizens, who hoped that the new ruler would reward them with revolutionary measures such as land distributions and the cancellation of debts. In the fourth century the strong enemy pressure compelled the Greeks to reorganise into larger units so that they would be better able to defend themselves. They had the choice of two options: they could organise a league of autonomous *poleis* or they could bind cities together in a territorial monarchy with a large Greek city serving as a fortified centre. The tyrants Gelon and Hieron I had already tried out the latter option (see above), but their family had lost its political power in 466. The Syracusan tyrant Dionysius I (405–367) made a new attempt. He captured the eastern half of Sicily and the southwestern part of the Italian mainland and abolished numerous Greek city states. The populations of those states he transferred to Syracuse and he settled mercenaries in the emptied cities and in a series of newly founded cities, which belonged to Syracuse. However, those efforts brought him, and later Syracusan tyrants with similar ambitions, into conflict with the Greek occupants of the city states, who fought stubbornly to preserve their autonomy. This situation came to an end in the third century BC, when all the Greek city states in southern Italy and Sicily passed under Roman control.

Figure 10.13 The temple of Hera at Poseidonia or Paestum, fifth century BC
Notes: Paestum (along the western coast of southern Italy, to the south of Naples) was a colony founded (*c.* 600 BC) by Sybaris, which had in turn been founded by Achaea, a region in the north of the Peloponnese. (Sybaris lay near Taranto. It was founded *c.* 720 BC and was destroyed by the neighbouring city of Croton *c.* 510 BC). Around 390 BC the Greeks living at Poseidonia were overpowered by Italians from the hinterland. From then onwards Poseidonia was an Italian city. In 273 the Romans turned it into a Latin colony (p. 162) and called it Paestum.
Source: Marburg photographic archive.

The Greeks in the western Mediterranean made original, important contributions to Greek literature, philosophy, art and architecture. It is they who first brought the peoples of Italy, Gaul and Spain into contact with Greek civilisation. In so doing they paved the way for the large-scale assimilation of Greek culture by the Romans, Gauls and other western Europeans that was to take place later (see p. 193).

THE HELLENISTIC ERA

Introduction
Alexander the Great
From Alexander to the Roman conquest
Greece
Athens and Sparta
Leagues of states in Greece
The Seleucid kingdom
The Ptolemaic kingdom
The government and the cities of the Hellenistic kingdoms
Economy and society
Greece
The Near East
Cultural aspects
General
Religion
Near Eastern religions
Philosophy and science
Science
The Jews in the Hellenistic era
The impact of Hellenistic culture in the Parthian kingdom
  and the Roman empire
Conclusion

INTRODUCTION

Alexander, who became king of Macedonia in 336, took up the plans his murdered father Philip II had been unable to realise and brought them to a successful conclusion (see pp. 109–11). As we will see below, he conquered the entire Persian empire. His conquests ushered in a new phase in the history of Greece as well as that of the ancient Near East. That phase is called the 'Hellenistic era'. In the present chapter we will restrict ourselves to the period of the Greco-Macedonian domination over the aforementioned regions. In the second and first centuries BC the Greco-Macedonian kingdoms one by one fell to the Roman and Parthian empires. However, that did not spell the end for what is known as 'Hellenistic culture'. In the following sections we will try to outline what 'Hellenism' embraces.

ALEXANDER THE GREAT

In 334, after quelling a revolt of Greek city states, Alexander and his experienced Macedonian army, enlarged with contingents from the League of Corinth, sailed across to Asia Minor. There he routed an army of the Persian satrapy and in so doing liberated the Greek cities along the west coast of Asia Minor. He then turned his attention to the Phoenician cities, where the Persian fleet was based, because he feared that the fleet might attack Greece during his absence. However, on his way towards those cities he first had to defeat the Persian land forces, which were commanded by Darius III. In the ensuing battle, at Issus, it was ironically the Greek mercenaries serving in the Persian army who offered him the fiercest resistance (see Map 11.1).

As for the Phoenician cities, the conquest of Tyre proved a particularly time-consuming enterprise: the siege of that city was to last no less than seven months. Next, Alexander marched along the coast to Egypt, where the Egyptians, who resented the Persian regime, welcomed him with open arms. During a visit to the oracle of Amon he was greeted as a pharaoh – in other words, as the son of the Egyptian god Amon, whom the Greeks identified with their supreme god Zeus. This made a deep impression on Alexander, who subsequently started to behave like a king of divine birth. Of great importance was his foundation of Alexandria, the city that was later to become Egypt's capital.

After this interlude in Egypt, Alexander advanced to the heart of the Persian empire. At Gaugamela (see Map 11.1), he once again defeated the Persian land forces (1 October 330 BC). This opened up the way to the empire's major capitals. Babylon, Susa and Persepolis offered him no resistance whatsoever. Within only a few months Alexander continued his campaign. The eastern satrapies did put up a fight, but they too were all defeated. Alexander showed his goodwill towards the subjugated population by marrying Roxane, a local princess. At the Indus river he defeated an Indian ruler, Porus. But by then his soldiers had had enough of all the fighting and they refused to march on any further. In 324 Alexander yielded to his men and returned to Babylon. One year later, at the age of 32, he died after a brief illness.

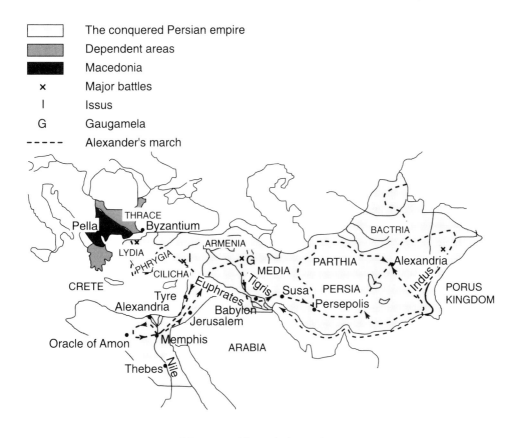

□	The conquered Persian empire
▨	Dependent areas
■	Macedonia
×	Major battles
I	Issus
G	Gaugamela
- - - -	Alexander's march

Map 11.1 Alexander's empire

Alexander saw himself as the legitimate successor of the Persian kings and started to behave accordingly. He adopted the Persian court ceremonial, which included kneeling before the king as an attitude of respect. To the Greeks and Macedonians this was totally unacceptable. They were accustomed to kneeling only before their gods and saw their king as the first among equals. As far as the administration of his empire was concerned, Alexander left many matters unchanged. Taxes continued to be paid in the same manner as in the past. Alexander allowed several Persian satraps to retain their authority, because he considered their Persian administrative experience to be of vital importance. His officers had to accept this. Alexander even urged his officers to take Persian wives. As he intended to make Babylon the capital of his empire, he ordered the rebuilding of the temple of Marduk – an act that would have befitted a true Babylonian king. His empire was to be a worthy successor of the empires of the ancient Near East. These plans turned Macedonia, formerly the heartland of his empire, into a backwater. All this brought Alexander into conflict with his generals, who were greatly displeased by this turn of events.

FROM ALEXANDER TO THE ROMAN CONQUEST

After Alexander's death, the lack of a suitable successor almost immediately led to the break-up of his empire into smaller states. An army assembly at Babylon appointed Alexander's feeble-minded half-brother Philip Arrhidaeus to the throne and decided that if Roxane, who was then expecting a child, should bear a son, that son would be made joint king. The effective power, however, came to rest with the Macedonian generals, who divided the power at conferences and above all on the battlefields. Some of those generals, such as Antigonus the One-Eyed, strove to keep Alexander's empire united under their own authority. Others, like Ptolemy, the satrap of Egypt, tried to consolidate their position as satrap within their own satrapy. It was the separatists who ultimately emerged victorious from the ensuing 'wars of the *diadochoi*' (successors). The most important of the kingdoms that were then formed are:

the 'Ptolemaic kingdom', founded by Ptolemy I (323–283);
the 'Seleucid kingdom', founded by Seleucus I (311–280);
Macedonia, which from 276 onwards was ruled by Antigonus Gonatas (276–239), one of the descendants of Antigonus the One-Eyed.

Later on, a few smaller kingdoms were formed alongside these large kingdoms, largely at the expense of the Seleucid kingdom. They included the kingdoms of Pergamum, ruled by the Attalids (early third century); Bactria, which was governed by Greek colonists; the Maccabean kingdom of the Jews (see p. 144) and Parthia, a small kingdom governed by Indo-Iranian invaders. Parthia became quite powerful and even managed to seize power in Mesopotamia from the Seleucids in the second century BC (see pp. 45 and 145). All these kingdoms are shown on Map 11.2 (p. 137).

Greece

Formally, Greece did not belong to any of these kingdoms. However, since the battle at Chaeronea (338, see p. 110), and since most Greek city states had agreed to join the League of Corinth (see p. 110), it had come under powerful Macedonian influence.

Athens and Sparta

On the whole, rebellions against Macedonia were rather unsuccessful. That also holds for the uprising that was provoked by the Athenian orator Demosthenes after Alexander's death. After suppressing this rebellion, the Macedonians installed a garrison in Athens and changed the city's constitution: from then onwards only people above a certain property qualification were to enjoy citizenship. This spelled the end of the Athenian democracy in the original sense (321 BC). Athens' days as an important participant in international politics were over. The city did succeed in throwing off the Macedonian yoke a few times after that, but each time she had to call in help from outside. In 307 the democracy was restored; it was to last until 86 BC, when Rome replaced it by an oligarchy.

Figure 11.1 Maquette of the city of Pergamum, one of the most important foci of Greek culture in the Hellenistic era

Notes: The city formed the centre of a small, but efficiently governed kingdom in the north-west of Asia Minor, which had shaken off the yoke of the Seleucids at the beginning of the third century BC (*c.* 260 BC). The kings of Pergamum had to fight many a battle against the Celts (Galatians), who invaded the Greek world in 279 and settled in central Anatolia. Pergamum had libraries, schools of rhetoric and a famous temple of Asklepios (Asclepius), the god of healing, where thousands of sick came to be cured. The city had developed from a fortress around 300 BC. Between 215 and 133 BC Pergamum was a loyal ally of Rome. In 188, after defeating the Seleucid king Antiochus III (who reigned from 223 until 187 BC), the Romans expanded the kingdom of Pergamum to the Taurus Mountains. In 133 BC the last king of the Pergamene royal house of the Attalids, Attalus III, bequeathed his kingdom to Rome because he had no children who could have succeeded him. This shows that the Hellenistic kings regarded their kingdoms as their private property.

Source: H. Rottier, *Stedelijke Structuren*, Coutinho, Muiderberg, 1980, p. 51. Maquette in the Staatliche Museen, Berlin.

Sparta's influence had also declined; the city had become a mere shadow of the great power she had once been, although she had managed to hold her own outside the League of Corinth. The number of Spartiates had decreased to 700, 600 of whom were poverty-stricken. The attempts of King Agis IV (244–241) and King Cleomenes III (236–222) to increase the number of Spartiates by raising *perioikoi* to the status of Spartiates had failed. What is more, they had led to a wave of revolts in southern and central Greece. To create the extra citizen holdings required to expand the privileged class, these kings had redivided the land – and that had inspired Greeks in other regions to demand the same.

Leagues of states in Greece

The Aetolian and Achaean leagues were more successful at maintaining their independence. These leagues had been formed in regions where the *ethnos* was the dominant political unit (see p. 73). They differed from leagues like the Delian League and the Peloponnesian League in that they were not led by a single *polis*. They were actually 'federations'. The citizens of those federations enjoyed double citizen rights, as inhabitants of their *polis* and as members of their league. But these leagues were also unable to prevent the intervention of the great powers in their affairs. In fact, they even invited the great powers to mediate in quarrels between individual league members. Greece thus became the plaything of the great powers, which all intervened in Greece's internal affairs, allegedly in order to safeguard the 'freedom and autonomy' of the Greek cities.

That is also how Rome entered the political scene in Greece: a number of city states sought her assistance against Macedonia. In 196, after the defeat of Macedonia, the Greek cities were formally declared 'free and autonomous'. However, Greece then passed under Roman influence. The Greeks were not happy with this situation.

Figure 11.2 The Great Altar of Zeus of Pergamum, built to commemorate Pergamum's successes against the Galatians
Notes: The sculptures include scenes showing battles between gods and other beings, symbolising the battle against the Galatians.
Source: Drawing based on a photo in the Marburg photographic archive.

After several years of friction, Rome once again intervened. In 148 the Romans made Macedonia a Roman province. Two years later they placed Greece under the supervision of the Roman *proconsul* of Macedonia (pp. 182–4; Map 13.2, p. 180).

The Seleucid kingdom

The Seleucid kingdom was the largest of the Hellenistic kingdoms. But as it was a very disparate realm, containing a wide variety of peoples and cultures, its fragmentation was a constant menace. Antiochus III (223–187) made a successful attempt to reinforce the kingdom. In 200 BC he wrested control of southern Syria and Palestine from Egypt. However, his ambition to conquer Greece brought him into conflict with Rome (191–188), which proved disastrous. In 188 BC he was forced to surrender his territories in Asia Minor to Rome's ally Pergamum and to pay a tribute of 15000 talents (see Appendix 2, p. 301). The Seleucid treasury was to suffer the consequences of this burden for a long time, as the sum was to be paid in instalments.

After the death of Antiochus IV in 164 BC, the king who quelled the revolt of the Jews (see p. 144), the Seleucid kingdom rapidly weakened owing to the ensuing dynastic struggles. In 129 Mesopotamia finally fell to the Parthians (see p. 145). By that time, the Seleucid kingdom had shrunk to an area roughly embracing what is now Syria. In 64 the Romans took over control and reduced the Seleucid kingdom to the province of Syria (see p. 207; Map 14.1, p. 204).

The Ptolemaic kingdom

The Ptolemaic kingdom (Egypt) flourished under Ptolemy I (323–283) and Ptolemy II (282–246). In the second century its strength was sapped by dynastic struggles, the loss of Palestine and enclaves in Syria (200) and growing unrest among the indigenous Egyptian population. In the second and, especially, the first century the Romans interfered increasingly in Egypt's affairs. In 30 BC Egypt lost its independence. The last queen of the Ptolemaic dynasty, Cleopatra VII, committed suicide when Egypt was captured by Octavian, who was later to become the Emperor Augustus (see p. 214).

THE GOVERNMENT AND THE CITIES OF THE HELLENISTIC KINGDOMS

It is often maintained that in the Hellenistic era large monarchies took the place of the small independent city states (*poleis*) of the Classical period. This is only partly true. The Hellenistic monarchies lay in areas where such states had flourished for centuries already, namely in Egypt, the Levant and Macedonia. Greece remained the country of the city states. Moreover, large monarchies had annexed Greek *poleis* or had dominated them already through dexterous politics before the reign of Alexander the Great. Lydia and Persia had for example annexed the *poleis* along the west coast of Asia Minor. The politics of the city states on the Greek mainland had been overshadowed by the Persians' interference from the Peloponnesian War onwards. Sparta had for example been assisted by the Persians in that war and in 386 the Persian king had dictated the terms of the 'King's Peace'. Later on it was the Macedonians who interfered in Greek politics. Their intervention had resulted in the League of Corinth, led by the king of Macedonia.

All the same, the Hellenistic era also witnessed important new developments. In the first place, the city states were now no longer able to play powerful roles in international politics as Sparta and Athens had done in the fifth century. Secondly, the protagonists in Greek politics were no longer the city states but the Leagues (see p. 134). A third new development was the establishment of new Greek cities all over the Near East. This development actually started with Alexander the Great, who founded many cities under the name of Alexandria from Egypt to what is now Afghanistan. The Seleucid rulers also established many new cities, which they gave Macedonian dynastic names, such as Seleucia-on-the-Tigris and Antioch-on-the-Orontes. The latter city they turned into their capital (see Map 11.2).

Some cities evolved from the colonies of soldiers and veterans which the Seleucids planted at several locations. In Egypt the soldiers were granted plots of land at locations scattered across the kingdom rather than in colonies. This is one of the reasons why no more Greek cities arose in Egypt after Alexandria, Naukratis and Ptolemais. The new cities were populated with Greek emigrants, Greek veterans, but also Oriental natives. Some of those cities became very large and attracted flocks of new immigrants. Alexandria evolved into a cosmopolitan centre of many different peoples – Greeks, Egyptians, Jews and Syrians. Alexandria, Antioch and Seleucia grew into cities with many hundreds of thousands of inhabitants.

Both the old and the new Greek cities enjoyed a special position within the various kingdoms. The kings set themselves up as the champions of the 'freedom and autonomy' of the Greek cities. The cities were allowed to govern themselves with their own chosen magistrates, a council and an assembly, as befitted a *polis*. Every city had its own territory, where the citizens owned arable land, which was often tilled by native dependent farmers. Some of these cities were exempt from taxation. But of course they were not truly independent – usually a royal governor kept an eye on things. In principle, only Greeks and Macedonians were granted citizen rights; the non-Greek occupants enjoyed a certain degree of autonomy in their own ethnic organisations (*politeumata*). We mustn't lump all these cities together though. The degree to which they underwent Greek influences differed considerably. The cities of Asia Minor, for example, had already been influenced by the presence of the Greeks for quite long by the time that the cities further east began to emerge; the former were consequently far more Hellenised than the latter. The relationship between Greeks and non-Greeks is still a poorly understood historical issue.

Besides the Greek cities there were still, of course, the ancient Near Eastern cities: Memphis, Thebes, Babylon, Uruk, Susa, the Phoenician cities, Jerusalem, etc. The kings' attitudes towards these cities were somewhat ambivalent. On the one hand they allowed the cities to retain both local autonomy (although they would often appoint a Greek or native governor to supervise their administration) and many of their local customs. The Near Eastern cities could for instance continue to administer justice and draw up contracts according to their native practices. In addition, they were not banned from rebuilding or embellishing their temples. They were also

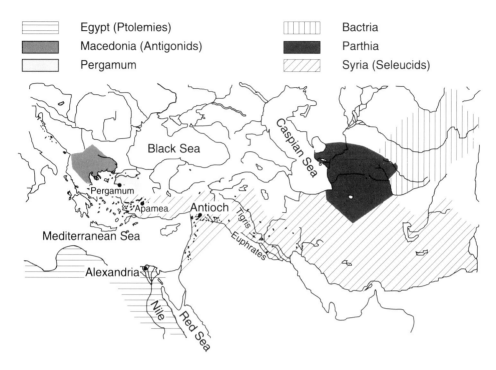

	Egypt (Ptolemies)		Bactria
	Macedonia (Antigonids)		Parthia
	Pergamum		Syria (Seleucids)

Map 11.2 The Hellenistic kingdoms, *c.* 200 BC

allowed to possess land, just like the Greek cities. On the other hand however, the kings did not grant the ancient Near Eastern cities a significant place in political and economic activity. Not one of the cities was made a capital. Many of the new capitals were founded near the ancient Near Eastern cities and were partly populated with people transported from those cities. Seleucia-on-the-Tigris, for example, was populated with deportees from Babylon, which was also deprived of part of its territory. In time, Greek communities emerged in several of the Near Eastern cities which were then usually given a new, dynastic name. Moreover the gymnasia, theatres and temples based on Greek models that arose within the cities gave them a decidedly Greek touch. But it is not always clear to what extent the administration of these cities was also based on Greek patterns.

Although the large states were all monarchies, their governments were not all the same. In Macedonia the king was still traditionally the first among his noble peers and was still appointed by an army assembly. In effect, however, kingship in Macedonia assumed an increasingly absolute character. In the Levant and Egypt the king had been an absolute monarch from the very beginning and that did not change. A great difference with respect to Macedonia was that in the Levant and Egypt the ruler was not a native. Alexander the Great had planned to involve the native population more in administrative and military affairs. He had intended to make a Near Eastern city, Babylon, the capital of his empire and to admit Persians to the office of satrap. His successors, however, did not support this policy; they relied on Greeks and

Macedonians where possible. When the great immigration of Greeks came to an end, the Hellenistic kings became increasingly dependent on native Orientals. Many of those natives had by then however become Hellenised to varying extents.

Ptolemy IV was the first to make use of native soldiers. He deployed Egyptian troops in his attempts to keep the Seleucid king Antiochus III out of Palestine. The victory of Raphia in 217 BC was won with their assistance. This greatly boosted the Egyptians' self-confidence.

The appearance of a new ruling elite in the Near East had little effect on the social structures in that area; it was only the upper layer that changed. In organisational terms, the Seleucid kingdom was very much like the Persian empire, while the Ptolemaic kingdom was in many respects a continuation of the Egyptian kingdom of the pharaohs. A noteworthy phenomenon was the ruler cult, to which we will return in the section on religion.

ECONOMY AND SOCIETY

Greece

The problems that Greece had experienced in the fourth century (see p. 109) continued in the Hellenistic era. The gulf between the haves and the have-nots widened, the poorer population continued to make demands for land reforms and the cancellation of debts and the *poleis* continued to be torn apart by social conflicts. The oligarchic governments of several city states were overthrown in bloody revolts and the rich were robbed. These uprisings were too radical and their triumphs were consequently short-lived; time and time again the oligarchs managed to return to power. In many cities only persons of above a certain property qualification enjoyed citizen rights and were entitled to sit on the councils.

When Greece came under Roman domination the Roman rulers supported the ruling elite, because they found a small oligarchy easier to control than an unpredictable democracy. For many of the poor, one of the few remaining ways of earning a living was by hiring themselves out as mercenaries in the armies of the great Hellenistic kingdoms; that way they stood a chance of being allowed to settle in a veteran colony. The populations of the cities in Greece consequently decreased even further. Cities like Athens and Corinth lost their positions as leading trade centres to newly emerged powerful cities like Alexandria in Egypt, Antioch in Syria, and to Rhodes.

The Near East

The conquests of Alexander the Great did not bring about any great economic or social changes in the Near East. The Egyptian economy remained a redistribution economy. Thanks to the many Greek papyri that have survived from the Hellenistic era we are better informed about the Egyptian economy of this period. The state controlled all agricultural activity by determining what crops were to be sown and providing the seed for those crops. Products were processed in state enterprises; private retail traders had to charge consumers set prices for their products. The chief

Figure 11.3 The dying Gaul – a typical example of Hellenistic sculpture: third century BC
Notes: The Gauls (Celts) originally came from the area that now comprises northeastern France, southern Germany and Bohemia. By 400 BC they had spread across France, the British Isles, Belgium, parts of Spain and the Po valley. In 279 Gallic tribes migrated from central Europe into Greece and Asia Minor. They settled in central Anatolia, where they had to put up many fights against the surrounding Hellenistic kingdoms. The kings of Pergamum (in northwest Asia Minor) won great fame in their battles against the Galatians.
Source: Rome, Museo Capitolino.

aim of Ptolemaic politics was to fill the treasury with precious metals by imposing high taxes and customs dues and exporting grain and other products. The high taxes made things very difficult for the peasants. Some no longer managed to make ends meet and fled from their land. Things were to become even worse in the Roman period.

In the Seleucid kingdom, too, economic conditions remained virtually unchanged. The land remained in the hands of the palace, the temples and private landowners. Most of the work was done by the native peasant population. We don't know much about their social status. Many were bound to the land they tilled: if that land was sold, they were included in the transaction. They had to work for the person or institution that owned the land, that is, the king, a temple, a private landowner or a citizen. A king would sometimes grant favoured private individuals large plots of land with entire villages on them. We know virtually nothing about small landowners. Slavery, which was such an important factor in Greek economy, was of much less significance in the Near East, because Near Eastern societies had from the outset always included a large dependent element and so there was no great demand for slaves.

Trade revived in the Hellenistic era because more money became available. Alexander had put the large quantities of gold stored in the Persian treasuries into circulation and the government's investments in armies and fleets, new cities and building projects boosted industry. There may well have been a demand for slaves in the industrial cities, as many Greeks worked there. Many of the people who were taken captive in the numerous wars were sold into slavery. Sometimes their families managed to purchase their freedom before they were taken to the slave markets, but most ended up as slaves in Rome (see p. 189) or in other slave-importing states.

CULTURAL ASPECTS

General

The Greek cities played a fundamental part in spreading Greek culture across the Near East. Tens of thousands of Greeks flocked to those cities, taking their language, their religion, their educational systems and their traditions along with them. School masters, rhetoricians and teachers of grammar, literature, geometry, the theory of music and other subjects settled in all of the Greek cities. The wealthy citizens employed private teachers to teach their children the literary culture of the elite. Children also received physical education. Many cities organised athletic contests modelled on the Olympic Games. Athletics started to be practised as a profession – a development that was to intensify in the Roman period. All these aspects of Greek culture were taught and practised in the gymnasia. Every self-respecting city also had a theatre, besides temples and offices for the city's administration.

Similar Greek buildings soon arose in the Near Eastern cities, too. The notables in those cities learned the Greek language and adopted Greek customs to varying extents. We must however bear in mind that it was mainly the upper classes in these Near Eastern cities that underwent this 'Hellenising' influence; beneath this thin Greek veneer the original culture lived on. In Babylonia, for example, chronicles, astronomical diaries, horoscopes and contracts continued to be written in the cuneiform script. Indeed, this period even saw a revival of Sumerian religious literature. In Egypt, temples continued to be built in the Egyptian style, their walls decorated with hieroglyphic texts. Large numbers of papyri written in Egyptian characters have survived from the Hellenistic era, besides those in Greek. Native authors who wrote about the history and culture of their own peoples in the Greek language betray a certain national pride *vis-à-vis* their conquerors. Such feelings are for example evident in the works of the Egyptian Manetho (see p. 10) and the Babylonian Berossus and in the writings of Flavius Josephus from Judah, who lived in the early Roman imperial age (*c.* AD 70).

There was very little merging of Near Eastern and Greek cultures into a new, Hellenistic culture. Greek and Near Eastern architectural styles were for example to be found side by side. The same holds for the scenes that were painted on the walls of Egyptian tombs. Sometimes a building or a wall painting shows elements of both styles, but they are then usually not combined into a harmonious ensemble. This cultural division must also be borne in mind in the following discussions of the religion, philosophy and science of these civilisations.

Religion

In the Greek world, the ancient myths about the Homeric deities had already been criticised in the Classical period; new ways of thinking had emerged that propagated more sublime conceptions of the gods and encouraged a more personal religious experience. We have previously mentioned for example the religious views of Xenophanes (see p. 85) and Plato (see p. 122) and the personal devotion of the initiates of the mysteries of Demeter at Eleusis. These trends continued in the Hellenistic era. More and more Greeks began to lose faith in the ancient Olympian gods. That is not to say that they became less religious or that the existence of the deities was widely denied. All the new Greek cities for example chose one of the Olympian gods as their patron deity, just like the *poleis* of the Greek homeland had done. And the Greek gods were honoured in the gymnasia. Nevertheless we get the impression that the gods acquired a more universal character. This is particularly true of the supreme god Zeus, who was sublimed into a general divine power in philosophical works. The declining faith in the Olympian pantheon is also apparent from the worship of the abstractions Fate and Fortune as personalised goddesses. In the past, Fate had been regarded as an impersonal, arbitrary power over which even the gods had no control.

Figure 11.4 Sculpture of Poseidon, the god of the sea from the island of Melos: second century BC
Source: Marburg photographic archive.

The contacts with the Near East had a profound influence on the Greeks' religious thought and practice. The Greeks started to identify their own gods with foreign gods (e.g. Zeus with other supreme gods such as the Syrian god of the sky Baal Shamen, the Egyptian Amon, the Babylonian Marduk and even the God of Israel). But the Greeks also included new gods in their pantheon, the best-known examples being the gods of the Egyptians. The cult of the Egyptian goddess Isis, for example, became quite widespread in the Hellenistic world and later also in the Roman world. The goddess was however greatly Hellenised to make her acceptable to the Greeks. That is clearly apparent from the way in which she is portrayed in the visual arts (see p. 146) and from the hymns that were dedicated to her. She was on a higher level than the Greek deities. She was even believed to be more powerful than Fate. Here we see a clear example of a trend towards henotheism. In Egypt, Isis remained the same Egyptian deity she had always been and people continued to worship her in the usual Egyptian manner. There was consequently a difference between the Egyptian and the Greek Isis cult.

The declining influence of the ancient gods is also apparent from the appearance of the ruler cult. The ruler was regarded as a god who moved among mortals, as a saviour and a benefactor. In a hymn to Demetrius Poliorcetes, the 'Besieger' who had freed Athens from the Macedonian garrison in 307, he and his father, Antigonus the One-Eyed, are honoured as divine saviours. The hymn explicitly states that Demetrius succeeded where the other gods had failed. What is rather odd is that in this same hymn he is referred to as a son of Poseidon!

It is believed that this spontaneously emerged ruler cult, which became particularly popular in the Greek cities, was a consequence of the Greeks' custom of paying divine honours to deceased notables and later also deceased relatives. At a certain stage the Seleucid and Ptolemaic kings instituted state cults, first for their deceased predecessors and later also for themselves and their wives.

Another way in which people sought security was by turning to mystery religions. Although cults like that of Eleusis had already existed for several centuries (see p. 82), mystery cults, revolving around Greek or Near Eastern deities (see p. 264ff), became far more widespread in the Hellenistic and Roman periods. A final example of Near Eastern influences on the West that should be mentioned here is that of Babylonian astrology. The Greeks and Romans copied the Babylonians in naming planets after deities. The Greeks called the Babylonian planet Marduk 'Zeus', while the Romans later named it 'Jupiter'. Likewise, Ishtar became Aphrodite and Venus, respectively. 'Chaldean' astrologers were renowned for their art of divination. Their influence is still noticeable today.

Near Eastern religions

In the cities and temples of the ancient Near East, Oriental deities continued to be worshipped with little evidence of Greek influences. Cult practices, prayers and temples all retained their traditional forms.

It was Asia Minor that felt the influence of Greece the most. Inscriptions found in that region show that the native languages were increasingly supplanted by Greek. As the west coast of Asia Minor had been Greek for many centuries, this is not all that surprising. However, in Asia Minor, too, the deities who were awarded Greek names often remained Near Eastern in character. Syrian religion became more Greek when Antioch was made the capital of the Seleucid kingdom. The degree of Hellenisation differed from one area to another, depending on the impact of the Greeks' presence. Sometimes the opposite would happen and Greeks would start to worship Near Eastern deities. Generally speaking, however, the religious practices of the Greeks and those of the Near Eastern natives remained distinctly separate.

Philosophy and science

The end of the *polis* as an independent political unit is also reflected in Greek philosophy. Man was regarded more as a world citizen (a 'cosmo-politan') than as a *polis* citizen. A consequence of this was that philosophers began to see man more as an individual than as a member of a citizen body. Attention shifted to man's personal responsibilities and personal ethics and to the question of how an individual can achieve happiness.

The principal schools of thought outside the Academy and the Lyceum, which still existed, were those of the Stoics, the Epicureans and the Cynics. The Stoics (so called after the Stoa, a colonnade in Athens where Zeno, the founder of this school of thought, taught his pupils) maintained that the cosmos was governed by a rational divine power, which permeated every aspect of the cosmos. This power, which was referred to as *logos* (word, reason), but also as *theos* (god), controlled everything; something of this divine power resided in man, too. All things had their own purpose and their own place in the natural order. Man therefore had to accept whatever happened to him in life with 'Stoic' equanimity and he had to 'live according to nature'. He was to free himself of strong emotions, he was to be self-sufficient and was to allow himself to be governed entirely by his reason, which most closely resembled the ordering power governing nature. 'Freedom' to the Stoics meant freedom from anxiety, which was superior to the old notion of political freedom enjoyed by a *polis*. The Stoics' doctrines opened up paths for the diffusion of Chaldean astrology, which was based on the assumption that there is a direct relation between the cosmos and life on earth.

Epicurus regarded pleasure as the highest ideal. This, he believed, was to be attained not in a dissolute life of partying, but by freeing oneself from one's passions and fears. He therefore condemned magic, superstition and fear of the gods, which terrorised people's lives. Like Democritus, Epicurus believed that everything consisted of atoms (see p. 85), but the movement of those atoms was in his opinion not governed by a controlling spirit, but by chance. That is also the main reason why all that man could aspire to was personal happiness.

The Cynics (dog-like, living like dogs) reacted against the contemporary conventional way of life. They taught that man must be entirely self-sufficient. The happiest man is he who can make do without anything. The Cynics saw little point in intellectual education. In their opinion the most virtuous man automatically made the best king; such a person did not require any education as he already knew how to rule his kingdom. The Cynics travelled around the Greek cities, begging for their living and holding moralising speeches in the markets.

Science

In the Hellenistic era a distinction arose between philosophy and the sciences. The sciences flourished in Alexandria in particular. They were greatly encouraged by Ptolemy I, who founded the 'Museum' in that city – a centre of scientific learning that also contained a library. Among the most famous scholars who worked there were Aristarchus of Samos, who propounded the theory that the sun was at the centre of the universe, Eratosthenes of Cyrene, who calculated the earth's circumference, and Archimedes of Syracuse, renowned for his calculation of the specific gravity of water and his designs for military machines. Medical science, for which Hippocrates had laid the foundations in the fifth century, also flourished and enjoyed great popularity. Many cities appointed doctors, who they paid to provide medical treatment.

As far as we know, the philosophers and scientists mentioned above were all of Greek origins, with the exception of Zeno, who was a Semitic scholar from Cyprus. Hence their theories were essentially Greek. The greatest scholars in the field of astronomy were however to be found in Egypt and Babylon. Astronomical observations were recorded in cuneiform script in Babylonia until the first century AD. We know that a Babylonian translated astronomical works written in the Persian era into Greek. No new scientific contributions are known from these regions from the Hellenistic era.

The Jews in the Hellenistic era

In the days of the Persian empire, after thousands of exiled Jews had returned from Babylonia, Judah had developed into a small temple state within the large satrapy known as 'Beyond the River' (see Map 4.3, p. 43). After the conquests of Alexander the Great this state first came under Ptolemaic rule. In 200 Antiochus III incorporated it in his Seleucid kingdom. There were however also large numbers of Jews living outside Judah. For a start, quite a few had remained in Babylon; many others had gone to Egypt, to serve in the Egyptian army or for other reasons. Alexandria had a very large Jewish community. These Jews are said to have lived 'in the Diaspora' (*diaspora* being the Greek word for dispersal).

The Jews, too, of course became acquainted with Greek civilisation, and some Jewish thinkers, especially in Alexandria, were greatly influenced by it. Many of the Jews in Alexandria could speak only Greek. For their benefit a Greek translation was made of the Old Testament (the 'Septuagint'). Jerusalem also underwent Greek influences. A gymnasium was built in the city and some citizens (even high priests) adopted Greek customs. But neither the Ptolemaic nor the Seleucid rulers ever tried to convert the Jews to the Hellenistic way of life.

In 168 BC the Jews rose against the Seleucids, when Antiochus IV Epiphanes invaded Egypt and the Romans forced him to retreat. A group of Jews in Jerusalem felt that this was a good moment to cast off the Seleucid yoke. However, Antiochus soon suppressed their revolt and garrisoned Syrian soldiers near Jerusalem. For the benefit of those soldiers he installed a cult object dedicated to the Syrian god Baal Shamen (Zeus Olympios to the Greeks) in the temple. To orthodox monotheistic Jews this was totally intolerable and a second uprising consequently broke out. This revolt was led by Judas Maccabaeus. As the power of the Seleucid dynasty gradually weakened in the incessant succession struggles that followed the death of Antiochus, the revolt was ultimately successful. In 152 the Maccabees claimed the offices of high priest and general from one of the pretenders to the throne. Ten years later Judah was granted exemption from taxation and acquired *de facto* independence following the disbandment of the Seleucid garrison. In 104 the Maccabees granted their leader the title of king (the Hasmonean dynasty). The Maccabees expanded Judah into a large kingdom and forced subject non-Jews to adopt Jewish customs, such as circumcision. The authors of the Books of Maccabees decried the Greek influences and Greek customs of the pre-Maccabean priests of Jerusalem. In spite of this, the Hasmonean kings, too, were becoming more and more Hellenised; they chose Greek names for themselves and even called themselves 'Phil-Hellene' (lover of Hellenism). Within their kingdom they sought support sometimes among the rather aristocratic Sadducees, at other times among the Pharisees, who were more popular among the common people. The Sadducees were members of the old-established rich families of priests who had long since dominated the temple in Jerusalem, while the Pharisees were learned rabbis who explained the Scriptures.

The Hasmonean dynasty was weakened by internal succession struggles, in which the Romans ultimately intervened. In 63 the Romans incorporated Judah in the province of Syria.

THE IMPACT OF HELLENISTIC CULTURE IN THE PARTHIAN KINGDOM AND THE ROMAN EMPIRE

The Parthian kingdom originated in the Persian satrapy Parthia (see Map 4.3, p. 43), which is known to have already existed during the reign of Darius I. In the middle of the third century BC the Parni, a Scytho-Iranian tribe, invaded the satrapy, drove away the Greek satrap, who had then only just acquired independence, and founded a new dynasty. In the course of the third and second centuries BC the Parthians, as the Parni were now called, conquered Iran and Mesopotamia. The members of the Parthian dynasty considered themselves to be the heirs to the Persian empire; the Persians, however, regarded the Parthians as foreigners.

The Parthian kings soon started to call themselves 'Phil-Hellene' on their coins to please the Greeks in their kingdom. The power of the Parthians was based on a strong cavalry, composed of Parthian nobles, but the kingdom lacked sufficient manpower and organisational expertise to form its own government. It was hence not long before large numbers of vassal kingdoms emerged alongside the satrapies. At the same time, the Greek cities in the kingdom acquired considerable local autonomy.

The language used for official purposes was Greek. A new Greco-Iranian style of architecture evolved, which found expression especially in the new cities. Some of these cities were built on the sites of former cities, such as Ctesiphon, the new capital which was built opposite Seleucia, and Hatra and Ashsur. According to Aramaic texts, the cult of the god Ashsur continued or was revived in Assur. Buildings designed in the new Parthian style arose in Uruk and Babylon, too. The new and rebuilt cities attracted many Iranian, Aramaic, Arabic and Jewish

Figure 11.5 Statuette representing Isis: Roman period, second century AD
Notes: In the Ptolemaic and Roman periods Isis was identified with Thermoutis, the snake
goddess of fertility and harvest.
Source: Rijksmuseum van Oudheden, Leiden.

immigrants. Mesopotamia became a cauldron of foreign peoples and cultures. The
ancient Sumero-Akkadian civilisation, which had lived on in a language that had gone
out of ordinary use a long time ago and whose last bulwarks Babylon and Uruk had
suffered severe damage in the wars, was ultimately obliterated by all these foreign
influences. What remained was an Iranian culture fecundated by Greek civilisation.
This culture was to receive a new impetus in the Sassanian era (see p. 274).

The parts of the Hellenistic world that came under Roman sway continued to feel
the influence of Greek culture for a long time yet. This was because the Romans
themselves had already been assimilating elements of Greek culture for many
centuries. The cultural traditions of the ancient Near East however gradually waned.
In economic terms, Egypt faced hard times under the Romans. Much capital disappeared to Rome in the form of extortionate taxes. The Ptolemies had also imposed
high taxes, but most of that money had been reinvested in the Egyptian economy.
The native Egyptians reacted to the exploitation of the Greco-Roman elite rulers by
adopting the Christian faith at a very early stage or by vehemently adhering to their
own religion. The latter came to a definitive end when the Christian emperor

Figure 11.6 Fragment of a mummy shroud from Thebes: Roman imperial age, second century AD

Notes: The deceased is represented in a Roman style. His head is surrounded by a halo. The halo motif has a long history of use. It is to be found on Greek vases and Etruscan mirrors from the fifth century BC, but became particularly popular in the Roman imperial age. First it was used only for gods and heroes, later also for emperors, notables and the deceased. In Christian art only Christ was originally represented with a halo; later on, the Virgin Mary and other important saints and also angels were shown with haloes.

To the right of the deceased is a mummified Osiris. Part of the sun boat and Re-Harakhte (Re-Horus of the Horizon), represented with a falcon's head and the solar disk, are visible on his chest.

Source: Rijksmuseum van Oudheden, Leiden.

Justinian closed the temple of Isis at Philae, the last heathen stronghold, shortly before AD 550.

CONCLUSION

Some historians claim that the Near Eastern world became entirely Hellenised after Alexander's conquests. That is not correct. Only the elite of the large cities became acquainted with Greek culture and adopted various elements of that culture. Nowhere in the Near East did Greek become the common spoken language, except in Asia Minor and in very large cities like Alexandria, where many Greeks lived together.

Something else that is often maintained is that Hellenistic civilisation is a blend of Greek and Near Eastern elements. That is not correct either. What actually happened is that a combination of diverse factors moved Greek civilisation into a new phase, in which it borrowed certain elements from the Near East. At the same time, the various cultures of the Near East assimilated Greek influences in varying degrees.

PART III

ROME

EARLY ROMAN HISTORY
(754–265 BC)

— *Chapter Twelve* —

THE WESTERN MEDITERRANEAN

The history of the civilisation of the western Mediterranean differs from that of the ancient world further east.

In the third and second millennia BC there were in the west no highly civilised centres of the kind that were then to be found in Egypt, the Levant, Crete and Greece. For these two thousand years the western Mediterranean remained shrouded in the veils of prehistory. Only between 800 and 500 BC, that is, in the period coinciding with the Archaic period of Greek history and the era of the Assyrian, Babylonian and Persian empires in the Levant (pp. 37–45), did civilisations comparable with those of the east emerge in the western Mediterranean. They are the civilisations of the Etruscans in central Italy, the Carthaginians in North Africa (Tunisia) and the Greeks in the Greek colonies in southern Italy, Sicily and southern Gaul (Map 12.1). The tribes living in the surroundings of these peoples were much less civilised. We know only very little about their traditions and social organisation.

The Etruscans

The Etruscans lived in city states that were associated in a loose federal organisation. All cultural life and administrative affairs were concentrated in the urban centres of these city states; Etruscan civilisation was very much an urban civilisation. The Etruscan cities became quite wealthy thanks to the high workmanship of their craft products, especially their metalwork and pottery. Metals and metal objects from Etruria were important merchandise all over the Mediterranean.

The Etruscans were a class of aristocrats who ruled over the native Italian population. Their origins were already a matter of debate in antiquity. Some scholars claim that they originated in Italy itself; others believe that they came from Asia Minor. The latter maintain that the Etruscans' art of divination, which involved observing the flight of birds (Latin: *auspicia*) and studying the livers of sacrificed animals, was also practised in Mesopotamia and Asia Minor (see p. 50), and that the few Etruscan words that have come down to us are reminiscent of languages spoken in Asia Minor. What we do know for certain is that these words are not Indo-European, whereas almost all the other languages that were spoken in Italy in these days did belong to the Indo-European family.

Etruscan civilisation was a blend including Near Eastern, Italian and Greek elements. The Greek elements reflect the influences of the Greek colonies that were founded in the western Mediterranean from the beginning of the Archaic period onwards (see pp. 126 and 127). Etruscan civilisation reached its height in the seventh and sixth centuries BC. In that period the Etruscans had control over central Italy, large parts of the Po valley and Campania in southern Italy (see Map 12.2). After 500 BC, however, the increasing competition of the Greeks (pp. 126–7) and the invasions of the Celts (Gauls) gradually undermined their power. Some time after 400 BC the Celts conquered the Po valley and repeatedly raided central Italy.

Figure 12.1 Etruscan tomb painting
Notes: The Etruscans buried their dead in *necropoleis* ('cities of the dead'). The tombs
were beautifully decorated and the deceased were accompanied by a wide range of goods.
Excavations in these *necropoleis* have taught us a good deal about the Etruscans.
Source: Marburg photographic archive, Rome, Villa Torlonia.

Carthage

Carthage was founded around 800 BC by colonists from the Phoenician city of Tyre (see p. 33). It was one of the military bases and trading posts that the Phoenicians founded along their shipping routes in the western Mediterranean (see Map 12.1; also see Map 9.1b, p. 75). When pressure from the Assyrians (p. 38) caused Tyre's power to decline, Carthage assumed control over the Phoenician network of trading posts and bases and founded a few new colonies herself, too. Those colonies, in North Africa, were essentially agricultural settlements.

Carthage was a prosperous city. Her wealth was partly based on her maritime trade in the western Mediterranean and across the Atlantic, between West Africa and the British Isles, and partly on her highly developed agricultural activities in her own African hinterland. The city's population was not large enough to enable her to man her mercantile ships, her war fleet and her army all at the same time, and Carthage's wars were consequently fought predominantly with hired mercenaries, mostly from North Africa and Spain.

As far as shipping is concerned, Carthage held a near monopoly in the southwest Mediterranean and on the Atlantic Ocean between West Africa and the British Isles. To defend this position, she had established a network of fortified bases in western Sicily, Sardinia, North Africa and Spain (see Map 12.1). Carthage was always prepared to engage in warfare whenever any of her bases were threatened. This is one of the causes of the constant wars between the Greeks and the Carthaginians in Sicily (pp. 126–7) and of the fierce battle between Carthage and Rome in the third century BC (pp. 178–80).

Carthage was governed by a class of large landowners and rich merchants that also included a few families which provided the army and navy commanders over several generations.

THE ORIGINS OF ROME

The first people to have settled at the site of what was later to become the city of Rome belonged to a tribe known as the Latins. They spoke Latin, an Indo-European language. The Latins had probably arrived in Italy some time in the last centuries of the second millennium BC. From the tenth to the sixth century, Latium, which contained Rome, was characterised by a homogeneous culture, which is attributed to the Latins.

According to Roman legend, Rome was founded in 753 BC by Romulus, who became the first king of Rome. From archaeological evidence we know that by that date there had for some time indeed been settlements on the Palatine hill and a few other hills along the Tiber. These hills lay in what was then the border region between Latium and Etruria; to the north of the Tiber lay the territory of the Etruscan city of Veii. The earliest Roman population was probably a mixture of Latins, Etruscans and Sabines (a tribe that lived in the hills to the east of Rome).

Towards 600 BC the influence of the Etruscans increased. It is only then that Rome grew into a true city, with a market surrounded by buildings and stone temples. After 600 Rome rapidly expanded into one of the largest cities in Italy. The

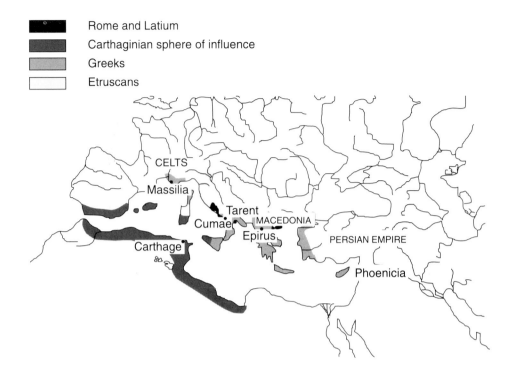

Map 12.1 The (western) Mediterranean in the fifth and fourth centuries BC

city was favourably situated, in a fertile, relatively densely populated region, at the junction of an important road linking Etruria to the Greek and Etruscan settlements in Campania, a shipping route (the Tiber) and a road to the salt-pans at the coast (salt was an extremely important commodity in the ancient world).

Tradition has it that Rome was first ruled by seven kings (seventh to sixth centuries BC). The first four are largely legendary figures. Later Roman authors were to attribute many Roman institutions and customs to those kings to demonstrate their great antiquity and venerability. The last three kings, Tarquinius Priscus, Servius Tullius and Tarquinius Superbus, ruled in the sixth century BC. They are believed to have come from Etruria. At that time Rome lay within the Etruscan sphere of influence.

State and society in early Rome

Archaeological finds, such as the objects with which the deceased were buried, and evidence in the works of later Roman authors suggest that the population of Rome in her earliest days was already characterised by some degree of social differentiation. There was an upper layer of aristocratic families who owned a relatively large proportion of the available land, there was a class of well-to-do peasants, and below them was a class of poorer peasants. The farms were still almost all self-sufficient family units. In the city of Rome there were also craftsmen. On the basis of later

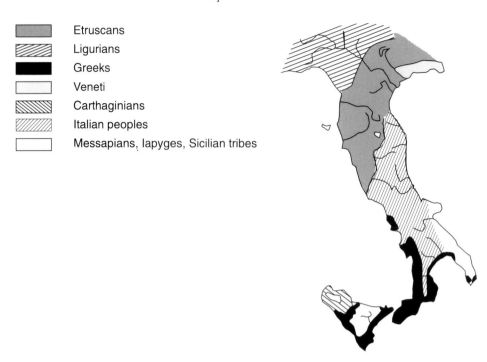

Etruscans
Ligurians
Greeks
Veneti
Carthaginians
Italian peoples
Messapians, Iapyges, Sicilian tribes

Map 12.2 Peoples living in Italy, *c.* 600 BC

evidence it is assumed that many of the peasants, even the more prosperous, were dependent on or protected by the aristocrats. Those peasants were called *clientes*, their aristocratic protectors *patroni*. The Latin word *clientes* means something like 'dependants'. The peasants and craftsmen who did not enjoy the patronage of the aristocrats were later to be referred to as *plebeians*. The aristocrats themselves were *patricians*. The *clientes*, on whom much of their power depended, were not classed as patricians. Only the members of the aristocratic families who claimed to descend from heroes of Roman legends and folk tales were patricians (cf. the *eupatridae* in Athens, p. 89).

From later evidence we know that the kings commanded the army, administered justice and led the ceremonies for the state deities. As in other states in the ancient world, those were the main administrative tasks.

The kings enjoyed absolute power (Latin: *imperium*) that covered all the fields with which the state concerned itself. They were assisted and advised by the *Senate*, a council consisting of the heads of the aristocratic families, and they could summon a public assembly, the *Comitia Curiata*. This *Comitia Curiata* was the organ that formally conferred the *imperium* on the kings and consequently sanctioned their position. Here we find the same three kinds of state organs as in the Archaic Greek *poleis*: an executive authority, an aristocratic council and a public assembly that had little effective power, but which was nevertheless the body that sanctioned the executive authority.

The *Comitia Curiata* consisted of thirty *curiae*, which each had a vote. A *curia* consisted of a number of *gentes* (singular: *gens*), that is, clans, groups of families, who

Figure 12.2 The she-wolf that allegedly suckled Romulus and Remus: 480–470 BC
Notes: The figures of the twins, Romulus and Remus, are later additions (AD 1510).
According to Roman legend, Romulus and Remus founded Rome. They were believed to have
been born from a union of the god Mars with Rhea Silvia, the daughter of a Latin king. They
were abandoned by a usurper, who deposed Rhea's father, and were kept alive by a she-wolf.
Source: Rome, Museo nuovo del Palazzo dei Conservatori.

claimed to be linked by a common ancestor and who shared certain traditions. A *gens*
was a group of several *familiae*. A *familia* was comparable with a Greek household
in the Homeric era (see p. 70). It consisted of a husband and wife and their children
(whether or not married), grandchildren, slaves and *clientes*.

Within the family, the *pater familias*, the male head of the family, enjoyed absolute
authority. He had power of life and death over his children and slaves. A woman
married into her husband's family and on her wedding day she and her dowry passed
under the authority of the *pater familias* of her husband's family.

The authority of the *pater familias* has been compared to that of the king. Just as
the king enjoyed unrestricted authority over the affairs of the *res publica*, the Roman
state, so the *pater familias* had absolute control over his *res privata*, his private household. And just as the king presided over the cult of the state gods, so the *pater
familias* led the simple daily offerings and prayers to the household deities, the *Lares*
and the *Penates*.

A note on Roman names

The organisation in *gentes* and *familiae* was reflected in the names that the Romans
were given. Each Roman had at least three names: a personal name (e.g. Publius,

abbreviated to P.), a name denoting his *gens* (e.g. Cornelius, of the *gens* Cornelia) and one or more surnames, intended to distinguish the family within the *gens* (e.g. Scipio).

The army and the *Comitia Centuriata*

Originally, the *gentes* were not only groups of families united by strong religious and cultural traditions, but also military units. It is thought that the earliest Roman army was organised on this basis. The aristocrats, at the head of their *gentes*, presumably dominated the battlefields in those days (see pp. 70 and 76). It was probably in the sixth century that the Romans started to fight in the same way as the contemporary Greeks and Etruscans, in a closed battle array of heavily armed infantrymen (a *phalanx*), surrounded by cavalrymen and lightly armed soldiers.

According to Roman tradition, the penultimate king, Servius Tullius (*c.* 578–535), adapted the organisation of civilians to the changed fighting method and divided the civilians into property classes (see p. 89 on Solon).

The wealthiest citizens served in the cavalry. Their horses were provided by the state – a curious form of subsidising of the rich (see p. 57). The members of this property group were called *equites*, after *equus*, the Latin word for horse. Almost all the patricians and a few wealthy plebeians belonged to this property group (and consequently to the cavalry). The wealthy peasants served as heavily armed infantrymen, the members of the lower classes as lightly armed soldiers. Propertyless citizens who could not afford to arm themselves did not serve in the army. This classification based on property was also employed in imposing property taxes (*tributum*) and in organising a new public assembly, the *Comitia Centuriata*, which consequently had the same organisation as the contemporary army. Below the cavalry there were five property classes, which were each subdivided into *centuriae* (*centuria* – a unit of 100 men). Each *centuria* had one vote. The *centuriae* – and consequently the votes, too – were divided between the five property classes so that the first class plus the cavalry could obtain a majority (see Diagram 12.2). They consequently pulled the strings at the *Comitia Centuriata*. The citizens without property (*proletarians*), who were excluded from the army organisation, sat on this assembly in one added *centuria*. In other words, they collectively had one vote. We note the same direct relation between wealth, military importance and political power as in some contemporary Greek *poleis* (see pp. 76–90; 116).

The *Comitia Centuriata* gradually superseded the *Comitia Curiata* in many respects, but the latter did continue to exist. Sometimes the citizens would meet in the new way, and their assembly would then be called a *Comitia Centuriata*; at other times those same citizens would meet in the old-fashioned manner, in a *Comitia Curiata*. We will return to the subject of the Roman popular assemblies on pp. 172–4.

THE EARLY REPUBLIC (509–265 BC)

State and society

Around 500 BC – the traditional date is 509 – the era of the kings came to an end. Tradition has it that the Romans expelled their last king, Tarquinius Superbus, because they had had enough of his cruelty and arrogance, but it is more likely that the real reason was the Romans' desire to break away from the Etruscan sphere of influence. For the first fifty years after they had expelled the Etruscan king, the Roman aristocrats progressively directed their look away from Etruria and towards their tribal relatives, the Latins. Rome became an important member of the Latin League of city states. It is believed that the members of this League had shared a form of communal citizen rights, the 'Latin rights' since the beginning of the fifth century. These Latin rights granted all the occupants of the League's member states the right to conduct trade with one another and to marry partners from all the member states.

When kingship was abolished in Rome the king's executive power was transferred to two annually elected magistrates, who were later, after 367, to be called *consuls*. These magistrates shared the former king's *imperium* (see p. 156), but their power was restricted because they could check one another's acts by right of veto and because their term of office was limited to one year. After that year any dissatisfied citizen could file complaints against them if they so desired.

The two ruling magistrates were assisted by two treasurers, or *quaestors*, and like the kings before them, they turned to the Senate for advice in administrative affairs. As they usually followed the Senate's advice, the Senate had a powerful say in

Figure 12.3 'Brutus': third or second century BC
Notes: The sculpture is now on display in the Palazzo dei Conservatori in Rome. According to Roman tradition, L(ucius) Junius Brutus expelled the last king and established the republic (509 BC).
Source: Rome, Museo nuovo del Palazzo dei Conservatori.

159

political affairs. The decisions of the popular assembly acquired the force of law only after they had been approved by the Senate.

The king's religious authority was passed on to the *rex* (king) *sacrorum* (of the *sacra*, the holy, sacred affairs) and the *pontifex maximus*, the president of the college of *pontifices* (priests). They were responsible for ensuring that the proper practices were observed when prayers and sacrifices were offered to the state gods to secure their favour.

Sometimes, in an emergency, for example when a war or a civil strife took a turn for the worse, the autocratic authority of the former kings would be temporarily restored. In such a situation the ruling magistrates could appoint a *dictator*, who was granted absolute power for six months.

After the fall of the last king the patricians dominated the political scene. It was they who furnished the magistrates and the senators; the *Comitia Centuriata* elected magistrates exclusively from the patriciate and new senators were almost always former magistrates (see below, p. 170). The patricians also provided the *pontifices* and the members of other important priesthoods. There were no true, separate priest castes; the priests were patricians who held the priesthood in addition to their secular offices.

The patricians also controlled every aspect of social and economic life: large numbers of peasants were their *clientes* or had been reduced to an even more dependent status by debts (debt slavery: see p. 90). The patricians were also the only members of society who were familiar with the unwritten laws and the ritual formulas with which pleadings had to be introduced.

However, it was not long before the patricians' powerful position was challenged by groups of dissatisfied plebeians.

The history of the Roman republic up to the third century BC is dominated by two lengthy historical processes:

1 the so-called 'struggle of the orders' between the patricians and the plebeians;
2 the expansion of the Roman empire in peninsular Italy.

Roman expansion in Italy (509–265 BC)

The period 509–338 BC was characterised by endless struggles in central Italy between Rome, the Latins, the tribes who lived in the hills around Latium, and the southern Etruscan cities. They fought one another in constantly changing coalitions (see Map 12.3). The main issues of contention were the fertile land in the valleys and coastal plains and the control of the land trade routes between Etruria and Campania. The struggles dragged on for many years because the contending parties were one another's equals in military terms. In her wars against the hill tribes, Rome was usually assisted by the other members of the Latin League, but her battles against the Etruscans she fought largely by herself. In the early fourth century BC Rome managed to annex the southern part of Etruria (including the city of Veii, to the north of the Tiber). With this act Rome gained decisive ascendancy over the other Latin city states in terms of territory and manpower.

In the next fifty years Rome had to defend herself not only against the hill tribes, but also against the Latin cities, which were afraid that Rome would try to extend

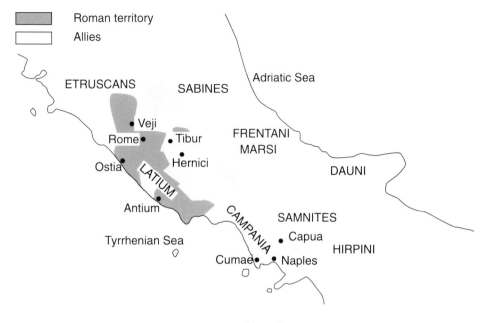

Map 12.3 Rome and her allies, *c.* 350 BC

her sway over their territory, too, and against Celtic gangs, who repeatedly pillaged Italy after 400 (see p. 152). Etruria suffered the most from these Celtic raids. It could be said that, by weakening the Etruscan cities, the Celts helped to pave the way for Rome's expansion in Italy.

After 350 the process of expansion in Italy really got under way. In 338 Rome subjected the Latin cities and concluded treaties with the most important city states in Campania. That brought the most fertile and most densely populated regions of central Italy within Rome's sphere of influence and vastly expanded her military resources. Rome now dominated the Latin League's member states. The Latin citizen rights continued to exist: within Rome's territory the Latins remained equal to Roman citizens (and vice versa) in business transactions and marriage law. Latins who took up permanent residence in Rome and renounced the citizen rights of their own city state were entitled to full Roman citizenship.

After 326 a multiplicity of minor local and regional conflicts in different parts of Italy merged into a number of protracted coalition wars (326–290), which came to involve all the peoples in Italy. Rome emerged from these wars as the mistress of the whole of peninsular Italy, with the exception of the Greek cities in the south. Those cities were subjected in the years between 282 and 270, in spite of the help that they received from a general of the Macedonian school, King Pyrrhus of Epirus (see Maps 12.1, and 13.1, p. 178). He helped the Greeks in southern Italy fight the Romans and assisted Syracuse in her battle against Carthage. In both wars he achieved spectacular successes. In 275, however, the Romans decisively defeated him at Beneventum (see Map 12.4).

Rome entered into a series of individual alliances with the city states and tribes

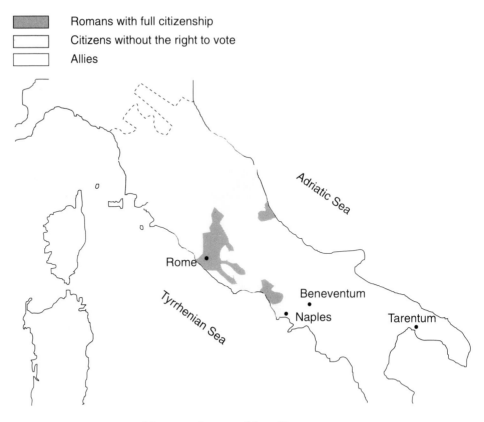

Map 12.4 Rome and her allies, 241 BC

she subjected in Italy: they were made subordinate allies. These allies were obliged to supply troops for Rome's wars and to support Rome's foreign politics but they did not have to pay any tributes. They also retained their autonomy in internal affairs and their own citizen rights. They were not granted anything comparable with the Latin rights.

Colonisation

Rome founded colonies in most of the lands she conquered. Her custom was to confiscate part of the territory of her subject opponents and to turn it into Roman public land, owned by the Roman state.

On this public land, Rome settled Roman and Latin peasants with military experience and propertyless Romans and Latins. These colonies were called Latin colonies (*coloniae Latinae*), to distinguish them from the few small colonies that Rome had founded as military bases at strategic points throughout her territory (the *coloniae Romanae* – Roman colonies).

The Latin colonies lay scattered across Italy, usually on fertile soil at road junctions and other strategic points. They were not independent city states; although they enjoyed local autonomy, they were subject to Rome. The colonists were granted Latin rights, which meant that they were entitled to full Roman citizenship if they were ever to return to Rome. The colonists of the small *coloniae Romanae* retained their full Roman citizenship.

The plots that the colonists were granted for their support varied in size from 0.5 to 10 hectares. In addition to this land, they could also rent part of the land that had not been divided among the colonists. That land was usually exploited on a communal basis. The colonists were also allowed to rent public land. This land consequently became an extra source of income for the Roman treasury, on top of the property taxes.

The public land became a source of competition at an early stage in Roman history. Besides the Roman and Latin colonists, local Italian peasants and wealthy Roman and Italian landowners were all entitled to rent public land. The wealthy had their land tilled by slaves and seasonal workers, many of whom were small proprietors who supplemented their income with the wages of this seasonal work. Some scholars believe that as early as 367, Rome passed a law limiting the amount of public land that any one individual could hold, so as to reassure the poor Roman citizens.

This colonisation policy was of great benefit to Rome. In the first place, she acquired a network of strategically based fortifications all over Italy and a means of solving internal conflicts in Rome and Latium by helping poor Roman and Latin citizens to start a new life under better conditions elsewhere. Secondly, the leasing of the public land meant extra income. Another great advantage of this policy was that it implied a considerable growth of Rome's military resources. This was because citizens who had hitherto been excluded from the army on the grounds that they had no property (see p. 158) now came to belong to the property classes from which troops were recruited. In some respects (the fact that the colonies were not new city states, the social upgrading of poor citizens, the military strategic considerations underlying the colonisation) the Latin and Roman colonies were more like the Athenian cleruchies of the fifth century BC than like the Greek colonies of the Archaic period (see pp. 75 and 99).

Municipia

Sometimes Rome would grant a subject city state with a culture and language akin to those of the Romans the status of a Roman city with local autonomy, as a reward for some service or for having voluntarily submitted to Rome's protection. Such a city was called a *municipium*. Its citizens had Roman citizen rights without the right to vote; some even enjoyed full Roman citizenship. This was another way in which Rome expanded her territory and her manpower resources.

Rome's colonisation policy greatly encouraged the adaptation of the Italian peoples to the organisation, language and culture of the Romans. This process is called 'Romanisation'. The notables who held the high offices in local government everywhere in Italy took the least time to adjust themselves to the Roman way of life. The vast majority of the Italian communities were governed by aristocratic or oligarchic landowning elites, just like Rome herself.

By around 265 BC Italy had become a patchwork of states and regions that stood in different relations to Rome and were bound to Rome in different ways (Map 12.4): the Roman heartland (with full Roman citizenship), the area of the former Latin city

Figure 12.4 The Via Appia, the first paved Roman road in Italy
Notes: The Via Appia, which led from Rome to Campania and then on to Brundisium (present-day Brindisi), was started in 312 BC. The paved roads facilitated the rapid movement of troops. These roads and the network of *coloniae* served as means for preventing attacks by the tribes living in central and southern Italy and for the provisioning of Roman armies. Along the road, just outside Rome, lay large funerary monuments of distinguished Roman families.
Source: Marburg photographic archive.

states and the *coloniae Latinae* with Latin rights; the *municipia* with citizen rights without the vote; and the allies, who had only their own local citizen rights. Rome's system worked well. The majority of the Italian city states and tribes loyally participated in her major wars in the period after 265 (p. 179) and played important parts in her expansionist campaigns in the third and second centuries BC. They never joined forces against Rome because their interests differed owing to the different terms of their alliances with Rome (Rome's 'divide and rule' policy).

The military character of Roman society

The wars that Rome fought in Italy in the fifth and fourth centuries BC were not as fierce as those which she waged on her enemies after 265 and were nothing like modern wars. They were essentially minor skirmishes and plunderings, which were fought only in the summer season (between March and November; seasonal wars). Only rarely did Rome engage in a pitched battle. Nevertheless, in these wars the Roman citizens came to regard warfare as an ordinary sideline and a lucrative, if hazardous, source of extra income, for it implied the possibility of acquiring booty and land (in the colonies). For the Roman elite, military fame was the chief status symbol, the best means of access to an honourable career in the state offices. Moreover, it was the elite, more than the rest of the population, who benefited from the booty. The many wars gave birth to a wealth of heroic tales and legends that were to influence Roman mentality for many centuries. Over and over again the Romans were exhorted to follow the examples set by their austere, valorous ancestors.

Warfare did not go against the Romans' religious principles. The Romans believed that as long as they made the proper sacrifices and said the proper prayers, their gods would bless their enterprises. All wars that were declared in the proper manner and were started with the proper rites were just in the eyes of the Roman gods.

The Romans usually regarded their wars as a form of defence. Large, nearby states were soon seen as a threat and many Roman wars hence started as preventive actions (what we could call 'forward defence') or as an act of support to small allies against great powers.

The struggle of the orders (c. 500–287 BC)

While Rome was engaged in her long struggle to extend her hegemony over Italy she also suffered a good deal of internal tension. As we have already seen above (p. 158), the patrician aristocracy had seized power in Rome after the fall of the last king, Tarquinius Superbus. But it was not long before the *plebeians* started to oppose their power. The plebeians were not a clearly defined social group. There were rich plebeians, plebeians of moderate means and poor plebeians and the activities in which they engaged differed. The rich plebeians were large landowners who had arrived in Rome or had been incorporated into the Roman citizen body after the patricians had closed their ranks. The plebeians of moderate means comprised land-owning farmers, who played important parts in Rome's military efforts, and merchants. The poor plebeians were small farmers, craftsmen and day labourers. See Diagram 12.1.

The rich plebeians demanded to be admitted to the governing elite monopolised by the patricians, the poor plebeians wanted relaxation of the harsh debt laws (a debtor could be reduced to slavery; see p. 90 on Athens in Solon's days). All the plebeians – especially the poor – demanded that the main rules of the unwritten law be recorded in a written code, arbitrary acts of the patrician magistrates be checked and the plebeians' assembly (*Concilium Plebis*) be recognised as an official popular assembly

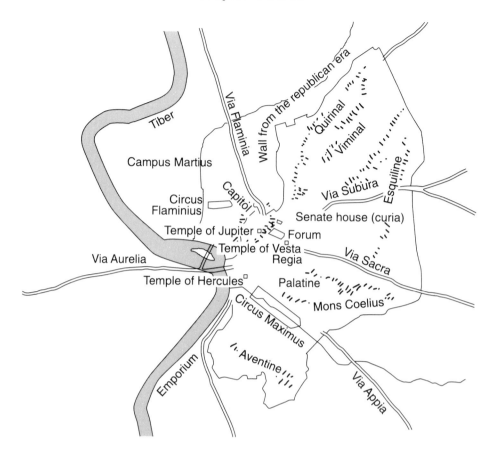

Map 12.5 The city of Rome in the republican era
Notes: The public assemblies convened in the Campus Martius (the field of Mars). That is also where the armies were mustered. The temple of Jupiter was the main centre of the cult of the state gods. Jupiter was the supreme god and the patron deity of Rome. The Regia was the house of the *rex sacrorum* (p. 160).
Vesta was the goddess of the domestic hearth. A fire burned in her temple, which was never allowed to go out. Her cult was administered by the Vestal Virgins, priestesses of high birth who were not allowed to marry.
All triumphal processions passed along the Via Sacra (p. 170).
The chariot races (popular games) were held in the Circus Maximus.
Emporium = quaysides and warehouses.

alongside the *Comitia Centuriata*. Since the fall of the last king the *Comitia Curiata* had become an empty phrase. The plebeians assembled near a group of popular temples on the Aventine hill (Map 12.5); their assemblies were led by *tribuni plebis* (*tribus* – quarter, district, tribe → district heads of the *plebs* – the people → tribunes of the plebs) and *aediles* (temple guards, that is, the guards of the temples on the Aventine). The plebeians were in a powerful position because their middle ranks (mainly the land-owning farmers) formed the backbone of the army: it was they who provided a large portion of the heavily armed infantry, the most important part of the armed forces. Without them, it was virtually impossible for Rome to form an army.

History of the struggle of the orders

During the many years that the so-called struggle of the orders was to last, the situation in Rome became quite critical on several occasions. This was in most cases the consequence of the poor plebeians' debt problems, which sharpened the social contrasts. When things got really bad and the entire plebeian body seceded from political life and refused to participate in Rome's military enterprises, the patricians made political concessions, after which the rebellion would die down. New wars would then temporarily distract attention from the internal problems and the subsequent division of booty and the settlement of poor citizens in colonies would ease a lot of the tension. This form of 'social relief' proved effective especially in the years between 350 and 270 – the heydays of Rome's expansion in Italy. In 326 the problem of the debts was reduced by the abolition of debt slavery.

The most important political concessions that the patricians made to the plebeians were:

- 494 BC: the recognition of the tribunes as the official champions of the plebeians. The tribunes of the *plebs* were elected annually (for a term of one year) in the *Concilium Plebis*. They became a kind of 'anti-magistrates' as against the governing patrician magistrates. The latter were called *consuls* after 367. The tribunes had the right to intercede to prevent the implementation of what they considered arbitrary decisions of the patrician magistrates. They could, for example, veto

Diagram 12.1 Social structure of the early republic

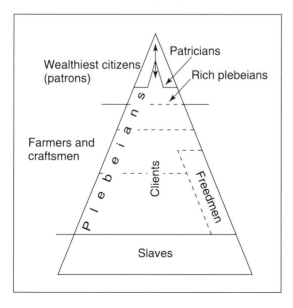

measures that went against the interests of the *plebs* and they could prevent arbitrary arrests. They were also the presiding officers at the *Concilium Plebis*.

- 451 BC: the first codification of a number of laws in the Twelve Tables. These laws consisted of a collection of concrete mandatory and prohibitory provisions and the penalties exacted if they should be violated ('if a person does this or that, then . . . '). Many of the penalties were based on the principle of an eye for an eye. Their main aim was probably to prevent blood feuds. These laws were of course rather primitive. Nevertheless, they were to form the basis for Roman civil law (see pp. 240ff.).

- 367 BC: the admission of wealthy plebeians to the highest administrative office, which was from this year onwards called the consulship. It was decided that one of the two consuls was to be a plebeian. Moreover, a new office was created: the *praetorship*. The consuls' main task was to command the armies while the praetors (there was first only one, but a second was soon added) were to concern themselves mainly with the administration of justice. (We will return to the matter of jurisdiction on p. 240.)

    It was probably in this same year that measures were taken to put an end to the concentration of public land in the hands of a small number of rich landowners (see p. 163).

- 287 BC: recognition of the *Concilium Plebis* as an official popular assembly. The decrees of this assembly (*plebiscita*) were recognised as having force of law (*lex*) and were binding on the whole Roman population (including the patricians, who did not attend this assembly). They did not require the Senate's sanction. From now onwards, the Senate only advised on legislative proposals before the assembly voted on them.

- A similar meeting was usually led by a consul and was called a *Comitia Tributa*. The *Concilium Plebis* was led by a plebeian tribune. The assemblies were convened by the presiding officer. The *Comitia Tributa* (and the *Concilium Plebis*) were organised on the basis of districts instead of property classes (cf. p. 92 on Cleisthenes in Athens). Each district (*tribus*) had one vote. There were thirty-five *tribus* (four within the city and thirty-one outside the city). The Romans soon began to mention their *tribus* in inscriptions, as a symbol of their citizenship. The law that was passed in 287, which is called the *Lex Hortensia* after Hortensius, the dictator who proposed it, is taken to mark the end of the struggle of the orders. After that year the contrasts between the patricians and the plebeians gradually faded, giving way to new social differences of a different kind.

THE INSTITUTIONS OF THE ROMAN REPUBLIC AT THE END OF THE STRUGGLE OF THE ORDERS

The magistrates

The magistrates embodied the Roman state. In the Athenian democracy the citizenry had embodied the state but in Rome this was not the case. New magistrates were elected every year and, as we have already seen (p. 159), their colleagues could stop their actions by a veto.

Within the sacred limits of the city of Rome (*pomerium*), the tribunes of the *plebs* had the right to veto the acts of their own colleagues and all the other magistrates. This right of veto was an important safeguard against arbitrary acts.

The magistrates were assisted in their tasks by small staffs of professional scribes, heralds, messengers, attendants and wardens, but there was no true civil service in the modern sense. The scribes were mostly slaves and freedmen (released slaves). The magistrates could also appeal to groups of advisers – members of their own class who had acquired specific expertise, for example in the field of law or in military strategics and tactics. These groups of advisers (*consilia*) usually greatly influenced a magistrate's policy.

The most important magistrates have already been mentioned above; to summarise, they were:

- *Consuls* (two). The consuls were charged with military command, maintenance of public order and general administration. They were elected by the *Comitia Centuriata*.
- *Praetors* (two; after 241 four; after 80 BC eight). The praetors replaced the consuls whenever necessary and were in most cases responsible for the administration of justice in Rome. They were elected by the *Comitia Centuriata*.
- *Tribunes of the plebs* (ten). The tribunes had the right of veto and the right of intervention. They presided over the *Concilium Plebis*. The tribunes of the *plebs* had to be plebeians; this office was not open to patricians.
- *Aediles* (four). The *aediles* were charged with the maintenance of order on the markets and other police matters, fire-fighting and the organisation of the games in Rome (games involving wild animals or gladiators and chariot races). Besides the plebeian *aediles* (see p. 166) of former days, who had been officially recognised as magistrates in the struggle of the orders, there were also two patrician *aediles*. Organising the games implied considerable personal investments on the part of the *aediles*. These investments were comparable with the liturgies in Athens (see p. 103).
- *Quaestors* (two; after 267 eight; after 80 BC twenty): management of the state treasury.
- The tribunes of the *plebs*, the *aediles* and the *quaestors* were all elected by the *Comitia Tributa*.
- The office of *dictator*, a special office, has already been discussed on p. 160.

Every five years the *Comitia Centuriata* elected two *censors* from among the former consuls, who were appointed for a term of one and a half years (which means that there were no censors for three and a half years). Their tasks were to select worthy new members to fill vacancies in the Senate (the Senate was to have three hundred members), register all the citizens and divide them into property classes (see p. 158), commission the execution of public works, lease state contracts for supplying the armies and farm the taxes. They had the right to remove unworthy senators from the Senate. At the end of their term of office they offered a *lustrum*, an expiatory sacrifice, to the state gods to atone for the offences that the Romans had committed against them. The aim of this purification process was to ensure that the state gods would continue to bestow their favour on the Roman population (in the eyes of the Romans this was a prerequisite for future success).

The highest magistracies were the consulship and the praetorship. Only these offices had *imperium*, the full absolute authority of the chief executive magistrate and general (see p. 156). All the other magistrates – including the *censors* – had powers within their specific fields of activity but no complete authority covering all the fields with which the state concerned itself. The magistrates with *imperium* were recognisable by their special clothing and insignia. Out in the streets they were accompanied by *lictors*, the bearers of bundles of rods and axes, the so-called *fasces*. Within Rome's sacred city limits (the *pomerium*) the magistrates' *imperium* was curtailed by the citizens' right of appeal (see p. 174) and by the powers of the tribunes of the *plebs*, but outside the *pomerium* they enjoyed absolute *imperium*, limited only by their colleagues' right of veto. This *imperium* they exercised for example over their armies in the field.

Armed soldiers were not allowed to enter the *pomerium*; they first had to change into civilian clothing and lay down their weapons. An exception was made when a consul was granted permission to lead his army through the town on a triumphal procession, as an honourable conclusion to a successful campaign. Dressed in the official purple robes of the former kings, the consul would then lead his troops in parade to the Capitol (see Map 12.5), where the chief temples of the supreme god Jupiter and various other state gods stood. There he would donate part of his booty as a thank-offering.

The notables who were appointed to the state offices were to hold those offices in a traditional order, starting with the quaestorship. After their term of office as a *quaestor* they could become an *aedilis* or a tribune of the *plebs*, then a *praetor* and finally a *consul*. This was called the career of the honorary offices (*cursus honorum*). They were called 'honorary offices' because the persons who held them were not paid for their services. That meant that they could only be held by the rich, who could afford to spend all their time on the tasks those offices involved and who could hire others to work for them on their estates. This is also the reason why censors regarded impoverished senators as unworthy and unsuitable for senatorship and the magistracies.

The Senate

The Senate was in effect the most important body of the Roman state. It included all the magistrates and ex-magistrates, because the censors tended to fill vacancies in the Senate with notables who had been appointed *quaestor* or *aedilis*. As a result, the Senate possessed a good deal of military, administrative and diplomatic expertise and experience. The popular assemblies almost always followed the Senate's advice. The Senate had complete control over state finances and foreign politics. A *consul* or a *praetor* presided over the Senate, but the tribunes were also entitled to act as the presiding officers. The ex-consuls were allowed to speak first and they were consequently the effective rulers of the Roman republic, who almost always determined Rome's politics.

Nobiles, senators and *equites*

The opening of the magistracies to the rich plebeians in 367 BC (see p. 168) led to the emergence of a new governing class. From now onwards a small circle of leading

Figure 12.5 Artist's impression of the Senate in assembly
Source: Copy of a drawing by Isings in a school edition of Livy, ed. P.K. Huibregtse,
Wolters, Groningen.

patrician families and rich plebeian families furnished all the praetors and consuls. Whenever a new *consul* or *praetor* was to be appointed, the *Comitia Centuriata* would always elect a member of one of these families. They were called the *nobiles* (nobles). These *nobiles* were the core of a wider circle of equally rich and distinguished senatorial families. This inner circle of nobles formed the actual oligarchic governing element within the Senate.

The senators (including the *nobiles*), in turn, formed the active administrative part of the highest property class in Rome, that is, that of the knights (*equites*) (see p. 158). At the beginning of the third century there were probably some two thousand *equites*. There were more than twenty thousand in the late republic.

The senatorial families and the other *equites* provided the officers for all the army units. The highest officers were magistrates, the middle cadre (the *tribuni militum*) consisted of the senators' young sons and other *equites*. The majority of the next rank of junior officers, the centurions, came from the army's rank and file.

There was not much difference in wealth or lifestyle between the senators and the other members of the property class of the *equites* (below, we will refer to the members of this class simply as 'knights' or '*equites*'). The senatorial and equestrian families were often related and knew each other well. The *censors* would almost always elect new senators from among the younger members of the rich, noble senatorial families who had acquired a good reputation and had behaved in a dignified manner in the field and in Rome. In Rome, such wealthy young nobles could prove their abilities in one or two of the lower governing bodies that assisted the magistrates and were charged with specific tasks such as the minting of coins, road repair work, the maintenance of public order and the administration of justice among the lower classes. (These governing bodies cannot be discussed in any further detail in this brief survey of ancient history.)

Occasionally a knight from a family that had not yet furnished any magistrates or senators managed to gain admittance to the *cursus honorum* by virtue of his remarkable military performance or excellent eloquence. The censors would then include him in the senate. If such a person was ultimately appointed *consul*, he was called a *homo novus* (a 'new man'). In the course of the third century the *nobiles* started to close ranks. After 200 only three or four 'new men' managed to penetrate into the governing circles of the Roman republic.

Increasing differentiation within the Roman elite

In the course of the third and second centuries BC a disparity emerged between the senators and the knights. In 218 BC a law was passed forbidding senators to engage in trade, banking and fiscal enterprises (tax farming). These sectors came to be controlled by their proxies or by a small group of rich *equites*. They set up large companies with vast staffs of specialised free men, slaves and freedmen, which concluded contracts with the censors for supplying the armies, road construction, public works in the city of Rome and tax collection. Whenever they collected a particular tax (e.g. a toll) or the taxes of a particular area, they would pay an advance sum to the state treasury, which they would then recover with profit from the taxable population. These knights were called *publicani*. The other knights remained landed gentry and continued to provide *tribuni militum* for the army as of old.

From the fourth century onwards the cavalry no longer consisted exclusively of members of the equestrian order. After 300 the cavalry included progressively more contingents supplied by allies in Italy and other areas.

The popular assemblies

After the struggle of the orders, Rome in effect had two popular assemblies: the *Comitia Centuriata* and the *Comitia Tributa* (or *Concilium Plebis*; see p. 168 on the *Lex Hortensia*). The *Comitia Curiata* (see pp. 156, 158) had for many years been an empty phrase.

No discussions were held at the popular assemblies. The assemblies were actually voting meetings, means for consulting the citizens. The citizens had the opportunity to form opinions on political issues and decide how they would vote at informal meetings (*contiones*), where politicians could advocate their views.

The officer who presided over a popular assembly had a very powerful position. After putting an issue or a legislative proposal before the assembly, he would first inform the assembly of the Senate's advice (see p. 168 on the *Lex Hortensia*) and

Diagram 12.2 The *Comitia Centuriata*

In the early republic, the subdivision of the five property classes into centuries and the order of voting were as follows:

Class I
12 centuries of *equites* (cavalry)
80 centuries of heavily armed infantry
    (40 cs. of seniors, aged 46 and older,
    40 cs. of juniors, aged 17–46)
6 centuries of *equites* (cavalry)

Class II
20 centuries of infantry
    (10 seniors and 10 juniors)

Class III
20 centuries of infantry
    (10 seniors and 10 juniors)

Class IV
20 centuries of infantry
    (10 seniors and 10 juniors)

Class V
30 centuries of infantry
    (15 seniors and 15 juniors)

Below this classification were five more centuries for those who were exempt from military service because they did not meet the lowest property qualification, including one century for unpropertied citizens (proletarians).

would then invite them to vote on the issue – that is, providing a tribune did not pronounce a veto. But that hardly ever occurred in the hundred and fifty years between the struggle of the orders and the civil strife of the late republic (from 133 BC). The great majority of the tribunes of the *plebs* were *nobiles* themselves, who always followed the Senate's advice.

Things were no different at elections. The presiding officer would present the list of candidates set up by the consuls then in office, after which one of the candidates was elected. The *Comitia Centuriata* was always led by a magistrate with *imperium*, in other words a *consul* or – if both *consuls* were engaged in warfare – a *praetor*. The *Comitia Tributa* was led by a *consul*, a *praetor* or a patrician *aedilis*, but only a tribune of the *plebs* could preside over the *Concilium Plebis*.

After 287 the citizens met as a *Comitia Centuriata* virtually exclusively for specific purposes, when a war was to be declared or a peace treaty was to be ratified or when new *censors*, *consuls* or *praetors* were to be elected. All other issues and elections were left to the *Comitia Tributa* (or *Concilium Plebis*).

The terminology (knights, *centuria* – unit of one hundred soldiers) reminds us of the army assembly which the *Comitia Centuriata* had once been, but that was a thing of the past. In the third and second centuries BC a *centuria* no longer had anything to do with an army company. It was, instead, a group of voters belonging to a particular

Figure 12.6 The Rostra (speaker's platform) on the Forum, Rome's central square
Notes: The public assemblies did not convene on the Forum, but people did meet there to form and exchange opinions. Orators and politicians would address the population on such occasions. The Rostra was decorated with the beaks of ships captured in a victorious naval battle in the fourth century.

property class. The *centuriae* of this popular assembly moreover differed in size. A *centuria* of propertyless citizens included thousands of members, whereas a *centuria* of the highest class sometimes comprised fewer than a hundred citizens. At the *Comitia Centuriata* the vote of the first *centuria*, of the knights, was of great importance, because the other *centuriae* would almost always follow its example. The citizens who met in a *Comitia Tributa* were organised according to the district in which they lived (*tribus*). Each district had one vote. In principle, the poor citizens had a greater influence at the *Comitia Tributa* than at the *Comitia Centuriata*, because within their *tribus* it was the power of their number that counted. In practice, until well into the second century BC, the *Comitia Tributa*, too, almost always followed the Senate's advice and abided by the presiding magistrate's opinion.

After 287 the *Comitia Tributa* also served as a court of appeal (in the fifth and fourth centuries BC appeal cases had been one of the responsibilities of the *Comitia Centuriata*). Appeal cases were brought before the *Comitia Tributa* by a *consul* or a tribune of the *plebs*. Only in the late republic (end of the second century and the first century BC) were separate courts with juries set up specifically for this purpose. But it was only very important cases that were tried by such jury courts. The vast majority of cases were handled by lower governing bodies (see p. 172), by jurors whom the praetors appointed per case, and by the magistrates who were responsible for the maintenance of public order.

An oligarchic government

The Roman republic had no constitution and few written laws. Only issues that had provoked dissension, for example in the struggle of the orders, were provided for by

Figure 12.7 A Roman noble with busts of his ancestors
Notes: For distinguished Roman families the ties with the ancestors were very important. The busts representing the deceased ancestors were given honourary positions in their homes and were carried in procession at funerals. The Roman is wearing a toga, the official dress of Roman men.
Source: Rome, Museo Capitolino.

written laws. Otherwise all state procedures and acts were based on unwritten rules and political codes of conduct which were honoured by the governing class and respected by all the citizens. The Roman polity was essentially oligarchic. It was the *nobiles* who pulled the strings. They dominated the popular assemblies via their many clients, their personal relations and the authority that they enjoyed among all classes. This authority they owed to a deep-rooted traditional respect for the old-established families and to their successful command in the great wars of the third and second centuries BC (see pp. 178–84). These wars had temporarily suppressed the growing feelings of discontent. Not only had they provided booty, they had also won the Romans great fame and had created strong feelings of solidarity among the Roman population *vis-à-vis* its enemies. The *nobiles* moreover respectfully protected the interests of the members of the highest property class, who dominated the *Comitia Centuriata* and were therefore very important for the *nobiles*, because it was the *Comitia Centuriata* that elected the consuls and the praetors. Such considerations, private friendships and vertical ties between clients and their patrons were of overriding importance in politics, far more so than political views or programmes. There were consequently no political parties. *Ad hoc* coalitions of *nobiles* would form around particular issues or candidates at elections. Those *nobiles* would mobilise their networks of relations, friends and clients to advance their interests or to help their favourite candidate win an election.

A new type of client

The patron–client relationship had changed somewhat since the beginning of Roman history (see p. 160). In the third, second and first centuries BC (and in fact also in the imperial age), clients were essentially poor citizens who were assisted by a notable in times of hunger and hardship and who were supported by him if they became involved in a conflict (e.g. a legal matter or a business conflict). Freedmen were in this way protected by their former masters. In return, the clients supported their patron at elections and in political conflicts, they escorted him in public and greeted him at his home at the break of day (on which occasion he would grant them a small sum of money or some food). A large group of clients was an important status symbol.

Some demographic data

Rome never became a democracy comparable with that of Athens. In actual fact, the Roman citizenry had already become too large for a democracy by the third century BC. It is thought that about two hundred and sixty-five thousand male adults (of over 16 years of age) had Roman citizenship in 264 BC. That means that only a small proportion of the Roman citizens, mostly occupants of the city itself, could attend the popular assemblies on a regular basis (see Diagram 14.3, p. 215).

In the hundred and fifty years preceding 264 BC Rome's citizenry had expanded tremendously. One of the causes of this was the incorporation of central Italian and southern Etruscan tribes and cities into the Roman citizen territory. Another was Rome's policy of granting citizen rights to children of mixed marriages (e.g. of a Roman citizen with a member of an Italian tribe), immigrants from Latium and the Latin colonies (see p. 162) and freed slaves. When a slave's freedom was purchased or a slave was released as a reward for worthy behaviour he became a Roman citizen with limited citizen rights. He was not allowed to hold state offices and was not liable for military service. These limitations did not apply to his descendants, who consequently enjoyed full citizenship.

FURTHER EXPANSION AND NEW SOCIAL TENSIONS (264–133 BC)

ROMAN EXPANSION BETWEEN 264 AND 121 BC

The Punic Wars

Contacts had existed between Rome and Carthage since the end of the sixth century BC. Carthage conducted trade with Italy and occasionally tried to fish in troubled waters. She had little to fear from Italy as long as the country remained divided. This changed around 270, however, when Rome acquired hegemony over the whole of peninsular Italy and came to represent a formidable power close to Carthage's sphere of trade and influence (see p. 154). Whereas Rome and Carthage had still fought side by side in the war against Pyrrhus in 282–275 (p. 161), after that time they began to distrust one.another and to fear one another's might.

In 264 Rome became involved in a problem in Sicily. Since 289, a group of Campanian mercenaries who had settled at Messina after doing service for a tyrant in Syracuse had been enriching themselves as pirates. They were now hard-pressed by Syracuse, which intended to put an end to their piracy. The pirates enlisted the help of Carthage, Syracuse's traditional enemy, and Rome, Campania's 'patron'. Both powers responded to the appeal and consequently impinged on one another's sphere of influence. This led to the First Punic War (264–241; Punic–Phoenician–Carthaginian). Syracuse defected to Rome after the first year of the war.

This war was a protracted and severe struggle because both parties were well versed in military tactics and neither was prepared to give in to the other. After their first successful campaigns, the Romans contemplated conquering all Sicily, but Carthage was of course anxious to retain her bases on that island.

Most battles were fought on land and at sea on and off Sicily. The Romans finally won the war thanks to their superior power on land and because they built strong fleets, which also enabled them to defeat the Carthaginians at sea. In this war the Romans achieved supremacy over the seas around Italy. In building their naval forces, the Romans received much help from their maritime (Greek) allies along the coasts of southern Italy.

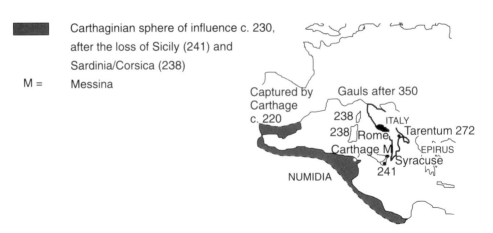

▮	Carthaginian sphere of influence c. 230, after the loss of Sicily (241) and Sardinia/Corsica (238)
M =	Messina

Captured by Carthage c. 220 Gauls after 350
238 ITALY
238 Rome Tarentum 272
Carthage M EPIRUS
Syracuse
NUMIDIA 241

Map 13.1 Roman expansion, *c.* 500–220 BC

In 241 Sicily became Rome's first province. Instead of making the states on Sicily her allies, as she had done with the Italian tribes and cities, Rome placed all the states, with the exception of Syracuse, under a *praetor's* authority. She allowed them to retain local autonomy, however. The Roman Senate probably opted for this form of government because Sicily would be in the front line if any more wars should break out against Carthage. We may regard this as a form of military control in a war-threatened area. This was to prove an influential precedent: most of the territories that Rome conquered from this stage onwards were ultimately converted into provinces, even those that were not in any front-line position.

In the twenty years between 238 and 218, Rome took Sardinia and Corsica (238) and restored order on the Adriatic Sea (229), where pirates from Illyria (now Albania and part of former Yugoslavia) were causing havoc. The Romans also subjected the Gauls in the Po valley (222).

Carthage sought to compensate for the loss of Sicily, Sardinia and Corsica by reinforcing her position in Spain. In the subsequent wars against the Gallo-Iberian tribes, which lasted for many years, the Carthaginian army in Spain became one of the best-trained professional armies of that time. It consisted chiefly of Spanish and North African mercenaries.

In 218 a new struggle broke out between Rome and Carthage, the Second Punic War (218–201), which evolved into a coalition war with far-reaching consequences. It was one of the fiercest and most intensive wars in Roman history. The competent Carthaginian general Hannibal, who had commanded the Carthaginian army in Spain since 221, embarked on a spectacular campaign through southern Gaul and over the Alps into Italy, where he won the support of the Gauls in the Po valley, who had only just been defeated by Rome.

In the years 218–216 Hannibal gained major victories over the Romans and their Italian allies. The greatest was that which he won in the battle at Cannae (216), in which over forty thousand Roman and Italian soldiers were killed (see Map 13.2). Hannibal owed his success to his brilliant tactical manoeuvres and his troops' great experience. After the battle at Cannae Hannibal received support from a number of southern Italian states, which had lost faith in the Romans' chances of victory, and from Philip V (221–179), the king of Macedonia. Philip, too, was anxious to see the Romans defeated. He regarded Rome's intervention in the Illyrian piracy issue, just before he had come to power, as a prelude to an attempt to invade the Balkans – and they were his territory. Even Syracuse, Rome's ally in the previous war, sided with Carthage.

Nevertheless, Carthage ultimately lost the war. The Romans mobilised all their manpower resources (see Diagram 14.3, p. 215), including the troops of most of their Italian allies who, contrary to Hannibal's expectations, honoured their alliances with Rome. One of the Romans' land forces successfully attacked the Carthaginians in Spain and in so doing undermined the basis of Hannibal's success (Hannibal obtained the bulk of his troops and army supplies from Spain). As the Roman fleet commanded the seas around Italy, it was very difficult for the Carthaginians to provision Hannibal by sea. The Roman commanders meanwhile waged a war of attrition on Hannibal himself, in which they exhausted his troops. In a series of minor skirmishes and sieges they ultimately confined him to the toe of Italy.

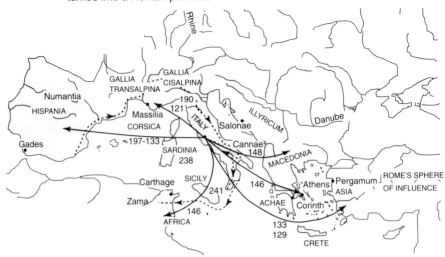

Routes followed by Hannibal between 218 and 201 BC

Year marked by arrow: year in which a territory was definitively turned into a Roman province

Map 13.2 The expansion of the Roman empire between 218 and 120 BC

Notes: Immediately after the Second Punic War Rome became involved in the struggle for influence in Greece and started to consolidate and strengthen her positions in Spain.

The struggle over Greece proceeded as follows: in 200–197 Rome successfully fought Macedonia. In 196, after the Romans' victory, the Roman general Flamininus proclaimed the Greeks free and autonomous; Greece was not turned into a Roman province. The Romans regarded the Greeks as 'clients' of the Roman people, who were allowed to govern themselves.

In 192 the Seleucid king Antiochus III (223–187) tried to acquire influence in Greece. That brought him into conflict with the Romans, who did not tolerate another 'patron' in Greece besides themselves. In 188 Rome won the war. Antiochus had to retreat behind the Taurus mountains (Cilicia) and pay Rome a tribute of 15,000 talents (Appendix 2). His territories in Asia Minor were divided between Pergamum and Rhodes (Rome's allies).

In 171–168 the Romans definitively defeated Macedonia. The land was divided into four republics (Roman satellite states). After uprisings in Macedonia and Greece (149–146) the Senate turned Macedonia and Greece into a province (Macedonia-Achaea).

Around 205 the first signs of victory for the Romans began to appear. The Roman general P. Cornelius Scipio, who had driven the Carthaginians out of Spain between 210 and 205, crossed over to North Africa, where he won over new allies in Numidia, one of Carthage's neighbour states (see Map 13.1). In 202, in the great battle at Zama, he defeated Hannibal, who had been called back from Italy to defend his home town.

In 201 Carthage made peace. The peace treaty compelled her to surrender all her outlying provinces and her war fleet to Rome and to pay an indemnity of 10000 talents (Appendix 2, p. 301) in instalments. The Roman treasury was to benefit from those instalments for over forty years. Syracuse lost her status of a free ally and was reduced to the same rank as the other subject city states on Sicily.

This war established Rome as the greatest power in the Mediterranean.

Diagram 13.1 Battle order of a Roman legion at the time of the Second Punic War (218–201 BC).

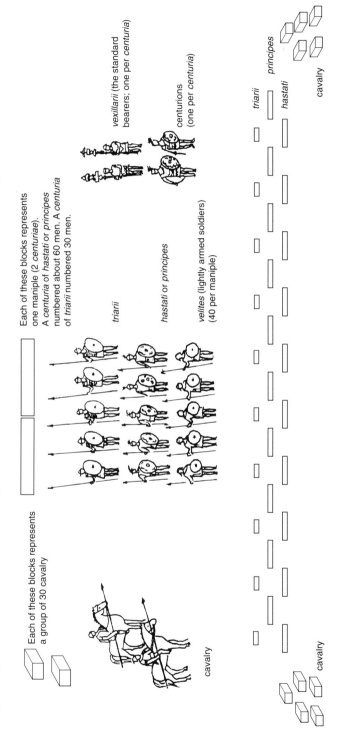

Each of these blocks represents a group of 30 cavalry

cavalry

Each of these blocks represents one maniple (2 *centuriae*). A *centuria* of *hastati* or *principes* numbered about 60 men. A *centuria* of *triarii* numbered 30 men.

triarii

hastati or *principes*

velites (lightly armed soldiers) (40 per maniple)

vexillarii (the standard bearers; one per *centuria*)

centurions (one per *centuria*)

triarii

principes

hastati

cavalry

cavalry

Notes: The commanders signalled their orders to the soldiers (optionally via messengers). They could for example order the maniples to increase or reduce the intervals between them or to form into a square. In the latter case the rear line (*triarii*) would turn round and march away from the middle line and the maniples of the middle line (*principes*) would march to the sides. The maniples could also form a closed front; the maniples of the *principes* would then fill the gaps between the maniples of the *hastati*. The commanders could also order their men to increase the distances between the three lines. And they could create a very wide front by ordering the *triarii* and *principes* to march left and right and align with the *hastati* in the middle. These possibilities made the Roman legions far more manoeuvrable than the Greek or Macedonian *phalanx*.

Source: H.E.L. Mellersh, *Soldiers of Rome*, 1964, p. 65.

Wars in Spain, the Po valley and the Hellenistic East

After 201 the Romans engaged in a series of wars that started as sequels to the Second Punic War but eventually led to a tremendous expansion of Rome's sphere of influence. Rome came to be the capital of a vast empire (see Map 13.2).

Between 197 and 190 the Romans once again brought the Gauls in the Po valley under their control. The Gauls had already been subjected between 235 and 222, but in 218 they had rebelled against the Romans and had sided with the Carthaginians.

The Gallo-Iberian tribes in the interior of Spain were subjected in two protracted, difficult wars (197–178 and 154–133), which claimed many victims on both sides. The Romans then split up the Iberian peninsula into two Roman provinces.

In the years 125–121 Rome also captured the strategic coastal strip between Italy and Spain, which she formed into the province of Transalpine Gaul (see Map 13.2). The Po valley, southern Spain and southern Gaul became important regions for Roman and Italian merchants and emigrants. Many Roman and Italian veterans remained here after their military service, while peasants from all over Italy flocked to these regions in search of a better livelihood.

In a series of brief, successful wars between 200 and 146 BC (see p. 180 and the text accompanying Map 13.2) against Macedonia, the Leagues of Greek states and the Seleucid kingdom, Rome established her hegemony over the southern Balkans and Asia Minor. The Romans managed to win these wars with comparative ease and rapidity thanks to the discord dividing their opponents, which enabled Rome to defeat them one by one. The Hellenistic kingdoms never joined forces against Rome. Rome moreover had the best-trained military manpower in the entire Mediterranean. In the Second Punic War and the wars that were to follow, a remarkably high percentage of the Romans and their Italian allies were under arms (see Diagram 14.3, p. 215), gaining military experience.

Two forms of Roman expansion

In the first half of the second century BC the Roman Senate, which in this period still controlled foreign politics (see p. 170), maintained a different policy towards the west (Spain, the Po valley, Gaul) than towards the east and North Africa. All that Rome initially (in the first half of the second century BC) demanded from her conquered opponents in the east and North Africa was that they acknowledged Rome's hegemony and paid the requested tributes. These tributes filled the Roman treasury and effectively weakened the conquered states, as they consequently had less money to spend on mercenaries and fleets. Rome meanwhile enjoyed the material advantages of her victories and did not have to worry about establishing an administrative system in those distant regions and the difficulty of control that that would have entailed. Moreover, many Roman notables cherished a deep respect for Greek civilisation, which they regarded as a superior sister culture. They felt that the Greeks deserved to retain their autonomy. Their attitude can be compared to that of the Assyrians towards Babylon (p. 38).

In the east and in North Africa Rome pursued a divide-and-rule policy. Her aim was to weaken the powerful Hellenistic states (Macedonia and the Seleucid kingdom) and Carthage, and at the same time strengthen and support their weaker neighbours, such as Pergamum in Asia Minor and Numidia in North Africa. Ptolemaic Egypt played no part in international politics after 170. From that year onwards it was constantly torn apart by succession struggles and social unrest. The only reason why Egypt retained its independence was that Rome did not incorporate it in her empire and did not allow any other state to assume control over it.

This divide-and-rule policy was fairly successful in Asia Minor, but Greece and Macedonia remained restless. On four occasions between 200 and 146 Rome was forced to engage in wars in those areas (see Map 13.2). In 146 Rome had had enough and put an end to the unrest once and for all. She turned the whole region into a province (Macedonia Achaea) and placed it under a Roman governor. Moreover, as a warning to other cities she destroyed the Greek city of Corinth, which had been a centre of anti-Roman activity since 149. The population was killed or sold into slavery.

That same year Rome also liquidated the last remains of the Carthaginians' power in North Africa after Carthage had come into conflict with her neighbour Numidia, one of Rome's allies (Third Punic War, 149–146). Carthage was destroyed and her entire population was killed or sold into slavery. Her territory was turned into the province of Africa.

In 133 BC the last king of the Attalids bequeathed the kingdom of Pergamum to Rome. In 129, after suppressing a revolt of mercenaries, slaves and poor tenant farmers in the western half of the kingdom, the Romans turned that area into the province of Asia (see Map 13.2). The rest of the kingdom they left in the hands of local vassal rulers loyal to Rome.

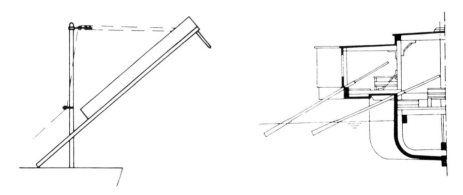

Figure 13.1 Boarding bridges used by the Romans during the First Punic War
Notes: In the First Punic War the Romans managed to gain naval supremacy over the Carthaginians' highly experienced naval forces by turning a naval battle into a 'land' battle. This they did by lowering the illustrated boarding bridges, known as 'crows', onto the Carthaginian ships so that they could cross over to conquer the Carthaginian ships. These crows however unbalanced the ships and many Roman ships were consequently wrecked in storms. The Romans therefore soon stopped using this device.
Right: cross-section through a double-deck war galley (a quadrireme). Each oar was pulled by two men. The rowers were propertyless citizens and men drawn from the cities of Rome's maritime allies.

Towards the west the Roman Senate pursued a different policy. The territories that the Romans conquered in the Po valley, Spain and southern Gaul were immediately turned into Roman provinces. Here there were no recognisable, well-developed states as in the east and North Africa, but only loosely organised tribes, which were not accustomed to the diplomatic play of Rome and the Hellenistic world and constantly renewed their efforts to throw off the yoke of Roman control. In the central and western parts of the Iberian peninsula in particular, rebellions broke out time and time again. In a series of harsh wars Rome slowly moved the boundaries of her empire further north and west, until in the end only the northwest corner of Spain was still free of Roman dominion (133 BC).

The decisive victories in North Africa (146) and Spain (134–3) were both won by a member of the Cornelius Scipio family, P. Cornelius Scipio Aemilianus. The Roman population hailed him as a great hero, but he never misused his popularity. He remained entirely loyal to his fellow-rulers in the Senate.

In the wars between 264 and 133 the Romans' traditional shifts in command proved a great disadvantage. In principle, the consuls (and praetors) could command their armies only during their one-year term of office. The exigencies of prolonged warfare however called for a new solution. In order to increase the number of commanders and to give capable generals the opportunity of remaining in command after their one-year term of office, the Senate created the 'pro'-magistracy. 'Pro' means 'comparable with' or 'in the place of'. A proconsul's *imperium* was comparable with that of a consul, only it was not necessarily limited to one year and he could exercise it only over his own army and on his own battlefield. It ended when the Senate called him back or when the predetermined term of his command came to an end.

The administration of a province

In every new province they established, the Romans left the local administrative system as they had found it and placed a governor above it, to keep an eye on things. At first the governors were all praetors, but around 190 the Senate started to appoint ex-consuls and ex-praetors as proconsuls and propraetors. Their *imperium* was limited to their province, their term of office usually to one or two years.

A governor's main responsibilities were the defence of his province and the administration of justice. After some time, the governors came to share their judicial duties with the local rulers. The governors had a small staff of councillors (e.g. Romans and Italians who had gone to live in the province), scribes and deputies, and were assisted by *quaestors*, who supervised expenditures and tax collection. The taxes were collected in cash or in kind by the local councils and were handed over to the agents of the *publicani* (see p. 172), who had already deposited an advance in Rome's treasury. The provincial quaestor received part of that advance to cover the provincial government's costs. In effect, it was the governor's councillors who preserved the continuity of the provincial government, for they remained whereas the governors were replaced every year or every two years.

The lion's share of the day-to-day administrative work was done by the local rulers. For the bulk of the provincial population they represented the immediate authorities. In the western provinces the local rulers were aristocratic members of Gallic and Iberian tribes. In the eastern provinces they were mainly the councillors and magistrates of the Greek cities which had emerged all over the Near East in the Hellenistic era (see p. 136), but also local sovereigns, temple priests and village chiefs.

The Romans encouraged an oligarchic form of government in the Greek cities. In Italy, the Roman Senate had found that well-organised councils of noble landowners constituted very effective local governments for the cities of Rome's allies, her colonies and her *municipia* (see p. 163) and it therefore decided to extend this system to the provinces. The oligarchically bent rich in the Greek cities on their part usually accepted the Romans' sovereignty. They realised that a pro-Roman attitude would secure them a privileged position in local government and would safeguard their property. Under Rome's domination the civil strife between the rich and the poor that had afflicted many Greek cities between 240 and 150 was suppressed.

In Italy, and also in the western and eastern provinces, the city councils that were responsible for local government gradually came to consist of wealthy notables who sat on the council for life and were appointed to the local administrative offices by the citizens of their city. The councils had between one hundred and six hundred members, depending on the size and the population of the city and of the rural areas governed by that city.

Disadvantages of Roman control

In the second and first centuries BC most of Rome's provinces groaned under Rome's control. In their provinces, the governors, their staff and the *publicani* were able to take advantage of their positions to enrich themselves because Rome exercised very little control over their activities. The Romans' administrative system did not include provisions for checking on magistrates far away from Italy. Governors and their assistants 'sold' the law and favoured cities and individuals who gave them generous 'gifts', while *publicani* employed greater profit margins than they were entitled to according to traditional standards. The provincial population also had to suffer the ruthless practices of Roman veterans and Italian merchants and slave traders. Italian merchants, for example, extorted low prices for the goods they purchased but charged exorbitant prices when they sold them. And the slave traders sold many former captives, rebels and well-educated provincials into slavery in Italy or Sicily.

In 149 BC, after a number of serious scandals (in Spain), Rome decided to take measures against the governors' extortionist practices. A permanent jury court was established in Rome for the specific purpose of handling complaints of extortion in the provinces. The complaints were to be lodged by Roman notables acting as the 'patrons' of the provinces. These patrons were chosen from among notables who, as a general in a war or a governor, had formed a special bond with their province, or who belonged to a family from which the Senate had chosen governors for a particular province for several generations. The jury consisted of senators.

NEW SOCIAL TENSIONS

The consequences of Rome's expansion

In the many years of Rome's expansion between 264 and 121 BC, vast quantities of money, goods and slaves poured into Italy. Within two or three generations this led to major changes in the cities (especially Rome) and in rural areas.

Increasing amounts of tributes and taxes flowed from the subjected territories into Rome's treasury, financing further expansionist campaigns. The *tributum*, the property tax that had burdened the Roman citizens in Italy, was no longer collected after 167 BC.

Grain was imported into Rome on a regular basis by sea from the fertile coastal plains of Sicily and North Africa (it was much cheaper and more efficient to transport bulk goods by water than overland, across Italy). The abundant availability of this staple foodstuff led to a tremendous increase in Rome's population as it attracted many occupants of rural areas to the city. Other foodstuffs were obtained from nearby Italian regions. Those regions focused more on cattle-keeping and the production of wine, olive oil and fruit than on cereal cultivation.

Most of the booty (slaves, money and goods) fell into the hands of the rich and powerful. They spent vast amounts of money in Rome and had expensive country estates built for themselves, but most of their wealth they invested in land in Italy, on which they put slaves to work. Large farms and estates consequently arose in fertile regions with good transport possibilities, where trained slaves produced the goods which would sell well in Rome and other cities.

More and more of the public land in those regions thus came into the possession of the rich, who settled slaves on that land. This meant that the free farmers (land-owning farmers, tenant farmers and land-owning farmers who leased extra land) were no longer able to exploit the public land and so lost a large portion of their income (see p. 163). Those who were forced to neglect their farms for the long periods that they had to spend in military service were even worse off. Many farmers eventually gave up, sold their private land and migrated to the towns, in particular Rome. Others ran up debts, lost their land to their creditors and joined the ranks of the proletarian day labourers who hired themselves out in the countryside and in Rome and other towns. Yet other farmers emigrated to the Po valley, southern Spain or southern Gaul (where they accelerated the process of Romanisation).

Similar changes took place among the Italian communities, especially those in southern Italy and Latium. As large parts of southern Italy had been devastated in the battle against Hannibal between 216 and 203 (see p. 179), the farmers in those regions were at an extra disadvantage. Many had run up debts because they had had to borrow money to rebuild their farms. Moreover, the communities in southern Italy that had sided with Hannibal after the battle at Cannae (216) had been forced to surrender their best land to Rome. That land had become Roman public land and had passed into the hands of wealthy investors. Large numbers of southern Italians drifted to Rome or towns closer by in Italy, or to the Po valley, Spain or southern Gaul. Rome moreover received a great influx of people from the Latin city states, who moved to the city so as to obtain full Roman citizenship (see p. 163).

Diagram 13.2 The consequences of Rome's expansion in the second century BC

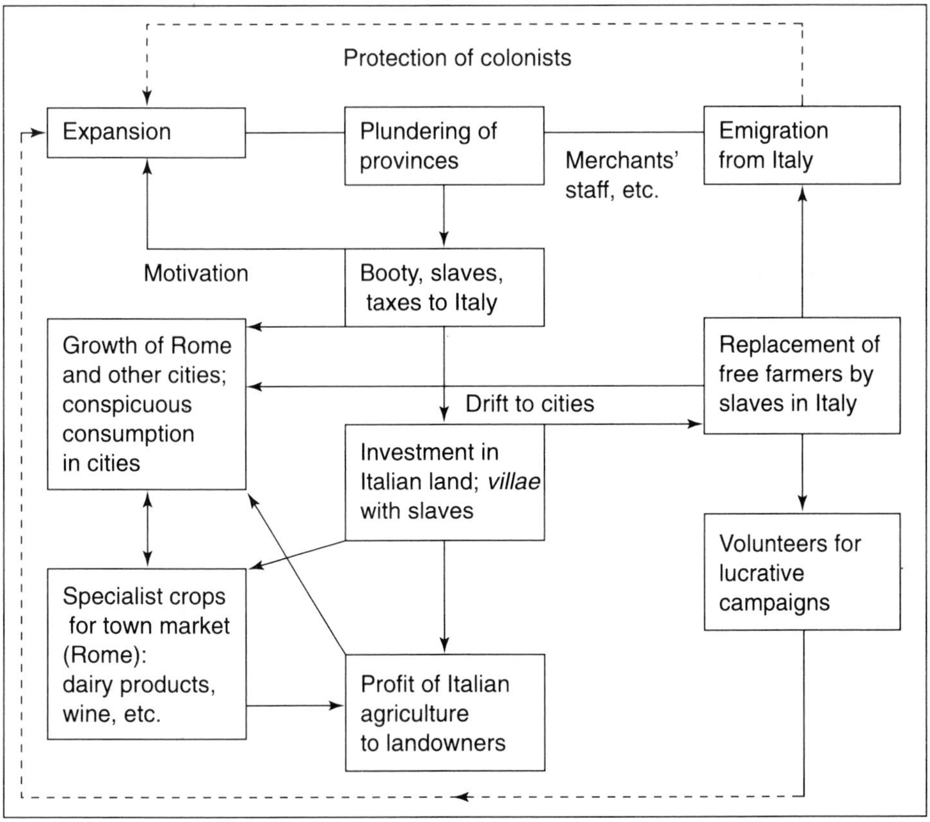

Note: villae are medium-sized plantations producing cash crops and foodstuffs for their own labour force

The consequence of all this was that the urban and rural proletariat grew all over Italy, while the number of free farmers decreased. The best chances of survival for the small-time free farmers with their old-fashioned farming practices aimed at self-sufficiency on a household basis were in regions without good transport possibilities, which were of little interest to wealthy Roman and Italian investors. Some small proprietors in the fertile, accessible areas also, however, managed to hold their own by supplementing their income with war booty and wages earned in casual labour.

For the Roman state the decrease in the number of free farmers was a serious development. Usually, the bulk of the soldiers were recruited from among the citizens who could afford to arm themselves. The state treasury lacked the funds to equip entire armies. However, as the free peasantry declined, the number of citizens qualifying for recruitment decreased. The situation was aggravated by the fact that many (peasant) soldiers were killed on campaigns or stayed behind in conquered regions.

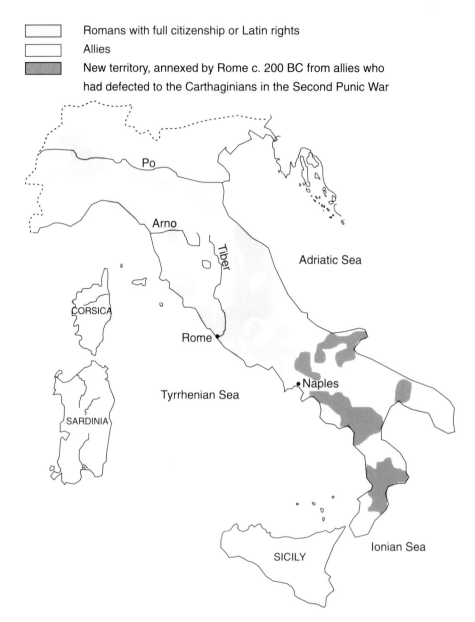

Romans with full citizenship or Latin rights

Allies

New territory, annexed by Rome c. 200 BC from allies who had defected to the Carthaginians in the Second Punic War

Map 13.3 Rome and her Italian allies, 91 BC
Note: This map clearly reflects the massive expansion of the citizen territory.

Some farmers managed to improve their material position by volunteering for – preferably lucrative – campaigns whenever they got the chance. They constituted the semi-professional backbone of the Roman armies in the numerous wars of those days.

Slavery in Italy and Sicily

In the third century BC there must already have been vast numbers of slaves in Italy and Sicily, partly because so many captives and other people subjected in the Punic Wars had been sold into slavery. It was however in the second century BC that slavery really expanded in Italy and Sicily. According to a plausible estimate, two million of the six million inhabitants of Italy were slaves at the height of this development, between 150 and 70. Those slaves were former war captives, deportees from subject regions, victims of pirates and slave traders, foundlings picked up by slave traders, poor people who had sold themselves and their children into slavery because they saw no other way out, and those who had been born into slavery. Slaves were the property of their masters; they were 'instruments without a voice'.

Large concentrations of slaves worked in the mines, in the quarries and on the large estates that specialised in the cultivation of crops specifically intended for sale (cash crops). Many slaves were also employed in the workshops or did the dirty and heavy work in the public services in the cities and in the homes of the rich, as domestic personnel. Small-time farmers and craftsmen who were doing quite well for themselves had one or two slaves. There were great differences between the slaves themselves. A notable's well-educated domestic slave often enjoyed a position of trust as a secretary or a family tutor and stood a good chance of being released from slavery some day. The slave of a small-time farmer or craftsman was regarded more or less as a member of the family, but the fate of the masses of slaves who worked in the mines and on the large agricultural estates was wretched. Even worse off were the slaves who were forced to perform as gladiators at the games; they had to fight one another to death in the arenas in Italy.

Occasionally a slave would be released. For many slaves the chance of being freed from slavery was their only hope and a reason for working hard and not rising in revolt. Freed slaves (freedmen) were granted Roman citizenship without the right to hold offices. They were not liable for military service either. Their sons did enjoy full citizenship (see p. 176).

Slave revolts

Between 150 and 70, conditions in Italy and Sicily (and probably also in Asia Minor) became more conducive to slave revolts. The number of slaves increased tremendously within a relatively short space of time. The new slaves were set to work on the large estates in groups. The memory of their days of freedom was still fresh in their minds and they were in a position to rise as a group. Around 134 and 104 BC, major slave revolts broke out on Sicily and in the years 133–129 slaves joined the uprisings in the former kingdom of Pergamum, in Asia Minor (see p. 183). The rebellious slaves were certainly not acting according to some international plan; as

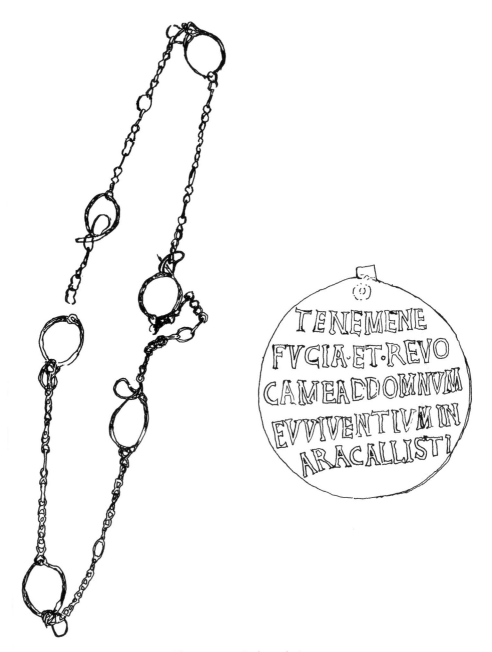

Figure 13.2 A slave chain

Notes: In rural areas slaves were sometimes chained together to prevent them from running away. Example of the tokens that some slaves wore around their necks. The tokens bore a text. This text reads: *Tene me ne fugia[m] et revoca me ad dom[i]nu[m] meu[m] Viventium in ar[e]a Callisti* – 'Stop me from running away and return me to my master, Viventius, who lives in Callistus' court'.

far as we know, they were not in contact with one another and had no communal reform programme. They were not even motivated by a desire to abolish slavery. All they were interested in was regaining their own personal freedom. The greatest slave revolt that ever broke out in Italy occurred later, in 73–71 BC, under the leadership of Spartacus (see p. 206).

The slave revolts on Sicily were a serious problem for the population of Rome because Rome obtained much of her grain from Sicily. The Roman legions therefore made great efforts to firmly suppress those revolts.

Piracy

A side-effect of the slave trade was piracy, which rapidly spread across the Mediterranean. Slaves were profitable merchandise for pirates. Since Rome had acquired supremacy over the Mediterranean and their own power had declined, the Hellenistic kingdoms were no longer able to secure the safety of the sea and the coasts. And as for Rome, the Roman Senate made no effort to curb piracy as the senators themselves stood to benefit by a good supply of slaves because they needed many for their estates. They were particularly interested in skilled workers from the well-developed Hellenistic world, to whom they could entrust the cultivation of their cash crops and domestic chores.

Some demographic data

The import of slaves and the influx of foreigners into Rome and the ports led to a considerable increase in the Italian population. Around 100 BC Italy probably had some six million inhabitants. The number of Roman citizens also increased, largely as a result of the inflow of Latins and foreigners into Rome (p. 186) and the release of slaves (see p. 176). Between 215 and 143 BC the number of adult male Roman citizens (above the age of 16) increased from about three hundred thousand to about four hundred thousand. The percentage of free peasants among those citizens however decreased (see Diagram 14.3 on p. 215).

The city of Rome

The great numbers of former peasants, ex-soldiers reluctant to return to a farming existence after their military service, foreigners, slaves and freedmen who flocked to Rome swelled the city's population. The newcomers found work in the building industry and transport or as craftsmen. The rich spent large sums of money in Rome. New occupational groups emerged, which satisfied the increasing demands of the wealthy public. The elite, impressed by the culture, level of learning and luxurious conditions with which they became acquainted in the Hellenistic cities, strove to alter their own way of life accordingly. In Rome this led to a demand for teachers, artists, architects, doctors, secretaries, bankers, legal advisors and manufacturers of luxury goods. This demand was met largely by former slaves from the Hellenistic east who set themselves up in business after being released from slavery by their masters.

Among the legal advisors were Romans from the highest orders (senators and *equites*). They assisted in litigation and provided magistrates with advice. This was considered a respectable *métier* for a Roman gentleman, unlike professions in commerce or manual trades.

Inadequate organisation

The Romans made very few efforts to adjust their public institutions to the altered conditions. The promagistracy (proconsulship and propraetorship, p. 184) was created and the number of praetors and quaestors was increased (p. 169), but otherwise the magisterial apparatus was not extended. Neither did the Romans establish a standing army along the frontiers of their empire to prevent or settle border conflicts. Many administrative matters were arranged via relations with important *nobiles*. Their patronage covered a wide range of interest groups in Rome, and entire cities and regions in Italy and the provinces. The traditional Roman way of thinking in terms of patron–client relationships extended to Rome's international relations. Rome saw herself as the patron of her allies and vassals in the Hellenistic world and the *nobiles* were the patrons of large groups of people, cities and regions in the Roman empire.

The discrepancy that came to exist between the public sector and the vastly expanded private sector is also reflected in contemporary Roman law. Public law still amounted to little, comprising as it did only a few rules relating to the magistrates, the Senate and the popular assemblies, but private law had grown tremendously (see p. 240). The public sector remained largely dependent on unwritten rules and customs.

A CHANGE IN MENTALITY

It is believed that the old Roman family ties (see p. 157), traditions and customs lived on for a fairly long time in rural areas and in small cities, not only among the lower classes, but even among the political class that governed the Italian communities. In Rome itself (and perhaps also in some ports) a major change in mentality however took place in the second and first centuries BC. We don't know much about the lower classes, but we may assume that they, too, felt the impact of the spiritual disruption generally associated with the influx of large groups of newcomers into a city. We are somewhat better informed about the ruling classes in Rome. In their public and private lives, the Roman notables slowly drifted away from the old Roman traditions. They surrounded themselves with ever more luxury and developed a more individualistic attitude. In theory, the old family ties and the power of the *pater familias* (see p. 157) still existed, but in practice they were gradually eroded. This is apparent from the position of women, for example. Progressively fewer elite women married in the old-fashioned way, formally passing under the authority of the *pater familias* of their husbands' families. Less conventional forms of cohabitation emerged and divorce became quite common.

Greek influences

One of the most influential factors in the change in mentality among the Roman elite was the latter's increasing familiarity with the culture and lifestyle of the Hellenistic cities in the eastern provinces (and in southern Italy and Sicily). Roman notables acquired first-hand acquaintance with the Hellenistic world as governors and generals, and Greek doctors, secretaries and teachers worked in their homes. Most of these Greeks were brought to Rome by Romans returning from the East or were imported as slaves. Others voluntarily settled in Rome or were sent there as envoys or hostages by their home towns. Among the latter was the Greek historian Polybius (c. 203–c. 120). He came to Rome as a hostage around 168 and later became a friend of the Cornelius Scipio family, one of the most distinguished families of *nobiles*. He wrote a history of Rome's expansion from 218 onwards, in which he also looked back on the 150 years that had preceded it. He attributed Rome's success to her balanced mixed constitution, which he considered a successful blend of the three elements of monarchy (the consuls), democracy (the popular assemblies) and aristocracy (the Senate).

The birth of a Roman literature

The years around 200 BC saw the birth of a Roman literature that was largely modelled on Greek literature. Roman authors started to imitate Greek literary genres (epic, drama, histories and scientific prose) in their own, Latin language. The earliest epic and historical works originated in the heroic age of the Second Punic War (218–201). Roman poets celebrated the valorous deeds of their people and Roman historians absolved Rome from guilt in the war.

The Greek educational system (primary school, secondary education in literature, grammar and other subjects and higher rhetorical education; see p. 122) was introduced in Rome. Here it was usually bilingual – the pupils were taught both Greek and Latin.

Some Roman authors criticised the changes they saw around them. They interpreted the increasing luxury and the influence of the Greek way of life (clothing, athletics, luxury goods) in their circles as signs of moral decay. The increasing individualistic pursuit of private interests they saw as greed and evil ambition. Cato (234–149) is the best-known exponent of these feelings. He wrote about the Romans' virtuous and glorious ancestors and about agriculture and vehemently criticised the growing Greek influences.

In one respect the decline of the former collective moral standards indeed implied a major threat. As Rome did not have an extensive legal system, much depended on a homogeneous acceptance of the unwritten laws which applied in politics. The disappearance of that homogeneity was to lead to much discord and uncertainty after 140 BC.

The change in mentality had consequences for foreign politics, too. Self-seeking individual *nobiles* increasingly set their own interests and glory before the wellbeing of the Roman state. At the same time, more groups came to have an interest in

Rome's conquests. *Publicani* sought new areas for taxation, merchants ransacked the new additions to the empire for cheap merchandise and poor citizens saw the expansionist campaigns as ideal opportunities for acquiring booty with which to improve their economic position.

THE CENTURY OF THE CIVIL WARS (133–30 BC)

SERIOUS PROBLEMS AND DISCONTENT

In the second half of the second century BC the Roman republic was confronted with a number of serious problems which interacted with one another and created an unstable political climate. The decline of the free peasantry led to a shortage of recruits, because proletarians were not yet admitted to the army on a large scale.

The proletarians felt deceived. They formed part of the people that was conquering the world but all they were getting out of the conquests was poverty. The rural proletarians yearned for a redivision of the public land with themselves as the chief beneficiaries. At first, the urban proletariat in the rapidly expanding city of Rome still managed to find sufficient casual labour, for example in the building industry and in the harbours. But by 140 BC many of the major building projects had been completed and less booty, with which further projects could have been financed, was pouring into Rome. The lucrative wars in the East and North Africa were over after 146 and only the costly, bloody campaigns in Spain continued. In fact, the wars in Spain even reached a climax around 133. After 140, crop failures, transport problems and the slave revolt in Sicily (see p. 189) moreover caused grain prices to rise. The charity that the rich patrons distributed among their clients was probably no longer adequate.

Feelings of discontent arose among the higher echelons of society, too. The *equites* who operated as *publicani* (see p. 184) wanted more influence in administration and jurisdiction, especially in the permanent jury court that was established in 149 to handle cases of extortion in the provinces. If they were to be admitted to that jury they would be able to see to it that governors who were too lenient towards tax payers in the provinces were punished.

A great threat to Rome was the growing resentment of her Italian allies. The Italians were well aware that, as Rome's allies, they had contributed as much to Rome's expansion as the Romans themselves, but they profited far less from the conquests. They had to pay their own soldiers, they received a smaller share of the booty and they were precluded from holding offices in provincial administration and from operating as *publicani*. The Italians were also vexed by the Roman magistrates' ruthless behaviour in Italy, against which they were far less capable of protecting themselves than Roman citizens. For the latter it was much easier to bring charges against a magistrate after his term of office. The Italians began to long for full Roman citizenship, which would make them equal to the Romans in every respect and would shift the financial burdens of levying and maintaining troops to the Roman treasuries.

THE GRACCHI

Tiberius Gracchus

Tiberius Sempronius Gracchus was a *nobilis* from one of the most distinguished families in Rome. He was a brother-in-law of Scipio Aemilianus (see p. 184). His aim was to solve the shortage of recruits and at the same time improve the material lot of the unpropertied citizens. In 133 BC, when he was a tribune of the *plebs*, he set up a bill reviving the old law of 367 (see p. 168) that limited the amount of public land that any one individual could own or use (the maximum was 125 ha). The public land that would become available once this bill had been passed he intended to split up among the landless. His plan found great support among the small peasants and rural proletarians, but met with fierce opposition among most senators, who regarded it as a threat to their investments in public land. They moreover saw Tiberius Gracchus as a potential autocrat, as they feared that he would use his popularity among the lower rural population to make a bid for power with their support. Some compared him to Greek tyrants of the past.

Tiberius Gracchus took his bill to the popular assembly (strictly speaking, it was a *Concilium Plebis*: see p. 173), where it was passed against the will of the Senate. He saw to it that a fellow tribune, who pronounced his veto after the bill had been read out (p. 173), was deposed. He became an even greater threat to the Senate when he stood for re-election as a tribune, for fear of prosecution for fabricated charges after his term of office, and started to interfere with the Senate's affairs (see p. 170). He tried to persuade the popular assembly to accept his proposal to use the treasures which Pergamum had bequeathed to Rome (p. 133) to finance his land programme. But before he could realise his plans he was murdered in public by a group of senators who saw his bid for re-election as a prelude to an attempt to gain absolute control and did not tolerate any interference in affairs which were traditionally the Senate's prerogative, that is, state finance and foreign politics.

After Tiberius' death his land scheme was nevertheless implemented, probably so as to prevent the risk of revolts among the poor rural citizens.

The redivision of public land emphasised and intensified the Italians' resentment. Large amounts of public land were confiscated from Italian landholders, and as it was not so easy for them to appeal to a Roman judge the lack of Roman citizenship was felt ever more acutely. After 129 the redistribution of public land gradually came to an end, but the Italians' discontent remained a burning issue.

Gaius Gracchus

Ten years after the death of his older brother, Gaius Sempronius Gracchus was elected tribune of the *plebs*. He was a great orator and a far more radical politician than his brother had been. His aims were to continue the redistribution of public land in Italy and to settle landless citizens in a colony which he intended to found at the site of the former city of Carthage (which had been destroyed in 146, see p. 183). The senators who had opposed his brother (the majority in the Senate) distrusted Gaius even more and fiercely resisted his plans. They feared that such an overseas colony would evolve into a closed rank of private supporters for Gaius Gracchus. The fact that he was re-elected as tribune of the *plebs* also caused them much concern (he was in office in 123 and 122).

Gaius tried to break their resistance by securing the loyalty of different interest groups by granting them political favours. To this end he had the popular assembly (*Concilium Plebis*) pass various bills. One of the new laws granted the *equites* the right to compose the juries which tried extortion cases (see p. 185). The population of Rome he made happy with a fixed low wheat price by arranging state subsidies for the purchase of grain. Gaius also proposed to grant the Italians Roman citizenship, but that proposal was rejected. All the ranks of the Roman citizenry were against granting the Italians any more benefits of Rome's expansion than they already enjoyed.

In 121 Gaius Gracchus and some three thousand of his followers were murdered by the conservative senators and their backing of clients and political allies.

Gaius' plans for the foundation of a colony in North Africa came to nothing, but all his other reforms were retained. The grain subsidies came to be a heavy burden on the state treasury.

Political consequences of the Gracchan reforms

The political struggle of 133–121 affected the elite's internal cohesion and undermined the old political codes of conduct. Violence had become a means for achieving political aims. Hostility grew between the senators and the *equites*. This development coincided with the emergence of a perceptible distinction between the two groups. In 129 the senators and the *equites* (knights) became two separate orders. Political distinctions arose within the Senate itself, too. There was a group of senators who were of the opinion that reforms were necessary. These senators, who were known as *populares*, wanted the popular assembly to pass proposals for reforms, if necessary against the will of the senatorial majority. The *populares* were by no means all idealistic reformers. Many of them were only interested in strengthening their own position within the Roman elite. The word *populares* comes from *populus* (people). They were so called because they tried to realise their political aims via the popular assembly.

But in the Senate the *optimates* were in the majority. They wanted things to remain as they were where possible. The word *optimates* comes from *optimi* (the best). The *equites*, the Italian notables and the lower classes in Rome did not steer a fixed course in the ensuing political struggles. In determining their political preferences they were usually guided by ties of patronage or concrete private interests. There were no political parties with a more or less fixed group of followers and an ideologically founded programme.

MARIUS' MILITARY REFORMS

In the years 113–100 BC wars against the Numidians in North Africa, who, after being Rome's allies for a century, had now revolted, and troubles with migrating German tribes demanded Rome's full attention. It was in these years that Rome first collided with the Germans, in this case the Cimbri (from Jutland) and the Teutones (from central Germany), who had left their homelands in search of better occupation areas. Corruption scandals in North Africa and crushing defeats in the wars against the Germans brought discredit on the *nobiles*. The defeat at Arausio (now Orange, near the Rhone in southern Gaul) in 105 was as disastrous for Rome as the defeat at Cannae in 216 had been.

Diagram 14.1 Social structure in the Late Republic

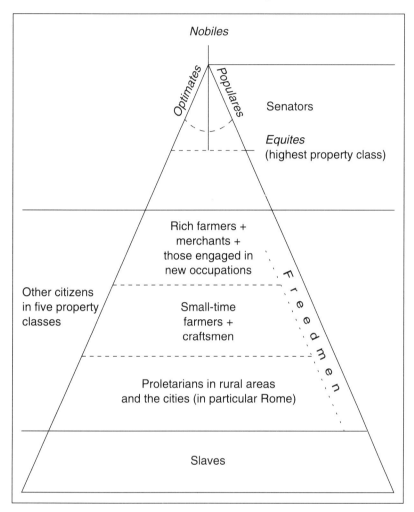

The competent general Gaius Marius (157–86 BC), a 'new man' from the equestrian order, who was elected consul six times between 107 and 100 (a testimony to the voters' lack of confidence in the old rulers), reformed the army and brought the wars to a successful conclusion. He subjected his recruits to a gladiatorial training programme, equipped them with better and more varied arms and introduced more efficient fighting tactics. He composed legions of six thousand (uniformly armed) men, organised into ten cohorts which could operate as independent units in a battle. This system afforded greater tactical possibilities than the former *phalanx* organisation. Marius' system was to be retained, with only minor changes, until well into the imperial age. It was soon to prove its worth, for in 102 Marius defeated the Teutones in southern Gaul, and in 101 he routed the Cimbri in northern Italy.

Figure 14.1 A Roman officer in the first century BC

Another of Marius' reforms was the admission into the army of proletarian volunteers, who were armed by the state. This was the culmination of a development that had started in the second century BC, when progressively poorer citizens had been recruited for lack of sufficient manpower. The old property qualification for service in the heavily armed forces had been increasingly often ignored after 218 (the outbreak of the Second Punic War) and in the second century BC the state had had to contribute more and more towards equipping the armies. The soldiers in effect became semi-professional soldiers, who enlisted for the sake of improving their material position and were armed by the state. This, alongside Gaius Gracchus' grain subsidies, came to be the treasury's heaviest burden.

The new burdens on the state treasury prompted further imperialistic campaigns: Rome went in search of fresh areas on which she would be able to levy taxes. So yet another incentive to expansion was added to those already mentioned above, with respect to the changed mentality. Rome's imperialism increasingly became a matter of material benefit for the treasury, the notables, the *publicani*, the merchants, the soldiers, the populace in Rome and everyone who profited indirectly from Rome's conquests.

Marius and the other contemporary political leaders did not fix periods of service or arrange pensions for the new proletarian soldiers. The soldiers were simply

Diagram 14.2 The basis of power of important generals

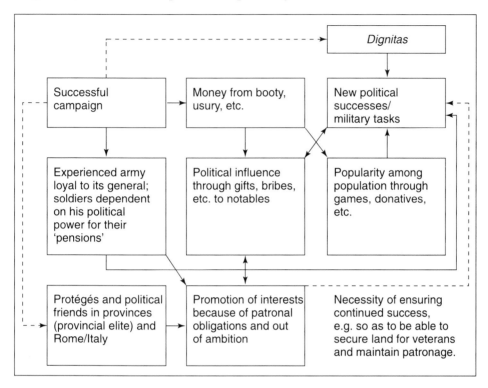

Note: Period: the civil wars.

Dignitas: dignity; high status obtained through major achievements, especially military achievements.

Not indicated in this diagram is the continuing expansion of the Roman empire, its capital and the retinues of the powerful politicians and generals.

Authors writing around the time of the civil wars complained about the unbridled greed and ambition of the powerful politicians; this diagram illustrates their complaint.

discharged when a war was over, just as in the past. But the proletarian soldiers had no farm or anything else to fall back on and they became a political threat. Unpropertied citizens would volunteer for military service for the sake of improving their economic position and, after the war for which they had been enrolled was over, they desired a plot of land for their support.

The Senate however always tried to prevent the distribution of land among ex-soldiers. They were afraid that that would lead to the formation of military colonies, which would support their former commander as one man. The majority of the senators had previously opposed Gaius Gracchus' colonisation plans for more or less the same reason. One of their greatest fears was a disturbance of the balance of power within the oligarchy. The generals were almost always important *nobiles* who already had large numbers of clients and ramified networks of relations. If colonies of veterans should be added to those numbers, the generals would have a very powerful backing indeed. Competent generals who won wars and were able to grant their soldiers booty and land would be in a position to use their soldiers as private support in political struggles. The first signs heralding this development already appeared in Marius' own time. In 103 and 100 BC serious conflicts broke out concerning the foundation of colonies for Marius' veterans who had fought in North Africa and against the Germans. Marius himself remained loyal towards the Senate and did not wish to use his troops as a political weapon, but a few radical *populares* amongst his followers were differently disposed. In their capacity as tribunes of the *plebs* they used violence to persuade the popular assembly (*Concilium Plebis*) to pass land and colonisation bills. The consequence was that Marius' veterans were granted land in Tuscany, the Po valley and North Africa. This affair widened the breach between the *optimates* and the *populares* within the Senate.

THE SOCIAL WAR (91–88 BC) AND THE FIRST CIVIL WAR

Citizenship for the Italian allies

Discontent had been smouldering amongst the Italian allies since the time of the Gracchi (see Map 13.3, p. 188). In the years 100–91 BC attempts to arrive at a peaceful solution failed and in 91 BC the Italian allies took up arms. In a short, but savage war, known as the Social War (91–88), they attempted to force the Romans to grant them citizenship. Rome won the war in military terms, but did not want to alienate herself from her Italian allies for good. And so, between 88 and 84 BC, she admitted the Italians to the Roman citizenry. The number of adult male Roman citizens consequently increased from about four hundred thousand in 88 BC to 1.03 million in 83 BC. The Italian contingents were abolished; from this point onwards Italian soldiers served in the Roman legions and received their pay from Roman coffers. Italy came to consist of self-governing communities of Roman citizens. The differences that had previously existed between the Romans and the Italians gradually disappeared. The terms *colonia* and *municipium* (see pp. 162 and 163) now both referred to communities of Roman citizens. They differed only in terms of the privileges they enjoyed; the *coloniae* were the more privileged.

The Romanisation of Italy, which had started many years earlier (*c.* 300 BC), was greatly accelerated by this development. This went hand in hand with the spread of urbanisation. Italy evolved into a country full of small and medium-sized cities with impressive centres modelled on Hellenistic examples (see p. 133 and Fig. 11.1), from which the surrounding rural areas were governed. Those rural areas contained the estates of local and Roman notables, which were worked by slaves and tenant farmers, and the farms of the remaining independent small land-owning farmers.

In the fifty years that followed the Social War the Italian notables came to form a third order, below the senatorial and equestrian orders. Just as new senators were occasionally chosen from the equestrian order, so too new knights were from time to time recruited from the Italian elite.

Decline of the popular assemblies

Roman citizenship in effect came to be a legal concept, a set of private and civil rights. Its political dimension diminished because only a small percentage of the citizens still voted in the assemblies on a regular basis. Most Romans (old citizens) and Italians (new citizens) who lived outside Rome only went to vote when a patron drummed them up, to help him win an election or get a bill passed.

Usually the popular assembly (in particular the *Comitia Tributa* or the *Concilium Plebis*) was dominated by a group of citizens living in Rome, who gave their votes to successful men who granted them donatives, organised games and behaved in a popularist fashion. They used tribunes with whom they were friendly as their henchmen. The latter would see to it that the popular assembly passed bills and measures that were to the advantage of their 'bosses'. The tribunate became a vehicle of the demagogic politics of a small number of powerful politicians.

The First Civil War (88–82 BC)

The political tension that had been building up since the middle of the second century BC (see p. 196) ultimately exploded in civil wars. Conflicting interest groups rallied around generals who competed for power and used their troops as political weapons. They availed themselves of tribunes, clients and wide networks of political and private relations in Rome, Italy and the provinces. Via these networks the civil struggles in Rome were propagated to the furthest corners of the empire.

The First Civil War (88–82) broke out when the armies that had fought the Italians (91–88) were still in the field. Its cause was a conflict between the two most important generals and politicians of those days, the aforementioned Marius and L. Cornelius Sulla (138–78 BC), who had served under Marius in the wars against the Numidians and the Germans, and had been the most successful Roman commander in the Social War.

Marius and Sulla competed for the supreme command in a new foreign war, against Mithridates, king of Pontus from 120 to 64 BC. Pontus was a Hellenistic kingdom in the north of Asia Minor (Map 14.1) which the Romans had hitherto left alone.

Around 100 BC Mithridates had built up a powerful empire along the eastern shores of the Black Sea, from Pontus up to and including the Crimea. He saw the conflict between the Romans and the Italians as a good opportunity to attempt to reduce the Romans' influence in Asia Minor. At first, Mithridates received much support from the exploited natives in the Roman provinces Asia and Achaea. He initiated the war in 88 by killing Romans and Italians all over Asia. But when, soon after this act, Mithridates proved himself as much an oppressor as Rome had been, many natives, in particular the notables in the Greek cities, moved over to Rome again (see p. 185).

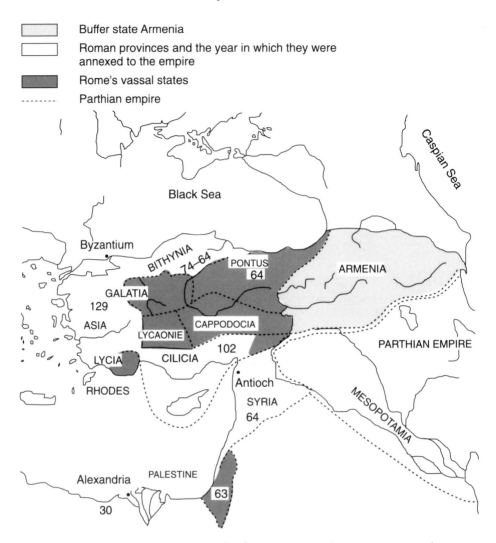

Buffer state Armenia

Roman provinces and the year in which they were annexed to the empire

Rome's vassal states

Parthian empire

Map 14.1 Rome's conquests and influence in Asia Minor, 133 BC onwards

The Senate granted Sulla, who had been elected consul for the year 88, the command against Mithridates (it was common practice for the Senate to allocate military command, for the Senate controlled foreign politics), but a tribune who sympathised with Marius persuaded the popular assembly (*Concilium Plebis*) to transfer the command to Marius. The *populares* in the Senate, most of the knights who were active as *publicani* and bankers, the majority of the Italian elite, Marius' veterans and the greater part of the urban proletariat in Rome supported Marius. The *publicani* in particular expected to gain more from him than from Sulla.

Sulla was supported by many *optimates* with their private backing and the soldiers who had served under him in the Social War. He responded to this transfer in command by marching his army into Rome and occupying the city – an outrageous act!

Sulla then secured important magistracies for his chief supporters, resumed his command and departed for the East. However, after he had left, in 87, Marius and his followers seized power in Rome and executed some of Sulla's followers. Marius was not to enjoy his triumph for very long though, for he died shortly after (early 86).

In the years 88–84 Sulla won the war against Mithridates in Greece and western Asia Minor and returned to Italy with an experienced army that was completely devoted to him. Mithridates was allowed to retain his original territory in Pontus. Sulla would not allow himself the time to defeat him there too.

In the years 83–82 Sulla defeated the Marians in a fierce, bloody civil war in Italy. In 82 he had himself proclaimed dictator, without the traditional restriction to six months of office (see p. 160). He shamelessly enriched his soldiers and settled some eighty thousand of his own and Marius' veterans on land in Italy which he confiscated from his political enemies and from communities that had chosen in favour of Marius. Sulla then began a reign of terror in which he is thought to have liquidated about a hundred senators and sixteen hundred knights. He introduced a series of new laws with which he hoped to restore stable government. Statutory rules started to take the place of unwritten standards of political conduct now that the consensus regarding such matters had disappeared within the elite (see p. 193).

Sulla ejected the knights from the juries, but as a form of compensation he admitted three hundred knights who sympathised with him to the Senate. This raised the number of senators to six hundred and marked the definitive end of the Senate's internal cohesion.

Sulla created five new permanent criminal courts that were to handle different kinds of offences. These courts were presided over by *praetors*. The tribunate was stripped of many of its powers. The persons who had held this office were moreover no longer allowed to stand for election to higher offices. By these measures Sulla hoped to dull the cutting edge of the populares' demagogic politics. In 79 Sulla voluntarily resigned. He died shortly after (in 78).

THE YEARS 79–49 BC

The thirty years between Sulla's resignation and the outbreak of the Second Civil War (49–45) witnessed the aggravation of the internal problems and a number of major wars. The powerful politicians in these years were Gnaeus Pompeius (Pompey, 106–48), Marcus Licinius Crassus (*c.* 112–53) and Gaius Julius Caesar (102–44). Pompey restored order in North Africa (*c.* 80 BC), Sicily (that same year) and Spain (78–71 BC), where defeated Marians who had fled to these areas after the First Civil War had been continuing their struggle with the assistance of local rebels.

In Spain the competent Marian commander Sertorius gave Pompey a hard time, but ultimately the latter managed to defeat him, and it was Pompey who finally established peace and order in Spain. In organisational terms he performed yeoman work. His reorganisations paved the way for Spain's Romanisation. Here, too, this process went hand in hand with the emergence of Roman-style cities, just as in Italy.

Figure 14.2 Gnaeus Pompeius (Pompey) (106–48 BC)
Notes: Pompey started his career as an officer in his father's army in the Social War (91–88 BC).
He then served as a junior commander in Sulla's army in Italy in 83, at the head of a private
army that he had recruited from among his father's veterans. After that, he led campaigns into
North Africa, Sicily and Spain. Pompey did not pursue the usual *cursus honorum*; in 70 BC
he achieved the consulship without having held a lower office, which was quite exceptional.
After that year he was granted more extraordinary commands, first against the pirates (67) and
later against Mithridates of Pontus (66–63). In 60 he allied himself with Caesar and Crassus. In
57 and 52 he was granted extraordinary powers to solve problems in Rome (grain supply,
restoration of order). In 49–48 he was defeated by Caesar in the Second Civil War.
Source: Marburg photographic archive.

Italy remained restless. Sulla's attempts to solve the old social and political
problems (see p. 196) had been unsuccessful and the civil war and Sulla's reign of
terror had caused much suffering. Italy was full of discontented men seeking revenge
and bankrupt veterans who had failed to make a living for themselves as farmers.

Spartacus' slave revolt (73–71 BC)

Crassus is best known for his suppression of the greatest slave revolt Italy had so far
experienced. For two years tens of thousands of pillaging slaves had roamed Italy,
led by the former gladiator Spartacus. They yearned for freedom and an acceptable
economic position. Some of them wanted to return to their home countries. Their
revolt was not motivated by any ideologically founded programme (see p. 191). In
71 Crassus' legions repressed the slaves' revolt in a bloody battle.

After 71 no more major slave revolts broke out in Italy, Sicily or the other
provinces for over three centuries. Slaves were treated in a slightly better manner and

there were no longer such large, homogeneous concentrations of slaves who, having been in Italy or Sicily for only a short time, still avidly recalled their days of freedom. The proportion of slaves who had been born into slavery and had hence never known a different life steadily increased. The slaves hoped to be released some day. Their hopes were not unfounded, for in Rome and elsewhere in Italy manumission became increasingly common; it served as a means of diverting discontent and as an incentive for encouraging slaves to work hard.

Pompey, Crassus and Caesar

In 70 BC the two most important political magnates and generals of the time, Pompey and Crassus, were both elected consul. They undid the restrictions that Sulla had imposed on the tribunate. Pompey in particular was to benefit from this. On two occasions (67 and 66) tribunes with whom he was friendly succeeded in persuading the popular assembly (*Concilium Plebis*) to grant him important commands with powers that exceeded those of a consul and a proconsul and applied in several provinces. The majority of the Senate was of course very much against this.

Pompey abused his special powers to further strengthen his political position and expand his backing of soldiers and protégés in Italy and the provinces. He and his supporters almost came to constitute a state within the state. In 67 BC he acquired authority over all the coastal regions in the empire and within three months he did away with the pirates, who had evolved into an autonomous power and were ravaging all the coasts. They had even established contacts with Mithridates, Spartacus and Sertorius (Pompey's opponent in Spain). We have already seen above (p. 191) how they had managed to acquire such power.

In the years 66–64 BC Pompey settled accounts with Mithridates of Pontus, who had been at war with Rome again since 74 BC. In 64/63, acting on his own authority, Pompey reorganised Asia Minor into a system of Roman provinces and vassal kingdoms (see Map 14.1) and annexed Syria (the last remaining part of the Seleucid kingdom) and Judah to the Roman empire. Syria was turned into a province and the Jewish territory became a vassal state. That put an end to the independent Jewish kingdom of the Maccabees, which had existed since 142 BC (see p. 145). The Euphrates came to mark the border between the Roman empire and the kingdom of the Parthians, who ruled over Mesopotamia and Iran.

In the meantime, in Rome, Caesar had risen to power. A *popularis*, he continued along the course marked out by the Gracchi and the Marians. His generosity and popular behaviour won him the favour of the lower classes in Rome. In 61, while he was a governor in northern Spain, he won a war against the last free tribes in the northwest of that country (see Map 14.2). That stirred his military ambitions.

Crassus had started his career as Sulla's second-in-command, but had gradually gone over to the *populares*. He had become the champion of the *publicani*, who looked to him to defend their interests in the Senate.

The resentment against Pompey, Crassus and Caesar's power grew among the *optimates* in the Senate. In 63 BC the Senate successfully crushed a conspiracy led by Lucius Sergius Catilina (Catiline), a bankrupt patrician. As a senator, he lacked authority in the Senate and his desire to achieve the consulship had consequently

Figure 14.3 The Mausoleum of Caecilia Metella, along the Via Appia, as represented in an eighteenth-century drawing

Notes: Caecilia Metella was the daughter of Q(uintus) Caecilius Metellus Creticus and the wife of M(arcus) Licinius Crassus. The Caecilius Metellus family played an important part in Roman politics between 150 and 50 BC. The Licinii Crassi were also a powerful family. Such important families often intermarried for the purpose of strengthening their political positions. They also built large funerary monuments to emphasise their high status.

Source: Marburg photographic archive

Figure 14.4 M(arcus) Tullius Cicero (106–43 BC)
Notes: A great orator and prose writer who is particularly well-known for his speeches,
rhetorical treatises, philosophical works and letters. Cicero is regarded as one of the
founders of written classical Latin.
Source: Marburg photographic archive.

remained unsatisfied. Out of rancour he organised a coalition of discontented parties
all over Italy and established contacts with a rebellious tribe in southern Gaul (we
recall that Sertorius had formed a similar combination of dissident Romans and
rebellious tribes; see p. 205). The consul M(arcus) Tullius Cicero (106–43), a *homo
novus* (new man) from the equestrian order who had made a successful career in
politics thanks to his great rhetorical skills and the support of a number of important *nobiles* (including Pompey), played an important part in this affair. He exposed
Catiline before he had been able to do much harm and crushed his conspiracy.
Cicero was not an *optimatis*. At first he supported Pompey, but after 60 BC he tried
to steer a middle course between the different governing groups.

The *optimates* thought that they would now also be able to put Pompey, Crassus
and Caesar in their places and obstructed all their aims and ambitions in the Senate.
They successfully prevented a distribution of land amongst Pompey's veterans and
refused to ratify Pompey's arrangements in the East.

The first Triumvirate

In 60 BC the three politicians privately agreed to assist one another in their political
struggles. This agreement is known as 'the first Triumvirate' (to distinguish it from
the second, of 43 BC; see p. 212). Together, they secured the election of Caesar to the
consulship in 59. With violence, and without consulting the Senate, Caesar persuaded
the public assembly to pass a bill granting land to Pompey's veterans. As for himself,
with the help of a sympathetic tribune he saw to it that the popular assembly voted

■■■■ Annexed to the Roman empire by Pompey and Caesar

▢ The Roman empire in 62 BC

⟵ Caesar's campaigns against the Pompeians and the *optimates* in the Second Civil War (x = places where battles were fought). Pompey fought battles at Dyrrhachium (D) and Pharsalus (PH), where Caesar won. Pompey then fled to Egypt. Caesar followed him, restored order in Egypt in 47, and returned to Rome via Asia Minor. In passing, he defeated one of the sons of Mithridates of Pontus who had rebelled against Rome.

In 46 BC Caesar defeated the *optimates* in North Africa and in 45 he settled accounts with the army of Pompey's two sons in Spain. Pompey himself had been killed in Egypt in 48.

GT   *Gallia Transalpina*

GC   *Gallia Cisalpina*

Map 14.2 The situation under Caesar and Pompey

him an important command in Gaul. Like Pompey before him, he used his command to pursue private ambitions. In the years 58–50 BC he conquered all of Gaul up to the Rhine. Caesar became one of the richest men in Rome and acquired a large backing of formerly pro-Marian families, Italian notables, knights and opportunistic senators. The successful Gallic campaign turned his army into the best-trained and most disciplined fighting machine of those days; his men were entirely devoted to him. Pompey's and Caesar's foreign adventures clearly reflect the consequences of the change in Rome's imperialist policy outlined above: the pursuit of private interests, power and wealth of a small number of political magnates had become the chief motivation for expansion (see Diagram 14.2).

Chaos in Rome

Rome was in these years the seat of fierce political struggles involving mob violence and political mock trials. There was progressively more scope for demagogues to manipulate the masses, because with every new generation the lower classes of citizens in Rome became more alienated from the old state institutions as the distance between them and the ruling *nobiles* increased.

One of the men who saw the masses in Rome as a vehicle for acquiring more power was the demagogue Clodius, a *nobilis* born into a patrician family. He left the patriciate so as to be able to become a plebeian tribune (see p. 169), in which capacity he promised the people the earth. In 58 he managed to persuade the popular assembly (*Concilium Plebis*) to convert the subsidising of grain into the distribution of free wheat. The effect of this was a massive influx into Rome of impoverished citizens from all over Italy and slaves who had been freed by their masters as they had become unprofitable (they were effectively written off as workers). In less than ten years the number of people receiving free wheat in Rome rose to about three hundred and twenty thousand.

To stem this chaos, the Senate granted Pompey special powers in 57 and 52 BC: in 57 to improve the supply of grain to Rome and in 52 (when he was appointed sole consul) to control the mob violence. Both tasks he successfully fulfilled.

In the meantime Crassus disappeared from the scene. In 56, when the Triumvirate was renewed, he had had himself appointed to an important command against the Parthians at the eastern border of Syria (Caesar remained in Gaul and Pompey in Rome), but in 53 BC he lost the war against the Parthians, dying on the battlefield.

In Rome, Pompey and the *optimates* started to grow towards one another after 52, for fear of the rising star of Caesar, who was achieving great successes in Gaul. In 50 they entered into a mammoth alliance with the intention of bringing about Caesar's downfall.

Many people in Rome began to yearn for a powerful leader who would restore order as a kind of arbitrator, but without immediately doing away with the existing state institutions. In 52–50 the orator, politician and philosopher Cicero wrote two works on the state in imitation of Plato. In his opinion the solution to Rome's problems lay in concord between the higher orders (in particular the senators and knights) and a curtailment of the greed and ambition of the powerful. The existing polity should be turned into a mixed constitution (see p. 193 on Polybius), and the state should be ruled by senators who were well prepared for their tasks and who were selected for their virtues. Cicero still thought entirely in terms of the old city state, which was not surprising: nobody in Rome had yet come to realise that the organs of a city state were not suited to the administration of a large empire comprising a wide diversity of peoples and cultures and having a capital with almost a million inhabitants.

THE SECOND CIVIL WAR (49–45 BC) AND ITS AFTERMATH (44–30 BC)

The year 49 BC saw the outbreak of a civil war between Pompey and the *optimates* on the one hand and Caesar and his followers on the other. Caesar won this war in a series of daring and spectacular campaigns which, between 49 and 45 BC, took him to all the corners of the Roman empire (see Map 14.2).

In passing, in 47 BC, he restored order in Egypt, which was then torn apart by succession struggles. Caesar subsequently helped Cleopatra to ascend the throne as Egypt's queen.

In 47 BC Caesar was appointed dictator and in 44 he was even made dictator for life. He appointed magistrates on his own authority and admitted his agents and henchmen into the Senate. In the end, in 30 BC, the Senate had about one thousand members. Caesar was more lenient than Sulla; he spared the lives and wealth of most of his opponents.

Between his campaigns, he launched his programme of reforms. He tightened the control of the governors in the provinces, limited the number of recipients of wheat to one hundred and fifty thousand and settled about forty thousand veterans and tens of thousands of proletarians and freedmen from Rome in colonies (two of which were founded at the sites of the former cities of Carthage and Corinth, which had both been destroyed in 146 BC and were rebuilt as Roman cities).

Caesar governed the Roman empire like an absolute monarch. That was the reason for his assassination, in March of 44, by the *optimates* Brutus and Cassius. But Caesar's murder did not lead to the restoration of the old regime, for after his death his adherents, supported by his soldiers, seized control in Rome. They were led by Marcus Antonius (Mark Antony), Lepidus and Gaius Octavius, one of Caesar's young grandnephews (born in 63 BC), whom he had posthumously adopted as his son in his will (Caesar had no sons of his own). After his adoption, Octavius' full name became Gaius Julius Caesar Octavianus (Octavian). Brutus and Cassius fled to the eastern provinces.

When Caesar's inheritance brought Antony and Octavian into conflict with one another, the Caesarians' enemies seized their chance to build up military power. One of Pompey's sons (Sextus Pompeius) built a strong fleet and established himself on Sicily, from where he could obstruct the supply of grain to Rome (see p. 191). Brutus and Cassius composed an army in the eastern provinces.

The Senate, which regarded Antony as the strongest party, supported Octavian in his struggle against Antony. In 43, after a few battles in the Po valley, the Caesarian leaders came to terms and formed the Second Triumvirate. The three men saw to it

Figure 14.5 The Senate House, built in Caesar's time
Note: It was restored in late antiquity (during Diocletian's reign, AD 284–305).
Source: Marburg photographic archive.

that the popular assembly granted them dictatorial powers in Rome, Italy and the provinces. In the years 42–36 they then settled scores with the *optimates* and Pompey junior in a series of major battles at sea and on land and a reign of terror. One of the victims was Cicero, who had revealed himself hostile to Antony.

The greatest battle was fought at Philippi, in Macedonia, where Antony (and Octavian) decisively defeated Brutus and Cassius. After this battle Lepidus ruled over Africa and Antony over the eastern half of the empire, while Octavian set about restoring order in Italy. In 41–40 Octavian ruthlessly confiscated land from eighteen selected communities in Italy, on which he settled almost one hundred thousand veterans who had fought for the Triumvirs and their opponents and whose services were now no longer required. These confiscations, together with those during the reign of terror against the Caesarians' opponents, were the greatest Italy had ever known.

Figure 14.6 G(aius) Julius Caesar (102–44 BC)
Note: An important politician, statesman, general and prose writer (he justified his behaviour
in Gaul and in the Second Civil War in two books).
Source: Rome, Museo del Terme.

In 36 Octavian liquidated Pompey's son and sidetracked Lepidus. Lepidus' troops
defected to Octavian, who now had control over the entire western half of the empire.

Since 42 Antony had been behaving like a Hellenistic absolute monarch in the
East and had started to work together with Cleopatra, the queen of Egypt (see p.
212). In 36 Antony suffered a costly defeat against the Parthians, which made him
dependent on subsidies granted by Cleopatra, in return for which he had to comply
with all her demands. Via Antony, Cleopatra hoped to gain control over rich regions
so as to be able to revive the faded glory of the Ptolemies (she was the last of this
dynasty to rule over Egypt).

In 33–32, in a shrewd propaganda campaign, Octavian managed to win the
support of the Caesarians and almost everyone else in Italy and the western
provinces in his struggle against Antony and Cleopatra's 'Eastern despotism'.

In 32 the Italian communities took an oath of allegiance to Octavian (the *coniuratio
Italiae*). Octavian defeated Antony and Cleopatra in 31 BC in a naval battle off Actium
and in 30 he conquered Egypt. Antony and Cleopatra committed suicide in Alexandria.
Octavian then returned to Italy, where he used his copious Egyptian booty to *buy* land

for the tens of thousands of superfluous soldiers. There was no longer any need for him to confiscate land for this purpose. Octavian had brought the civil wars to an end and was the sole surviving ruler. He owed his victory to a group of faithful friends (among whom were Maecenas and Agrippa) who helped him in every respect and won his naval and land battles for him, to Caesar's soldiers, who regarded him as Caesar's own son, and to Caesar's agents and henchmen, who supported his enterprises financially and in any other way they could. But to acquire a permanent, stable position, Octavian had to seek the support of a wider circle (including, in particular, the notables), without however estranging his soldiers and the Caesarians.

Octavian set out from a good starting position: almost everyone was now prepared to accept a moderate form of monarchic rule if that would mean a definite end to the civil wars. The civil wars after 44 had caused much dismay. Never before had so many Roman soldiers been under arms and never before had so many men died in civil strife (see Diagram 14.3).

Diagram 14.3 Numbers of citizens under arms

Year	Estimated number of adult male citizens	Size of the armies in the field (some figures are estimates)	%
225 BC	300,000	52,000	17
213	260,000	75,000	29
203	235,000	60,000	26
193	266,000	53,000	20
183	315,000	48,000	15
173	314,000	44,000	14
163	383,000	33,000	9
153	374,000	30,000	8
143	400,000	44,000	11
133	381,000	37,000	10
123	(not known)	32,000	(not known)
113	(not known)	34,000	(not known)
103	400,000	50,000	13
93	id.	52,000	13
83	1,030,000	143,000	14
73	id.	171,000	17
63	id.	120,000	12
53	id.	121,000	12
43	1,480,000	240,000	16
33	1,600,000	250,000	16
23	1,800,000	156,000	9

Notes: We here observe the effects of the intensive Second Punic War (218–201 BC, p. 178 ff.), the granting of Roman citizenship to the Italians (p. 202) and the civil wars, which coincided with the continuing expansion of the Roman empire (pp. 203–12). These figures were inferred from data in the works of Roman historians and other ancient sources by P.A. Brunt and K. Hopkins. The 156,000 soldiers in 23 BC are Augustus' legionaries and guards. They had to be recruited from among citizens (p. 225).

Source: After K. Hopkins, *Conquerors and Slaves*, 1978, p. 33.

THE FLOURISHING OF CULTURAL LIFE DURING THE CIVIL WARS

For the arts and humanities the period of the civil wars was by no means a period of decline. In fact, it was only now that Roman architecture and the visual arts came into bloom, partly as a result of the inspiration provided by Greek examples.

In the realm of literature, the fifty years between 80 and 30 BC were characterised by great productivity. Cicero wrote not only about the state, but also about rhetoric and (ethical) philosophy. From a whole range of Greek works he selected that which best suited his purpose, which he then remodelled into a work of his own. Caesar wrote long memoirs to justify his deeds in Gaul and his behaviour in the Second Civil War. Roman poets, historians and writers of scholarly prose texts produced works in imitation of Greek authors which have remained classics to this day. The best-known historian of this period is Sallust, one of Caesar's followers and an opponent of the *optimates*. Writing in the style of the Greek historian Thucydides (see p. 126), he discussed different episodes of the Civil Wars, for example the Catiline conspiracy of 63.

Rome of the first century BC has been compared to Pericles' classical Athens. And indeed, we note the same convergence of money, talent and a broad interested public. The money that was spent in Rome was one of the fruits of Rome's expansionist campaigns. The talent was drawn to Rome from every part of the Greek and Roman cultural world, the well-paying patrons of letters who were to be found in that city acting as magnets for artists and intellectuals. And the broad interested public consisted of the Roman elite, who customarily received a thorough grounding in rhetoric and literature – a tradition which the Romans had adopted since the second century BC in emulation of the Greeks (see pp. 122 and 193).

THE EARLY IMPERIAL AGE
(27 BC–AD 193)

Augustus
Augustus' constitutional position and the real basis of his power
The settlement of 27 BC
The settlements of 23 and 19 BC
Changes in the administration
The Senate and the popular assemblies
The higher orders: senators, knights
The decuriones
The army
Ideal and religious aspects of emperorship
Latin literature in the Augustan era
Augustus' conquests
The early imperial age after Augustus (AD 14–193)
Wars and rebellions
Emperorship and the problem of the emperor's succession
Developments in administration after Augustus
The spread of Roman citizenship
Changes in the higher orders
Roman law
The western and eastern provinces
The western provinces
The eastern half of the empire
Agriculture, trade and crafts
The lower classes
Trade
Work and status
The position of women
Religion
Roman gods and religious practices
The introduction of foreign gods
The Christians

AUGUSTUS

Augustus' constitutional position and the real basis of his power

The struggles in Rome had left Octavian the sole surviving ruler in 30 BC. He was elected consul several years in succession and he also still enjoyed his triumviral powers. He was therefore legally entitled to remain in power. But more important than this legal basis were the support of the armies and the common acceptance of his position by all the social classes. They constituted the real basis of his power. Almost everyone accepted Octavian's leadership because he was the man who had finally put an end to the civil wars. This achievement had won Octavian powerful informal authority (*auctoritas*).

But Octavian was anxious to formalise his authority. He did not wish to remain dependent on the annual consular elections and on the dictatorial powers granted him in the days of the Second Triumvirate. The civil wars had cast a slur on those powers. And so, in a long process of trial and error, he searched for an alternative way of securing a more constitutional position that would be generally acceptable.

The settlement of 27 BC

In 27 BC Octavian laid down his powers and restored the government to the Senate and the popular assembly. They then granted him the name Augustus (majestic, he who has been promoted to greater power) and proconsular *imperium* in the three provinces where most of the troops were stationed: Gaul, Spain and Syria. Until 23 BC he was moreover re-elected consul every year. His three provinces he governed through deputies (*legati*) with propraetorial *imperium* (*legati Augusti propraetore*). These deputies were usually appointed every year or every two years from the senatorial order. They were assisted in their tasks by procurators from the equestrian order, who supervised expenditures and tax collection. From this point onwards these provinces were the imperial provinces, the others were the public provinces, that is, the old provinces of the 'Roman people'. The latter provinces are sometimes still called 'senatorial provinces'. These provinces continued to be governed by pro-consuls, who were appointed every year or every two years and were assisted by quaestors. The tasks and responsibilities of a *procurator* in an imperial province were the same as those of a *quaestor* in a public province. The proconsuls of the public provinces were ex-praetors (in the smaller provinces) or ex-consuls (in the larger provinces). The title of propraetor went out of use in these provinces.

The new provinces that were annexed to the empire under Augustus became imperial provinces (see Map 15.1). Egypt, which had been incorporated in the Roman empire in 30 BC, was in effect also an imperial province, although it differed from the other provinces because the Romans had retained the bureaucratic system they had found there. In the other provinces the governors (*legati* and proconsuls) supervised the local municipal authorities (see p. 185), which took care of most day-to-day administration. In Egypt, however, the governor was the head of a stratified civil service. The men who were appointed governors there came from the equestrian order (the *praefecti Aegypti*). The governorship of Egypt came to be one of the highest posts open to knights, a top position in the new equestrian career (see p. 224).

Figure 15.1 Augustus (27 BC – AD 14)
Source: Marburg photographic archive, Rome, Musei Vaticani.

Did Augustus still distrust the senators too much to admit them to this area? Senators were not allowed to travel to Egypt without the emperor's permission. The emperors who succeeded Augustus regarded Egypt as a major source of food for Rome (Egypt, Sicily and North Africa ranked among Rome's most important granaries) and of money for their private treasury. The sophisticated tax system that the Ptolemies had established to wring all they could from Egypt now came to fill the treasury of the Roman emperors. Italy was not a province. The emperor, the high magistrates in Rome and the Senate supervised the self-governing communities of Italy to varying degrees and administered the city of Rome. Rome and Italy did not pay direct taxes.

We have started to use the term 'emperor'. The word 'emperor' comes from the Latin *imperator*, meaning 'commander-in-chief'. This was a title given to a general after an important victory. The general would add this title to his name. Imperator was also one of Octavian's names. At first, the Roman emperors were informally referred to by the popular name 'Caesar', after Julius Caesar. At some time in the late imperial age 'Caesar' became the official title of the heir to the throne. The Romans of the first centuries of the imperial age also used the title *princeps* (first citizen), which was not an official term, but rather a form of address. The word principate, which is often used to refer to the Roman monarchy as it was in the first two centuries of the imperial age, is derived from this.

The settlements of 23 and 19 BC

Augustus saw that his monopolisation of one of the consulships meant that fewer senators could achieve this office, which was still the highest honourary office open to a senator. He realised that he would need other powers to regularise his position.

In 23 BC the Senate and the popular assembly granted Augustus tribunician power for life (he did not become an actual plebeian tribune) and supreme control over the governors of the public provinces (he of course already had supreme control over his deputies in his imperial provinces). This *tribunicia potestas* (tribunician power) and the *imperium proconsulare* (proconsular power), which had been granted him in 27 and which was extended in 23, were to remain the legal, official basis of imperial power until in the late imperial age. The Senate (also on behalf of the people) conferred these powers upon each new emperor. This conferment of powers was in fact tantamount to an official proclamation of a new ruler.

In 19 BC Augustus received the most important consular powers (with the exception of those relating to a consul's ceremonial duties) for life without actually having to hold the consulship. He had already been performing the tasks of a *censor* since 28 BC; as we have already seen, they comprised filling vacancies in the Senate and the equestrian order, conducting censuses, concluding contracts for tax collection and commissioning the construction and maintenance of public works.

Thus Augustus clothed his control in a combination of constitutional powers derived from traditional offices, which entitled him to legally exercise direct authority in all areas of government. This made it easier for the senators and other traditionally minded Romans to accept Augustus' regime. His political system was rooted in the old republican institutions – in theory at least.

Changes in the administration

In practice, however, major changes took place behind this façade. Augustus assumed control over jurisdiction in appeal cases (see pp. 174 and 241) and acquired supremacy over foreign politics and public finance because the Senate meekly accepted everything he proposed. The powers granted him in 27 and 23 BC had given him control over the governors in the provinces. For the occupants of those provinces this proved to be a favourable development, because Augustus kept the governors and tax collectors under surveillance, restricting their opportunities to exploit the provincials.

Local provincial notables remained responsible for collecting the direct taxes; they were placed under the supervision of the procurators (in the imperial provinces) and the quaestors (in the public provinces). The *publicani* continued to levy the indirect taxes (customs and duties).

These new conditions led to a busy correspondence between the emperor and citizens lodging appeals, governors asking for advice and cities (in Italy and the provinces) requesting favours. The imperial letters that were sent in reply had the force of law. This great flow of correspondence entailed a considerable amount of extra work and this led to the emergence of imperial secretariats. During Augustus' reign they were still staffed by the emperor's private slaves, led by experienced freedmen. Later on, these secretariats were to grow into offices.

The emperor also acquired his own financial sector, separate from the old public treasury, which had always been controlled by the Senate. That public treasury was called the *aerarium*. Its management was transferred from the quaestors to experienced ex-praetors. In the course of his reign, Augustus appropriated more and more control over the *aerarium*.

The financial resources available to the emperor besides his private funds were the funds of the imperial provinces: the *fisci* (singular: *fiscus*), which were managed by the procurators. These *fisci* were fed by the taxes levied in the imperial provinces. They were used to pay the soldiers in those provinces. So the procurators were actually the armies' paymasters general. The main taxes in the provinces were the indirect taxes (customs, duties) and a direct tax based on landed property and on the produce of the land (it comprised a fixed percentage of the roughly estimated yield).

The emperor's private resources grew rapidly, largely because families anxious to win the emperor's favour would bequeath money and property to him and because the emperor confiscated goods of the individuals he convicted. The imperial properties were managed by the emperor's freedmen.

The emperor acquired decisive influence over the careers of the senators and knights. Around 5 BC this influence was formalised. The emperor was allowed to nominate candidates for all the important offices and those candidates were almost always elected. Candidates who had not been nominated or commended by the emperor stood little chance of achieving the most important magistracies. The emperor could of course appoint whomever he liked in his own provinces and services.

The emperor's trusted advisors, united in his *consilium* (the *Consilium Principis* – the *princeps'* council) acquired considerable executive influence. The *Consilium Principis* was to some extent comparable with the advisory committees of the

Figure 15.2 Funerary monument of Gaius and Lucius Caesar, next to one of Augustus's triumphal arches

Notes: Augustus hoped that Gaius, the oldest of the two, would succeed him. Both brothers however died at an early age (Lucius in AD 2 and Gaius in AD 4). Augustus was ultimately succeeded by his step-son Tiberius, the son of his wife Livia from a former marriage, whom he had made the heir to his empire by adopting him as his son. Tiberius ruled from AD 14 until 37.

Next to the funerary monument is one of Augustus' triumphal arches. The monuments are in St Rémy-en-Provence.

Source: Marburg photographic archive.

republican magistrates and governors (see p. 169), only it was far more important. It was this council, and no longer the Senate, that prepared the emperor's decisions and discussed matters of policy and jursidiction.

The Senate and the popular assemblies

The importance of the popular assemblies declined substantially under Augustus. Hardly anybody attended them any more. After Augustus they convened only rarely. The last popular assembly seems to have taken place under the emperor Nerva (AD 96–98).

The Senate ostensibly acquired more power. Senatorial decrees came to be as binding as laws and imperial edicts. Augustus' successor Tiberius (AD 14–37) transferred the responsibility of electing magistrates from the popular assemblies to the Senate.

In practice, however, the Senate was guided in all things by the emperor's wishes: the Senate's decisions were almost always based on imperial proposals or letters. The senators knew very well how things were really run and were aware that their prospects of promotion depended on the emperor's goodwill. The Senate's real importance lay in the fact that it consisted of the wealthiest Roman landowners with the most experience in higher administration and in military command: a combination of economic power and indispensable scarce knowledge. The Senate moreover represented legality. Until AD 282 a ruler was the legal emperor only after the Senate had conferred upon him the combination of powers which Augustus had first acquired.

The higher orders: senators, knights

Augustus fixed property qualifications for admission to the senatorial and equestrian orders. In the past, the censors had also employed more or less traditional prosperity criteria, but now they were officially fixed. Only persons who had at least one million sesterces stood a chance of being admitted to the senatorial order; the property qualification for admission to the equestrian order was fixed at 400,000 sesterces (see Appendix 2 on Greek and Roman money, p. 301). Usually about 80 to 90 per cent of the property of the members of these orders consisted of land. The rest comprised houses, bank balances, moveable property and slaves.

In these days, an estate of average quality yielded a profit of about 6 per cent. That meant that a senator had an annual income of at least 60,000 sesterces. We get a good idea of how much that was when we compare it with a legionary's annual pay, which amounted to 225 denari (900 sesterces) in the first century of the imperial age.

Under Augustus (and his successors until in the third century) the senators continued to hold the most important administrative offices. They still followed the old *cursus honorum* (see p. 170), but all kinds of new posts emerged between the old honorary offices. After completing the praetorship, a senator could for example be appointed to a post with the treasury (the *aerarium*), to the office of legion commander, to that of *legatus Augusti propraetore* in a small imperial province or to that of proconsul in a small public province. The next office after the consulship was no longer the censorship (there were no longer any censors besides the emperor), but a governor's post in one or more of the large imperial provinces or in Asia or Africa and ultimately the important function of *praefectus urbi* (prefect of the city, the mayor of Rome) – a post that had been created in AD 6.

It was in these new offices in particular that the senators performed yeoman work. Some of the old honorary offices, such as the aedileship and the tribunate of the plebs, became honourable sinecures. The work formerly done by the magistrates who held those posts became the responsibility of the imperial services. The quaestors worked in the public provinces, the praetors still served a function in jurisdiction in Rome and were partly responsible for organising the games in that city, while the consuls had mainly ceremonial and representative tasks in Rome.

In Augustus's time the knights acquired an important position in administration. They furnished the army officers and could make themselves useful in the imperial provinces as procurators. After their service in those provinces they stood a chance

Figure 15.3 A luxury glass goblet
Source: Cologne, Römisch-Germanisches Museum.

of being appointed to one of the important administrative offices which Augustus created and reserved specifically for knights, namely those of prefect of the fleet, prefect of the grain supplies in Rome, prefect of Egypt (see p. 218) and prefect of the praetorian guard, the imperial bodyguard, which was permanently quartered outside Rome from Tiberius' reign onwards. Nevertheless, only a small percentage of the knights was actively engaged in administration; at the end of the republican era there were some twenty thousand knights. Under Augustus the Senate had six hundred members.

The *decuriones*

The local notables of the Italian communities and of Roman cities outside Italy started to constitute a kind of third order, that of the *decuriones*, also known as *curiales* (the members of the *curia*, the council house). The members of this order avidly supported Augustus as they benefited from his regime, for Augustus greatly improved their prospects of social advancement. The vacancies that had arisen in the Senate due to the civil wars and the dying out of the old families he filled not only with knights, but also with Italian notables. The names of many of the men who held the consulship during Augustus's reign betray Italian origins.

The army

The control over the armies, which were almost all stationed in the imperial provinces, Augustus reserved for himself. He also saw to it that the Senate granted all important military commands to his relatives and friends, so as to prevent the emergence of new military commanders from outside his own circle.

Augustus established a standing army of about three hundred thousand professional soldiers. One half consisted of legions of six thousand men (recruited from Roman citizens), the other of auxiliaries (*auxilia* – recruited from provincials). The auxiliaries comprised squadrons of cavalry and cohorts of six hundred or one thousand infantry. The legions were commanded by senators, the lower officers came from the equestrian order. The majority of the centurions in the legions (see p. 171) still came from the army's ranks and file, as in the past.

Augustus also created an imperial bodyguard (the praetorian guard) of about nine thousand men led by an equestrian prefect, which he quartered in camps in Italy. This guard was responsible for guarding and defending the capital. The guard prefect (*praefectus praetorio*) was a powerful man. Several guard prefects had a decisive influence on the appointment of new emperors after Augustus. This powerful position they owed to the fact that they commanded the largest military force in the vicinity of the capital (and the emperor's court) after Tiberius permanently stationed the guard near Rome.

In AD 6 Augustus established a body of seven thousand watchmen (*vigiles*) in Rome; they also constituted the fire brigade. He also created a police force of four thousand men (the four urban cohorts, the *cohortes urbanae*). The watchmen were recruited from freedmen and were commanded by an equestrian prefect. The urban cohorts were commanded by the urban prefect. The urban prefecture, which was also created in AD 6, came to be a very influential post. The urban prefect was the head of Rome's administration, but he also had an important position in the administration of justice and the maintenance of order in Italy.

Augustus fixed good terms of service for his soldiers and made provisions for their retirement. Praetorians did sixteen years' service, legionaries served for twenty years and auxiliaries for twenty-five years. When they were discharged, the soldiers were granted a plot of land or a sum of money. Moreover the auxiliaries received Roman citizenship. Soldiers were not allowed to have a wife, but they could have a mistress outside the camp. On their discharge they could legally marry their mistress and officially acknowledge their children. Their wives and children then acquired Roman citizenship too (if they did not already have it).

Augustus paid his soldiers' retirement bonuses from his private resources at first, but in AD 6 he established a special treasury for this purpose (the *aerarium militare*), which was maintained out of a 5 per cent death duty levied on legacies of Roman citizens exceeding 100,000 sesterces and a 1 per cent sales tax.

The pay scales employed in the army differed tremendously. Officers and junior officers received many times the amounts paid to ordinary soldiers (until AD 83 a legionary's pay was 225 denarii; after that it was 300 denarii per year).

Ideal and religious aspects of emperorship

Emperor worship

Augustus succeeded amazingly well in neutralising the sharp distinctions created by the civil wars and incorporating the different social groups into his political system. He made it impossible for anyone outside his own circle to acquire a powerful military position; he granted the knights access to the administrative offices; he gave Italian aristocrats the chance to rise to the equestrian order and the Senate, and he arranged good terms of service and pensions for his soldiers, which created a bond between the army and the emperor. Everyone in the empire benefitted from the restored peace.

Augustus wanted to be neither an Eastern despot, a master of slaves, nor a military dictator. He wished to be seen as a father and a benefactor, who respected the old state institutions, the citizens' private rights and the traditional privileges of the higher orders. Augustus presented his reign as a new epoch of success, peace, prosperity and plenty after the sufferings caused by the civil wars. He propagated the revival of the traditional rites and ceremonies for the state gods and of the old strict code of conduct, which (in his eyes) had assured the greatness of Rome. As vehicles in his 'propaganda', Augustus used the visual arts, legends and representations on coins, and inscriptions in well-frequented places. All his successors did the same and elaborated on the slogans introduced in Augustus's time.

During Augustus's reign emperorship already began to acquire religious traits. The emperor cult emerged in the eastern provinces, whose occupants had become accustomed to worshipping their kings in the Hellenistic era (see p. 142). From there it gradually spread across the whole empire. It played a prominent part in the military camps in particular, where it was employed as a means of binding the soldiers to the emperors.

Latin literature in the Augustan era

Echoes of Augustus's 'propaganda' are to be found in the Latin literature of his reign. This period is regarded as the golden age of Latin literature. The emperor and his friends (especially Maecenas) financially supported good poets and prose writers and organised private gatherings, at which writers were invited to read from their works. Many a creative mind and knowledgeable literature lover would meet at these gatherings. Some of the literary works that were written in these days have continued to exert an influence on European literature into our times. Among these works is the *Aeneid*, an epic inspired by the works of the Greek poet Homer (see p. 70), which the poet Virgil (70–19 BC) wrote towards the end of his life. It recounts the adventures of the Trojan hero Aeneas on his way to Italy after the Greeks had destroyed his home town Troy. According to Roman legend, Roman history began with

Figure 15.4 Part of the relief on the Altar of Peace consecrated by Augustus in 9 BC, showing the imperial family

Notes: Various 'propagandistic' scenes were represented on the Ara Pacis: Mars, a procession of the Senate and the people of Rome, the *dea Roma* (divine personification of Rome) seated on weapons, the goddess Italia (personification) surrounded by plenty, the imperial family attending a sacrificial ceremony and Aeneas, the legendary founder of the Julio-Claudian dynasty.

The scenes were intended to link the old-established Julio-Claudian dynasty, Augustus' family, with prosperity, presented as the consequence of military success, and Augustus' dynasty, the Senate and the people with the restored piety towards the state gods.

Source: Rome, Alinari.

Aeneas: he was believed to have been the founder of the Julio-Claudian dynasty, the family of Julius Caesar and his adopted son Augustus.

Another well-known writer from this period is Horace (65–8 BC), who won fame with his odes, satires and verse epistles. One of those epistles is the *Ars poetica*, a work discussing literature, which has had a profound impact on European literature. It owes much to one of Aristotle's works (see p. 125). Livy (59 BC – AD 17) wrote a history of Rome from its beginnings down to his own times. He believed that Rome would regain her former greatness if the Romans were to revive the virtues of their ancestors.

Latin literature continued to flower for some time after Augustus. One of the most famous authors of the period around AD 100 is the historian Tacitus (*c*. AD 55 – *c*. AD 120). He wrote about the emperors who ruled between AD 14 and 96, about the Germans and about Britain. Tacitus was of the opinion that a monarchy was the

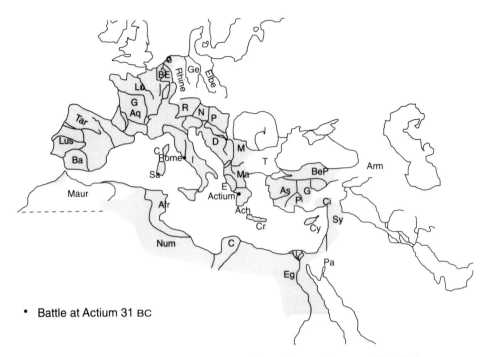

• Battle at Actium 31 BC

Gaul:
Be   – Belgica
Lu   – Lugdunensis
Aq   – Aquitania
Na   – Narbonensis

Hispania:
Tar   – Tarraconensis
Lus   – Lusitania
Ba   – Baetica
Sa   – Sardinia
C   – Corsica

Afr   – Africa
Num – Numidia
Maur – Mauretania
C   – Cyrene
Eg   – Egypt

Danubian regions and the Balkans:
R   – Raetia
N   – Noricum
P   – Pannonia
D   – Dalmatia
M   – Moesia
T   – Thracia
Ma   – Macedonia
Ach – Achaea
E   – Epirus
Cr   – Crete

Asia:
As   – Asia
Ci   – Cilicia
B e P – Bithynia et Pontus
G   – Galatia
Sy   – Syria
Cy   – Cyprus
Pa   – vassal states in Palestine and
         Jordan + Judah
Arm – Armenia, a buffer state

Map 15.1 The Roman empire under the emperor Augustus
Note: Some vassal states are not indicated.

only possible form of government, but he criticised its shortcomings and regretted the loss of the republican freedom.

Augustus' conquests

Augustus's officers conquered the northwest of Spain, the Alps and the Danubian plain, which had not yet been brought under Roman control (see Map 15.1). Between 15 BC and AD 9 several new imperial provinces were established to the south of the Danube. Augustus's aim was to expand his empire to the Elbe in the northwest, but he was unable to conquer Germany. Between AD 9 and 16 the Germans successfully fought for their freedom. When the Romans suffered a major defeat in the Teutoburg forest (AD 9) Augustus put a stop to his campaigns in Germany. He and his successor Tiberius realised that it would cost too much money and effort to subject this region. Tiberius' commander Germanicus left Germany in 17 and the river Rhine became the northern frontier of the Roman empire.

In 20 BC Augustus diplomatically worked out a *modus vivendi* with the Parthians: Armenia was to become a buffer state in which Rome and Parthia were to share influence.

Augustus readily entrusted important campaigns and diplomatic enterprises to his loyal friends and relatives. The most important of these were Agrippa, the husband of his daughter Julia (see Appendix 3, p. 302), and his step-sons Tiberius (who was emperor from 14 until 37) and Drusus. Tiberius played an important part in the conquest of the Danubian regions. Drusus gathered laurels in the Rhine-Meuse delta and in western Germany between 12 and 9 BC, the year in which he died. His son Germanicus commanded the fighting there from AD 13 until 17.

The end of Augustus's reign was also the end of the era of Rome's major conquests. The Roman empire entered a new phase. Up to 146 BC the Roman empire had primarily aimed at hegemony (see p. 182). After that date there followed a transitional period in which Rome, evidently desiring a more direct form of control, began to govern increasingly more regions as provinces. By the time of the Late Republic and Augustus's reign the Roman empire had become a territorial empire, with clearly defined frontiers. Augustus had made a determined effort to establish natural, easily defensible frontiers.

Under Augustus, Roman imperialism was no longer primarily motivated by the greed and ambition of generals, politicians and interest groups (see p. 193) as it had been in the Late Republic, but more by a combination of strategic and propagandistic interests. Establishing good natural frontiers was not Augustus's sole aim. Above all, he wished to use military success as a means of binding his soldiers to him and winning the esteem of the rest of the population. The new conquests were propagated as the successful consequences of the restoration of concord and the revival of the old Roman piety and valour. Contemporary Roman authors started to praise the Romans as the nation that was destined to subject and govern the peoples in the surrounding world.

Augustus's successors switched to a defensive strategy. Some emperors, such as Claudius (41–54) and Trajan (98–117), conquered a few new territories (see Map 15.2) for the sake of winning their soldiers' esteem, securing a frontier or annexing a potential source of wealth, but the heydays of Roman expansion were over. The Rhine, the Danube, the Euphrates and the Sahara came to mark the empire's definitive borders.

THE EARLY IMPERIAL AGE AFTER AUGUSTUS
(AD 14–193)

Wars and rebellions

For the greater part of the first two centuries AD peace reigned throughout the empire. The armies remained stationed in permanent camps and forts along the frontiers (see Map 15.3). The Romans endeavoured to maintain a buffer zone in the regions across the Rhine and the Danube and tried to play the tribes living there off against one another. For a long time they were quite successful. For the first two hundred years of the imperial age no major wars broke out along more than one of the northern frontiers at a time. That period did see a few dangerous wars in individual frontier regions. In 69–70, for example, the Batavi, who lived in the region traversed by the Rhine, the Waal and the Meuse, revolted against the Roman empire just when it was divided by succession struggles. The year 69 is known as 'the year of the four emperors'. Nero, the last emperor of the Julio-Claudian dynasty, had died without appointing a successor, and four rival pretenders to the throne were fighting one another at the head of their armies (see Diagram 15.1 and Appendix 3, p. 302).

In the years between 42 and 84 Britain was annexed to the Roman empire (see Map 15.2). The emperor Claudius (41–54) launched the first campaigns to Britain for the sake of winning military fame. But he did not succeed in establishing permanent control over Britain, for border conflicts and rebellions were to break out intermittently until 84, when the country was finally pacified.

During the reign of the emperor Domitian (81–96) the empire was alternately threatened by tribes in the regions along the Rhine and the Danube. To raise his soldiers' morale Domitian increased their pay from 225 to 300 denarii per year in 83. It was the emperor Trajan (98–117) who set things right in the aforementioned regions: in a series of major campaigns (c. 105–106) he subdued Dacia (present-day Rumania), which had been the greatest hotbed of raids and resistance in the years before 96.

A state of armed peace was maintained along the eastern Parthian frontier, which on several occasions was disturbed by wars over the buffer state Armenia (c. 55–65, 114–117, 161–166). But those wars were largely ineffective: the *status quo* that had been reached under Augustus was preserved until the end of the second century.

Fierce Jewish revolts broke out a few times in the southeast corner of the empire. The Jews in Palestine rose in revolt in 66–70 and 132–135 and those in Cyrenaica and Egypt and on Cyprus in 115–116. The latter revolt was a desperate response to increasing discrimination. The aim of the Jews in Palestine was to found a new powerful Jewish state. The first two Jewish revolts (66–70 and 115–116) caused the Romans quite a few problems, as they coincided with other wars. The Jewish war of 66–70 coincided with a revolt in Britain, the Batavian uprising and the internal strife in the year of the four emperors. In 69 the threat to the Roman empire became acute.

Abbreviations as on Map 15.1
plus from west to east

Brit – Britannia   Dac – Dacia
Gl – Germania Inferior   Ca – Cappadocia
GS – Germania Superior   Me – Mesopotamia

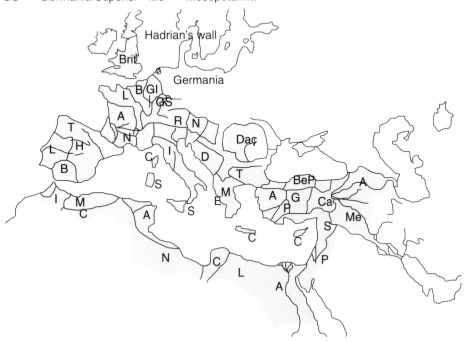

Map 15.2 The Roman empire under the emperor Trajan
Notes: Trajan conquered Davia (present-day Rumania), part of Arabia to the east of the Jordan and parts of Mesopotamia (in the Roman-Parthian war of 114–117). His successor Hadrian (117–138) returned the conquered areas in Mesopotamia to the Parthians. Britain was subjected between AD 42 and 84.

However, the emperor Vespasian (69–79) solved all the problems. He eliminated the last other pretender to the throne and quelled the rebellions. In 70 his son Titus razed Jerusalem to the ground.

In the last Jewish revolt (132–135) the Jews were led by Bar Kokhba, who passed himself off as the Messiah, the saviour of the people of Israel whose arrival was predicted in the Old Testament. After suppressing this rebellion, the emperor Hadrian (117–138) banned the Jews from Jerusalem. He turned the city into a colony for Roman veterans.

Emperorship and the problem of the emperor's succession

Thanks to Augustus's efforts, the monarchy rested on sound foundations. Augustus had secured the acceptance of imperial rulership by the higher orders, he had created

Diagram 15.1 The emperors of the Roman empire in the first and second centuries AD

The following emperors ruled between ad 14 and 193:

Tiberius	14–37	
Caligula	37–41	All related to Augustus
Claudius	41–54	see Appendix 3, p. 302
Nero	54–68	
	68–69	The 'year of the four emperors'. Four pretenders struggled for power after the murder of Nero, who had died without an heir
Vespasian	69–79	
Titus	79–81	Flavian dynasty (Vespasian was actually called
Domitian	81–96	Flavius Vespasianus, see Appendix 1, p. 299)
Nerva	96–98	
Trajan	98–117	
Hadrian	117–138	Emperors who adopted their successors or
Antoninus Pius	138–161	were themselves adopted
Marcus Aurelius	161–180	

Notes: Marcus Aurelius was succeeded by his own son Commodus, 180–192. Commodus was murdered at the end of 192. After a succession struggle, the empire was ruled by the Severan dynasty (193–235) (p. 276).

strong ties between the emperor and his armies and he had secured control over state finances (the *aerarium*, *fisci* and the emperor's private funds) and influence over the election of the highest officials.

The emperors' vast private resources enabled them to act as the chief benefactors in the empire, in particular in the capital Rome (bread and circuses!). The emperors gradually took over a large part of the patronage of Rome's population from the senators and deprived them of the possibility of using their clients as weapons in political conflicts. The senators' power came to rest exclusively on their private estates (and the people living on them). The poor in Rome were no longer solely dependent on their elite patrons, but could now also look to their emperor as a 'super-patron'.

The emperors also had ties with the local elites in Italy and the provinces, who took care of a large share of the day-to-day municipal administration and constituted the local authorities for the greater part of the empire's population. The Roman empire of the early imperial age was an empire of cities from which landed notables governed the surrounding countryside. Above these municipal authorities were the provincial authorities and the central government. This stratified system was reflected in social relations, too, with the imperial aristocracy of senators and *equites* ranking higher than the local elites.

Figure 15.5 Claudius (AD 41–54)
Notes: Claudius was the youngest son of Drusus, Tiberius' brother. Drusus had died at an early age, in 9 BC. Claudius, then, was a grandson of Augustus' wife Livia; Tiberius and Drusus were her sons from her previous marriage to Tib(erius) Claudius Nero, a *nobilis*. Claudius conquered Britain, expanded the imperial secretariats, improved Rome's harbour (Ostia) and was the first emperor to admit Romanised Gallic nobles with Roman citizenship into the Senate. In the last years of his life he was greatly influenced by his wife Agrippina, a granddaughter of Julia (the daughter of Augustus) and Agrippa. She persuaded Claudius to adopt her son Nero and make him his successor, even though Claudius had a son of his own.
Source: Rome, Museo Capitolino.

The emperor came to supplant the senators in the informal relations with the local notables, too. Ties between senators and local notables now had political influence only if there happened to be a vacuum at the top of the administrative system, for example in times of succession struggles.

The emperor's 'job' essentially comprised commanding the armies in wartime, administering justice, nominating and appointing officials at all levels and responding to the problems presented to him (petitions of cities and private persons, questions of governors, etc.). In our eyes this may seem a somewhat passive form of government, but in those days, with economic insight and means of communication being as they were, it was virtually the only form possible.

A difficult problem from Augustus's reign onwards was the issue of succession (see Diagram 15.1 and Appendix 3, p. 302). The reigning emperor had to prevent the risk of the armies, which had the greatest effective power, pushing forward their own favoured candidates after his death. That would mean a revival of the civil wars in the form of succession struggles. Hereditary succession within one imperial family was a good solution, because the soldiers could relate far better to the person of the emperor and to his family than to the government's abstract laws and rules. If for example a lack of sons precluded hereditary succession (daughters were not eligible for appointment to the throne in the Roman empire), the reigning emperor could

Figure 15.6 Agrippina
Source: Rome, Museo Capitolino.

choose a man who was popular with the troops and acceptable to the Senate for adoption as his son. The problem of selecting the most suitable candidate was then solved through hereditary succession via adoption. In Roman society adoption had always been a frequently used and commonly accepted means of securing a family's continued existence or of enhancing it with new competent members.

Augustus himself was the first emperor to adopt a successor, namely his step-son Tiberius, who reigned from AD 14 to 37 (Augustus had no sons of his own; see Appendix 3, p. 302). The emperors who ruled between 96 and 161 also adopted successors. By coincidence, none of those emperors had any sons of their own.

Most of the later emperors modelled their conduct on Augustus' example and respected the members of the higher orders, in particular the senators. They tried to act as the protectors and benefactors of citizens and not as the masters of slaves. Some emperors on the contrary behaved like absolute despots, such as Caligula (37–41), Nero (54–68), Domitian (81–96) and Commodus (180–192). Domitian even insisted on being addressed as 'master and god' (*dominus et deus*). Those emperors had a poor relationship with the Senate and were all killed by conspiracies of senators and other high officials. Oddly enough, the main cause of the antipathy that they aroused was their behaviour. In administrative matters and their election policy these emperors acted very much the same as the other emperors. But behaviour was an important issue in Roman society. The common people in Rome would

Figure 15.7 Gaius Caesar (Caligula)
Notes: A grandson of Agrippa and Augustus' daughter Julia, Caligula ruled from AD 37
until 41.
Source: Rome, Museo Capitolino.

Figure 15.8 Nero
Notes: The son of Agrippina and the adopted son of Claudius, Nero ruled from
AD 54 until 68.

for example watch their emperor's behaviour at the games closely (which the emperors were supposed to enjoy, like good fathers who were pleased to see their 'children' having a good time).

Developments in administration after Augustus

The political system that Augustus had so carefully constructed during his long reign was to endure for another two centuries after his death, with only a few minor changes.

The most important of those changes was the expansion of bureaucracy in administration. The local rulers (*decuriones* or *curiales*) passed on more and more tasks and decisions to the governors and the emperors, especially in the fields of criminal justice and security. This greatly increased the workload of the imperial secretariats and the governors' bureaux (*officia*). The quaestors and procurators in the provinces had to concern themselves ever more with jurisdiction in fiscal matters. The provincial bureaux recruited extra personnel from the administrative staffs of the nearby armies. The secretariats in Rome sometimes did the same, but they employed predominantly rhetorically and/or legally trained intellectuals. Many a legal advisor (see pp. 191 and 241) and graduate of the schools of rhetoric (see p. 193) was appointed to a post in the imperial bureaux, especially after the latter had acquired an official status under Hadrian (117–138). In Julio-Claudian times the bureaux were still staffed predominantly with slaves, supervised by freedmen (who enjoyed a great deal of influence), but by the second century their staffs already included a large proportion of intellectuals of free birth. The emperor Hadrian also replaced the freedmen at the head of the imperial bureaux by knights.

The staff responsible for the emperor's private estates also expanded, because the emperor accumulated ever more land through inheritance or confiscation (see p. 221). The imperial estates were amongst the most rapidly expanding landed properties in the empire. They included mines, quarries and workshops and were spread across many parts of the empire. The large group of slaves, freedmen and free citizens who worked on the imperial estates had their own hierarchical system. In some provinces they constituted a separate social group, the *Caesariani* (the emperor's men). Together with the staff of the imperial bureaux they formed the *familia Caesaris*.

This expansion of bureaucracy led to a steadily growing stream of post. In the imperial age the Roman empire had a well-organised public postal system. All the corners of the empire were connected by a vast network of paved roads, along which were inns where the couriers could exchange their horses or carriages on presentation of a special pass. The expense of maintaining the roads, inns and means of transport fell on the local authorities. This implied a considerable burden on their financial resources, especially in poor regions.

The spread of Roman citizenship

In the first two centuries AD Roman citizenship gradually spread through more and more provinces. Every year, thousands of veteran auxiliaries (and their families) and

Diagram 15.2 Social structure in the early imperial age

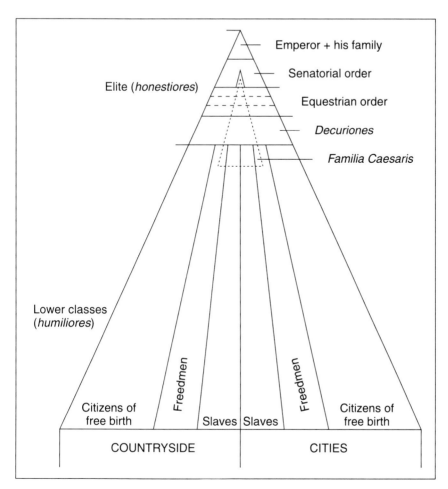

Emperor + his family

Senatorial order

Elite (*honestiores*)

Equestrian order

Decuriones

Familia Caesaris

Lower classes
(*humiliores*)

Freedmen

Freedmen

Citizens of
free birth

Slaves | Slaves

Citizens of
free birth

COUNTRYSIDE

CITIES

Source: After G. Alföldy.

many wives and children of discharged legionaries acquired Roman citizenship in the frontier provinces (see p. 229). The number of Roman citizens in the frontier regions around the military camps and in the cities in their hinterlands consequently rapidly multiplied. By the end of the second century, the legions (which had to consist of Roman citizens) were recruiting almost all their troops from their own hinterlands. Roman citizenship also spread rapidly amongst the elite in the Romanised cities in the west and in the Greek cities in the east. The emperors would sometimes enfranchise entire cities or regions that had become so Romanised that there was very little difference between them and Italian cities or regions. We will return to the Romanisation of the western provinces on pp. 243–4.

Changes in the higher orders

The local elites in the Romanised cities in the west and Greek cities in the eastern half of the empire came to belong to the order of *decuriones* (or *curiales*), like their Italian fellows. And like their Italian fellows, they too then stood a chance of climbing the social ladder.

When the time came for an emperor to fill vacancies in the Senate, he would always select young members of senatorial families and members of the equestrian order who enjoyed his favour, who had impressed him with their competence or who had contacts among his circles. Augustus had brought the number of senators back to six hundred again. Over the years, many a senator was removed from the Senate because he or his family had fallen into disfavour with the emperor, suffered severe financial losses (there was a property qualification for admission to the Senate!) or lost lawsuits. Moreover, quite a few old senatorial families died out. Consequently vacancies regularly occurred for 'new men' in the Senate. The vast majority of these vacancies were filled with knights.

The expansion of bureaucracy led to a corresponding expansion of the equestrian order. Ever more successful junior officers, intellectuals and *decuriones* managed to acquire positions in the imperial services, from where they could with relative ease rise to the equestrian order, because the emperor would often admit competent members of those services to that order. So the expansion of bureaucracy can be said to have improved the aforementioned groups' chances of social advancement. Some very wealthy provincial notables even managed to gain admission to the Senate. Usually the process of social advancement would span a few generations: a father would be granted Roman citizenship, his son would make his mark in the army and would rise to the equestrian order as an officer, after which his grandson would be admitted to the Senate after having followed a successful career in the offices that were accessible to knights.

The first notables from Spain and southern Gaul were already included in the Senate under the emperor Tiberius. They were descendants of Roman emigrants. The emperor Claudius admitted the first real Gallic nobles to the Senate (AD 47). After that this development gained momentum. In the second century large numbers of notables from the Romanised and Hellenised interior provinces (southern and eastern Spain, Gaul, North Africa, Sicily, Greece, southern and western Asia Minor, Syria and the Hellenistic cities in Egypt) were admitted to the Senate. An even greater number of notables and intellectuals from these regions rose to the equestrian order. Even military men from the northern and eastern frontier regions managed to gain admission to this order.

By AD 200 an aristocracy of service (an aristocracy serving in an administrative machinery) had emerged throughout the empire. It comprised three ranks (senators, knights and *decuriones*) and shared a common Latin-Greek elite culture and a common spiritual baggage of popular moralistic notions absorbed from a wide diversity of Hellenistic philosophical schools. The language of this elite was Greek in the eastern half of the empire and Latin in the west. Of great importance to this elite was the literary culture (Greek: *paideia*) with which they were brought up. It was this which distinguished them most from the masses who still spoke their

Figure 15.9 School scene
Notes: The pupils are holding their book rolls. Until in late antiquity the book roll (of papyrus) was the most common form of book. The texts were written on the rolls in columns. The reader unwound the roll as he read the columns. The rolls were not easy to read. The individual words were not separated by gaps and there was no punctuation. Book rolls were costly because each roll had to be written by hand. Some book sellers would dictate a text to thirty or more slaves at a time. That enabled them to produce several rolls simultaneously.
Such book sellers were to be found only in large cities in civilised provinces.
Source: Trier, Rheinisches Landesmuseum.

original languages or vernaculars. Anyone who lacked *paideia*, who could not speak pure, civilised Latin and/or Greek and who could not quote passages from the works of classical authors did not really belong to the upper ten. Even if he was rich and powerful, he would always give himself away and prove himself a parvenu. On the other hand, anyone who did not belong to this elite but nevertheless had *paideia* did stand a chance of climbing the social ladder. The literary elite culture was more or less the same all over the empire. From Gaul to Syria it encompassed a thorough grounding in Latin and Greek written rhetoric (in the eastern half of the empire virtually exclusively Greek; in the west only Latin or both Greek and Latin) and familiarity with classical literature. Also important were etiquette and knowledge of a code of conduct based on the instructions and recommendations of popular philosophers. Only a small group of students at the schools of philosophy (e.g. those of Athens, pp. 125 and 143) actually studied philosophy as a science. The educational system that the Romans had borrowed from the Greeks in the second century BC (see p. 193) spread across all the western provinces in the imperial age. In the Greek-speaking cities in the Hellenistic eastern provinces it had of course existed for several centuries already. This educational system was the vehicle by which the elite propagated their literary culture.

From time to time even the son of a former slave managed to rise to a high social position. A case in point is the emperor Pertinax, who ruled Rome for three months in AD 193. He was the son of a freedman who had been a private teacher as a slave and had established himself as an independent school teacher when he was released from slavery. Pertinax started off as a school teacher too, but a senator (a relative of his father's former master) secured him a post as an army officer just around the time when serious border conflicts broke out in the east (c. 161–166) and along the Danube (c. 165–180). Pertinax proved his worth, was admitted to the equestrian order and ultimately became a senator after a long career in equestrian offices. Around 180 he was a highly esteemed general and advisor of the emperor Marcus Aurelius (161–180). When the latter's successor Commodus (180–192) was killed by a court conspiracy before he had appointed a successor, Pertinax was placed on the throne.

However, such a career was very rare; generally speaking it was only in exceptional circumstances, such as a serious war, that a man of such humble birth could rise so high.

ROMAN LAW

All Roman citizens throughout the empire were protected by Roman law. Roman law, which was an original Roman achievement, had a profound influence on Western legal systems.

Roman law was formalistic. The Roman legal system revolved around the letter of the law and depended upon strict adherence to definitions and prescribed forms. There was for instance one rule for sale (which involved money), another for barter.

Roman law was essentially private law (including most criminal law), which had evolved in the practice of jurisdiction and was hence not derived from legislation. We have already seen above that public law was relatively poorly developed (pp. 174–5). From the early republican era onwards the sources of law were enactments (the *leges* of the *Comitia Centuriata* and the *Comitia Tributa* and the *plebiscita* of the *Concilium Plebis*, p. 172), judgements, precedents, the *mos maiorum* (customary law), the commentaries of legal advisors and the praetors' edicts. In the imperial age senatorial decisions and imperial letters and decrees took the place of the enactments. In the republican period it was the praetor who dismissed or allowed a claim. If he decided a claim was admissible, he would approach a *iudex* (sworn judge) or several *iudices* and draft written instructions specifying what definitions and rules would apply to the case. There were no public prosecutors. Bringing a defendant before the court was not the government's responsibility. Anyone wishing to lodge a complaint against an individual had to bring that individual before the praetor and the *iudex* himself. The *iudex* (or *iudices*) delivered judgement. At the beginning of their year of office, the praetors proclaimed what kinds of trials and procedures they would allow. This was known as the praetor's edict. In practice, a praetor would usually take over the greater part of his predecessor's proclamation, sometimes after slight adaptations. This led to the formation of a constantly expanding collection of edicts,

Figure 15.10 Hadrian (AD 117–138)
Notes: Hadrian was a major reformer in the fields of administration and the codification of law. He visited most of the empire's provinces in person. Hadrian put an end to the expansionist politics of his predecessor Trajan and set about consolidating and strengthening the frontiers instead. He was a great admirer of Greek culture. He is here shown with a beard, as also worn by contemporary Greek philosophers.
Source: Rome, Museo Capitolino.

adapted to practical requirements. Under the emperor Hadrian (AD 117–138) the jurist Julianus completed and systemised this collection. Nothing more was added to it after that.

A *praetor* usually based his proclamation on the advice provided by his private council of legal experts, his *consilium* (see pp. 169 and 221). These legal experts were Roman notables who studied law out of interest and gave free legal advice to magistrates and other individuals seeking their opinion on a point of law. They interpreted issues of customary law, legislation and case law (judgements and cases). Their written commentaries constituted one of the principal sources of private law. The various sources of private law were ordered and systematised on several occasions in the imperial age – first of all under the emperor Hadrian and again later, at the beginning of the third century and in the late imperial age. In the sixth century the sources were codified in the *Corpus Iuris Civilis* of Justinian (who was the emperor of the east Roman empire from 527 until 565). This work comprised a textbook (the *Institutiones*), the legal advisors' interpretations of private law (the *Digesta*) and the imperial decrees (the *Codex*). The textbook was based on a similar work from Hadrian's time; it is still used as a guide to jurisprudence today.

In Rome, citizens could appeal to a higher court. In the republican era, they could appeal to the popular assembly via a tribune of the *plebs*. Around the end of the second century BC the popular assembly delegated the task of hearing appeal cases to separate courts of justice. In the imperial age appeal cases became the emperor's responsibility. Many other legal cases from all over the empire were also referred to the emperor. The administration of justice came to be one of his most time-consuming tasks. To assist them in this task, the emperors therefore increasingly called in the help of others, for example the *praefectus urbi* (Rome's town prefect), the guard prefect and, from Hadrian's time onwards, the emperor's deputies in Italy. By about 200 the guard prefects had evolved into competent legal advisors.

The Romans had separate courts for different kinds of offences. The first of these courts was that which was established in 149 BC to handle extortion cases. Another five permanent criminal courts were instituted under Sulla (*c.* 80 BC; e.g. for cases of poisoning, embezzlement and violence). The courts were presided over by praetors. In the imperial age there were courts-martial in the military camps.

In Rome and Italy the administration of justice in the imperial age was hence in the hands of the praetors' sworn judges, the six special courts, Rome's town prefect, the guard prefect and the emperor. Local councillors administered justice at a lower level. In the provinces, the administration of justice was in the hands of the local rulers (lowest level), the governors and – for appeal cases, which prerogative was reserved for Roman citizens – the emperor.

There were also several lower colleges, which functioned only in the city of Rome, but they fall outside the scope of this book (see p. 172).

Much distinction was made between the different social classes in the administration of justice. Slaves for example, unlike higher classes, could be tortured during interrogations. In the course of the imperial age Roman law increasingly discriminated between the members of the three highest orders (senators, knights and *decuriones*), who were referred to as *honestiores*, and those of the lower classes, the *humiliores*.

THE WESTERN AND EASTERN PROVINCES

The western provinces

The Celts

Most of the western provinces were occupied by Celtic tribes (Celts = Gauls) and by peoples who were very much influenced by the Celts (Map 15.3). In terms of material culture and technology the Celts were not much inferior to the Greeks and the Romans. The Celtic occupants of the region between the Rhine and the Meuse (approximately what is now Luxembourg) and of Bohemia, for example, were talented iron craftsmen. What the Celts however lacked was an efficient military and political structure designed for long-term warfare. Celtic warriors were renowned for their personal valour, but they were poorly organised. The Celtic tribes probably consisted of clans that were led by aristocrats (see p. 158, on Rome's early history). To our knowledge, the lower peasantry was dependent on those nobles. A nobleman often had a personal retinue of warriors, who had voluntarily allied themselves with him. In times of war, the warriors' assembly would appoint one of the aristocrats as king.

Areas occupied by the Celts
Areas occupied by the Germans
X = Roman military base
.... Frontier of the Roman empire
n = Major Roman naval base

c. AD 200

Celtiberians   Ligurians   400 BC   279 BC   Galatians   M

Map 15.3 Areas occupied by the Celts and the Germans before the Roman expansion

Important centres in a Celtic tribe's occupation area were the *oppida* (plural of *oppidum*), or hillforts. They lay on easily defensible hilltops and had a small number of fixed inhabitants, but they were designed to serve as places of refuge for all the occupants of the surrounding areas with their goods and chattels in times of war. Inside these *oppida* were workshops and sanctuaries.

When Gaul came under Roman control, cities on Roman (and Greek) models took the place of many of the *oppida*. As peace then reigned throughout the empire, there was no need for the cities to be fortified; many had a spacious layout and were situated in valleys. These cities evolved into *foci* of Roman culture and served as the administrative centres of the surrounding rural areas. Together with those surrounding areas they constituted communities that resembled Italian and Greek city states. The country folk living outside the cities adhered to their old customs and

Figure 15.11 A Celt dressed in a hooded cape, breeches and leggings
Note: Probably a member of the tribe that lived near Trier (the Treveri).
Source: Trier, Rheinisches Landesmuseum.

traditions and continued to use their own languages for a long time. Celtic dialects continued to be spoken in rural areas in the western provinces through to the end of antiquity and even after. The old ties of dependence between the rural population and the notables lived on more or less unchanged (though sometimes Roman names were used to describe them).

The tribal noblemen flocked to the new cities and were quickly Romanised. After some time the cities acquired Latin rights. The nobles who became the cities' magistrates were granted full Roman citizenship and could consequently become officers in the Roman army. Together with enfranchised rich immigrants from other

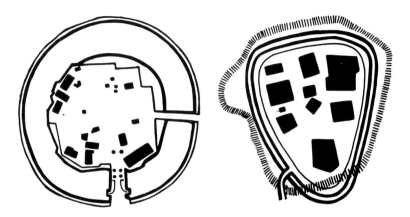

Figure 15.12 *Oppida*, pre-Roman hill forts
Source: H. Rottier, *Stedelijke Structuren*, Coutinho, Muiderberg, 1980, p. 64.

provinces and veteran junior officers of the frontier armies they came to constitute the elite of the new communities. We have already seen above that members of this elite started to be admitted to the equestrian order and the Senate in the mid-first century AD (p. 238). The urban councils in the western provinces were usually quite small (most had thirty to one hundred members) and were very oligarchic. Once the new elite had firmly established itself, its families monopolised the council for many generations. Only when one of those families was degraded or promoted to a higher class or when a family died out did a new family stand a chance of being admitted to the council.

Like the Italian cities, the cities in Gaul and Spain had theatres (for plays), amphitheatres (for gladiatorial and animal fights) and gymnasia, where people could practice athletics or attend lessons in Latin and Greek rhetoric.

Gaul in particular had been exposed to Greek influence for many centuries already. Much of this influence came from Massilia, the colony that the Greeks had founded in southern Gaul around 600 BC. In the imperial period Massilia was a centre of Greek rhetorical education.

We don't know much about the Celts' religion or traditions because their myths, legends and heroic songs were passed on orally. Celtic gods, which resembled Roman deities, were given Roman names in the imperial age, but retained their native character. The Druids held a special position in Celtic society. They were a kind of 'medicine men', sages who were familiar with the secret incantations and rites which the Celts believed had power over the lives of human beings and cattle and the success of crops.

The western half of the empire also included the North African provinces Africa, Numidia and Mauretania. These provinces were dotted with small towns, whose populations also included peasants. The higher classes had become Romanised as a result of the large-scale immigration of Romans from Italy (which started under Marius and Caesar; see pp. 202–12), but the lower classes had continued to use their own Berber and Punic (= Phoenician = Carthaginian) languages. In the first century

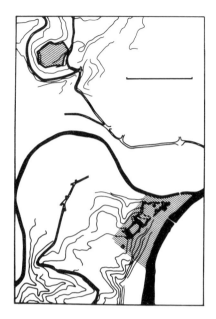

Figure 15.13 The Roman settlement of Namur
Notes: the settlement lay at the junction of the Sambre and the Meuse rivers. To the
northwest of the settlement lay the former *oppidum*.
Source: H. Rottier, *Stedelijke Structuren*, Coutinho, Muiderberg, 1980, p. 65.

Figure 15.14 Gateway of an *oppidum*
Source: Trier, Rheinisches Landesmuseum.

AD the *decuriones* of the North African cities were given access to the equestrian order and in the second century the first of their ranks were admitted to the Senate.

In the first two centuries of the imperial age the western half of the empire enjoyed unprecedented peace and prosperity. Conditions in Italy began to stagnate somewhat in the second century, but Gaul, Spain and North Africa continued to prosper until in the third century.

The eastern half of the empire

The Greeks in the Roman empire

The period from 30 BC until AD 230 was characterised by fairly peaceful and prosperous conditions in the eastern provinces, too. The most prosperous period in these parts was around the middle of the second century, but things continued to go well until about 230.

The Roman empire had had control over a large part of the Hellenistic world since the second century BC; the histories of Rome, Greece, Egypt and the western part of the Levant had merged into the history of the Roman empire. But that had not meant the end of the Greek and Near Eastern civilisations. They had lived on under the Roman control, just like the civilisation of Hellenistic Mesopotamia had endured under the sway of the Parthians (see p. 145). This is clearly apparent from the history of the cities. The Greek cities and their territories (some of which had once been independent city states) had retained local autonomy and their traditional institutions. The same holds for the Near Eastern cities, although many of those cities increasingly acquired a Greek character, largely as a result of the Hellenisation of their elite inhabitants. The Greek cities in Parthia likewise retained their Greek character for a long time (see p. 145).

The Greek-speaking eastern half of the empire experienced a period of unrest and impoverishment in the second and first centuries BC. The Romans ruthlessly exploited those regions and took away thousands of educated people to serve as their slaves. Moreover, many of the battles of the Roman civil wars were fought in those regions.

In the Greek cities the Romans promoted an oligarchic form of government. They put an end to the civil struggles that had afflicted the cities for so many years (see p. 185). After this, discord was to resurge within the Greek cities only during the Roman civil wars, when conflicts broke out between protégés of contending Roman generals or when rebels used their support of one of the struggling Roman parties as a cover-up for their own private pursuits.

The period from 30 BC until the end of the first century AD was a time of recovery, which was followed by an era of prosperity and cultural revival in the second and early third centuries. The notables who governed the Greek cities acted as benefactors and competed with one another and with notables in other cities in embellishing city gates, streets and squares and in arranging donatives and public entertainments. For the elite this aspect of their city was an important status symbol.

The period AD 100–230 saw major literary achievements in the Greek language,

Figure 15.15 A wounded Amazon: Greek copy (second century AD) of a
Classical Greek sculpture
Notes: The Greeks of the Roman imperial age turned to Classical examples for inspiration
in literature, philosophy and architecture, and also in sculpture.
Amazons were mythical female warriors. According to Greek legends they fought battles
with Heracles, the Athenians and the Greeks who besieged Troy (see p. 70 on Homer and
the Iliad).
Source: Rome, Museo Capitolino.

Figure 15.16 Depiction of Greek games: during Roman times athletics, chariot races, wrestling and boxing spread across all the countries of the eastern Mediterranean and also to the West
Notes: Professional sportsmen would travel from city to city to participate in the games. Sometimes they were paid handsome fees.
Source: Cologne, Römisch-Germanisches Museum.

especially in certain sciences and rhetoric. These were the days of the doctor Galen (*c.* 129–210) and the geographer Ptolemy (mid-second century), who had a profound influence on later Western European science. In this period, too, itinerant orators attracted great crowds of people to the theatres with their show speeches on moralistic and historical themes. The Persian wars of 490–479 BC were particularly popular themes. Contemporary Greek culture adulated the magnificent achievements of Greece's classical past (5th–4th centuries BC). The Greek-speaking public was familiar with those achievements and greatly enjoyed the variations on historical topics presented by the orators in their show speeches.

Most educated Greeks resigned themselves to Roman dominion and appreciated the positive aspects of the Roman imperial system. In their eyes there was a good symbiosis between the Romans, who were the best fighters and rulers and kept the barbarians outside the borders of the empire, and the Greeks, who had the most refined culture in the empire. They did not really look upon the Romans as a foreign people. Greeks and Romans tended to regard one another as kindred peoples.

The Greek-speaking elite appreciated the Romans' policies of enfranchising the occupants of the provinces who shared in the Greek literary culture and giving Greek-speaking notables the chance to be admitted to the Senate and the equestrian order (see p. 238).

Most senators from the eastern half of the empire were descendants of (former) Hellenistic kings, Italian and Roman emigrants, local aristocrats or Greek intellectuals. A good stepping-stone to the imperial aristocracy of senators and knights was a post in the provincial assemblies of the imperial cult. In all the provinces, both east and west, local governors periodically convened in provincial councils to worship the emperor and discuss matters of communal interest.

AGRICULTURE, TRADE AND CRAFTS

The lower classes

Between 80 and 90 per cent of the population of the Roman empire was involved in the production, processing and transport of agricultural products. Farm work was heavy and not very productive. Everything had to be done by hand – no mechanical aids were yet available. Crop yield ratios were low, except in areas where the soil was extremely fertile. This was the case for example in the Nile Delta, in the volcanic parts of southern Italy and Sicily and in some valleys and coastal plains in North Africa. Egypt, Sicily and North Africa were the granaries of the capital Rome.

In the Mediterranean parts of the empire, stock-keeping was practised at the farms (where the cattle was kept in byres, orchards and stubble fields) and by transhumant herders who moved their livestock to and fro between summer and winter pastures. The summer pastures were often in the hills and the mountains.

In the first two centuries of the imperial age the peasants and the landowners benefited from the peaceful conditions prevailing throughout the empire. Buildings and crops suffered little devastation through warfare. Most major building projects and the public entertainments and charity that were provided in the cities were financed by the regular, high profits that the landowners, who governed the cities, made on the produce of their land. In this way means were transferred from the countryside to the cities via the purses of the landowners.

A large proportion of the city dwellers were craftsmen. They sold their products to farmers who visited the town markets, members of the local elite and the foreigners who were drawn to the towns by cultural manifestations, games and religious festivals. The craftsmen were self-employed; they ran their businesses together with their relatives, one or two slaves and occasionally a day labourer (of free status). There were only few large workshops employing more than ten slaves.

Figure 15.17a A street lined with shops in a small Roman town
Source: David Macaulay, *City. A Story of Roman Planning and Construction*, Collins, London 1975.

Figure 15.17b Street scene in a large Roman city

Notes: The tall, storeyed buildings which increasingly dominated the aspect of streets in Rome in the late republican era had no chimneys and no running water. Their occupants washed at the public baths or at other communal water sources and cooked on braziers, which also served as sources of heat during cold times of the year. On the ground floor there were usually workshops and cafés or restaurants. The living areas were on the floors above.

Men lived mostly out in the streets. They ate in cheap restaurants (soup kitchens) and hung around in places where they hoped to find work. Those who had a business themselves were

The craftsmen were united in trade guilds (*collegia*), which enjoyed the patronage of the local elite. The vast majority of the craftsmen lived a very sober life, but they were not paupers. The paupers in the cities were the day labourers, the beggars, the tramps and the invalids. They were usually dependent on the charity of the rich.

Free peasants (small-time land-owning peasants and tenant farmers), slaves and day labourers worked in the rural areas. In those areas the social and economic conditions of former days still prevailed and there were consequently great differences between the rural areas of the individual provinces. In Egypt and the Levant little had changed in terms of social conditions since the Hellenistic era and earlier times; in Italy and some parts of Greece much use was still made of slaves and in the rural areas in Gaul, too, many of the social conditions of former days still remained (see p. 244).

A comparatively large proportion of the occupants of the rural parts of the frontier regions behind the Rhine and the Danube were small-time land-owning farmers. In those regions the difference in wealth between the tribal aristocrats and the farmers was probably not as great as that between the landowners and the farmers in Gaul, Spain and Italy. There were different types of farms, using different farming methods and employing different types of staff.

Mixed farming aimed at self-sufficiency of the farm owners and tenant farmers prevailed in isolated, relatively under-developed regions. Estates in those regions often consisted of a central farmstead surrounded by tenant farms. In fertile regions with good means of transport to city markets there were often many medium-sized and large farms that specialised in the cultivation of specific cash crops and employed trained slaves. Between these estates and specialised farms were tenant farms and the farms of small landowners. The small-time free peasants (both tenants and land-owners) and the day labourers in the rural areas and in nearby towns constituted a reservoir of labour that could be exploited for seasonal tasks at the large and medium-sized farms.

There was a complex legal structure: farm owners would for example lease an extra plot of land or fishing water alongside their own property; a tenant often possessed cattle of his own, and a slave who did not live on his master's estate would exploit a nearby small quarry for his own account. The free paupers in rural areas were day labourers, tramps and unpropertied tenants. In some regions there was a form of sharecropping: the landowner would provide the land and the means of production, and the produce of the land would be split between the owner and the tenant.

---

to be found in their workshops. Slaves worked all day, from early in the morning until late at night. In those days without mass media, information about what was going on elsewhere was picked up in the streets and squares, from travellers and the like. The rich lived in large houses laid out on one floor around a central garden and in luxurious apartments. They did not always reside in separate quarters. Many houses of the rich were to be found between other buildings.

Source: David Macaulay, *City. A Story of Roman Planning and Construction*, Collins, London 1975.

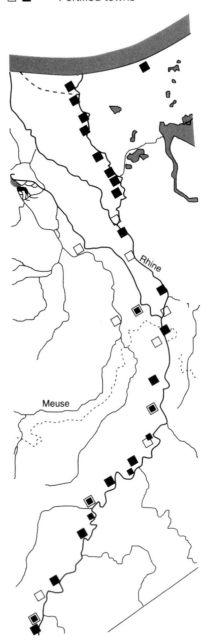

Map 15.4 The *limes* of the lower Rhine, AD 47–260
Note: *Limes* – fortified frontier.

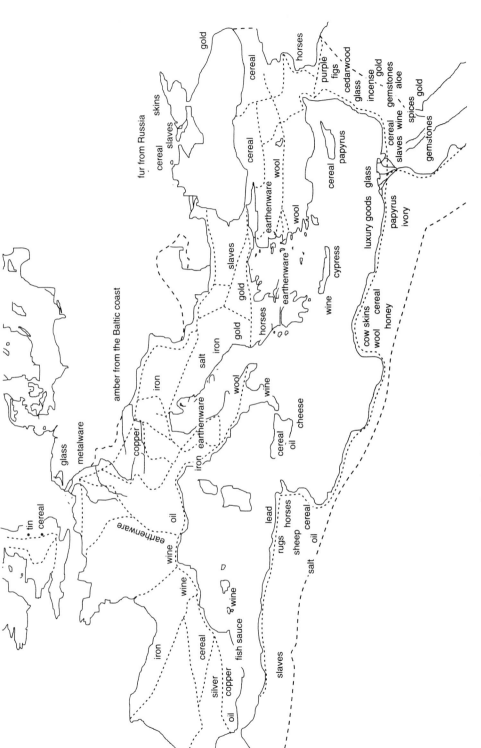

Map 15.5 Agricultural and industrial products and roads in the Roman empire

Debt was a serious problem. Small-time peasants who ran up debts were usually soon reduced to the status of proletarian day labourers. If a debtor failed to pay his debts, his property fell to his creditor.

Trade

Most trade by far was retail trade at local markets and in the streets where the workshops were. The workshops were also shops.

But long-distance trade was also relatively common, both by water (seas and rivers) and overland. The chief commodities were metals, artisanal products and articles of high value that were not too perishable and took up little room. Contemporary eulogists praised the possibility of safe travel throughout the Roman empire. The Roman fleets suppressed piracy and the local authorities (or the governors in cases of severe disorder) policed the land routes. Nevertheless, the Romans preferably travelled in convoys and caravans, because banditry was never entirely eradicated. The paved highways that crisscrossed the empire from frontier to frontier had been built primarily to facilitate the rapid movement of troops, but they had soon evolved into important trade arteries, too. To spread the risks, a merchant would almost always find a number of co-financiers to help finance his long-distance commercial enterprises. There was also some trade with regions beyond the frontiers. The distribution patterns of Roman products and coins give us a good impression of the distances covered by the foreign trade routes. They extended into Scandinavia, central Asia, Further India, Arabia and East and West Africa.

Figure 15.18 Paying tribute: relief from a funerary monument in the Moselle region
Source: Trier, Rheinisches Landesmuseum.

Figure 15.19 Roman shop-lined street from around the beginning of the
second century AD
Notes: The shops were also workshops. Above a shop was a storage area and above that were
three or four residential floors. The shops could be closed with shutters.
Source: R.J. van der Spek.

Work and status

The social class to which a Roman belonged was far more important for his status
than the kind of work he did. A slave always remained at the bottom of the hierarchical system, even if he worked as a doctor or an artist. At the top of the system were
the landowners, who did not have to support themselves with the fruits of their own
hands and were at leisure to devote themselves entirely to education, administration
and entertainment. Small-time traders and usurers enjoyed little respect. A small step
above them were the craftsmen and above them were the small farmers. Farmers
supplied material products and were more independent because they produced their
own food.

Figure 15.20 River ship transporting casks of wine
Source: Trier, Rheinisches Landesmuseum.

The position of women

We have little information on the women of the low social classes. Observations in classical literature suggest that agricultural and artisanal tasks were traditionally divided between the genders throughout the entire Roman world. Boys were trained in the male tasks by their fathers or other male relatives, girls in the female tasks by their mothers or other female relatives. Women's tasks included spinning, weaving, looking after small stock, preserving foodstuffs, tending to the vegetable garden, caring for children and all other domestic chores. The men did the heavy work and work that had to be done far from home.

In the circles of the Roman notables much had changed since the earliest days of Roman history (see p. 157). The elite's old family ties now existed in theory only. Loose alliances, which could easily be broken, had taken the place of marriage in the ancestral sense. Women would marry at an early age (of about 13 or 14). Men usually married when they were between 20 and 35. Divorce was fairly common. Most men who divorced their wives did so for opportunistic reasons, for example so as to be able to improve their position by marrying another woman, from a powerful and wealthy family. A woman was allowed to own property in her own right. That property was however managed by her husband or some other male relative. If a couple got divorced, the proper custom was for the man to return the woman's dowry to her.

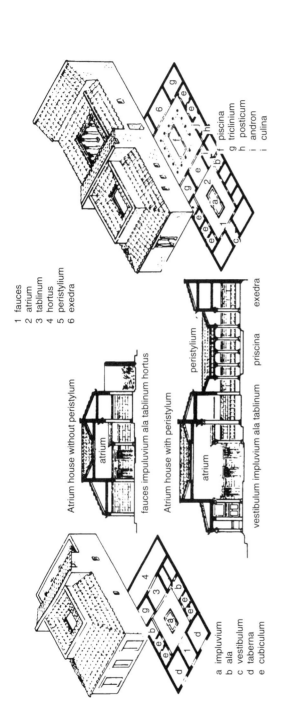

Atrium house without peristylum

faux impuluvium ala tablinum hortus

Atrium house with peristylum

peristylium

atrium

vestibulum impluvium ala tablinum   priscina   exedra

1 fauces
2 atrium
3 tablinum
4 hortus
5 peristylium
6 exedra

a impluvium
b ala
c vestibulum
d taberna
e cubiculum

f piscina
g triclinium
h posticum
i andron
j culina

Figure 15.21 Plan and elevation of typical Roman houses

Notes:

Atrium house without a *peristylum:*
1. *fauces* (entrance passage)
2. *atrium* (hall)
3. *tablinum* (reception room)
4. *hortus* (garden)
5. *peristylium* (colonnaded court or garden)
6. *exedra* (open-fronted garden room)

Atrium house with a *peristylum:*
a. *impluvium* (shallow catchwater basin)
b. *ala* (recess)
c. *vestibulum* (entrance court)
d. *taberna* (shop)
e. *cubiculum* (bedroom)
f. *piscina* (basin)
g. *triclinium* (dining room)
h. *posticum* (back exit)
i. *andron* (corridor)
j. *culina* (kitchen)

Figure 15.22a Portrait of a Roman boy from the middle of the imperial age
Source: Rome, Museo Capitolino.

Figure 15.22b A Roman lady at her toilet
Source: Trier, Rheinisches Landesmuseum.

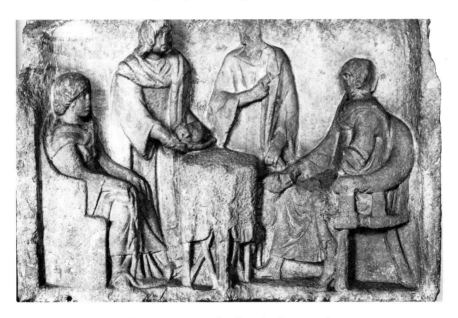

Figure 15.22c A family enjoying a meal
Source: Trier, Rheinisches Landesmuseum.

Women of the higher classes supervised the male and female slaves in their domestic tasks and accompanied their husbands to banquets, the theatre, the games and the temples, but they had no say in administrative or legal matters.

Something that still puzzles us is the low birth rates in the highest Roman classes (of senators and knights) in the imperial age. Senatorial and equestrian families died out one after the other. This has been attributed to a desire to limit the number of heirs.

A noble Roman woman had more freedom of movement and more rights (including the right to own property) than her Greek counterpart (cf. p. 114). She also had a greater chance of enjoying a good education. It was fairly common for daughters of the Roman elite to be educated by a private teacher and to attend primary and secondary schools. They did not attend schools of rhetoric; by the time they had reached the age at which pupils were admitted to those schools they were already married and consequently no longer received further education.

RELIGION

There was a vast multiplicity of religions and religious rites in the Roman empire. Every people, every city, every association and every family had its own cults, religious rites and patron deities. And all over the empire were temples, sacred groves, and trees and objects in which spirits were believed to reside.

Every region had its own means for divining the future and its own magic devices for warding off evil or invoking misfortune on enemies.

The vast majority of the religions were ritual religions, characterised by many deities. Most rites were intended to win the gods' favour; the idea was that a person who made an offering to a deity could claim a favour in return. Offerings and sacrifices, prayers, vows and incantations accompanied all acts in public life, work and private life.

The different peoples living in the empire often identified their own deities with those of other peoples. For example, a Greek visiting Syria and seeing a temple of a sky god or a storm god would call that god Zeus, like his own supreme god, who was originally also a sky god.

The rites were sometimes related to myths, stories recounting the deeds of the gods. Those myths were not dogmas – they were not generally held to be true, so it did not matter if they did not agree with one another. Some myths overlapped one another or even contradicted one another. Philosophical theories were expected to be dogmatically logical and pure, but stories about gods were not. Many gods were in one way or another associated with the forces in nature which controlled every aspect of man's life. Every people and every town had its own religious calendar indicating when offerings or sacrifices were to be made to the different deities and on what days their festivals were to be celebrated. People did not work on those days. Only the Jews had a fixed weekly day of rest (the Sabbath).

Roman gods and religious practices

The principal Roman gods were the supreme god Jupiter (the sky god, the head of the divine family and the patron god of Rome), Juno (his wife), Minerva (the goddess of handicrafts, learning and the arts) and Mars (the god of war and of vital force in spring). They were the protectors of the Roman state, the state gods. The Romans originally regarded their gods as powers which they could not represent visually, but in the fifth century BC, under the influence of the Greeks, they started to depict their principal gods as superhuman beings. In time, the Romans came to identify their gods with kindred Greek gods. Their gods retained their Roman names, but their appearance, their myths, their genealogy and the patterns of their deeds gradually acquired many Greek elements.

In addition to their gods in the form of superhuman beings (for which the Greek term 'anthropomorphic' is often used), the Romans had many other deities that were associated with specific acts, times and places. At harvest time, for example, they would pray to gods of threshing, winnowing, storage, etc. Those gods were called *numina* (singular: *numen*).

The Romans believed that their undertakings would be unsuccessful if the (state) gods were enraged, but that little could go wrong if the gods were satisfied. In the latter case they were at 'peace with the gods' (*pax deorum*). In order to retain that peace with the gods, the Romans always had to make the required sacrifices and recite the required prayer formulas in a painfully accurate manner. If the slightest mistake was made during a ceremony, the whole ceremony was repeated. Every five years the censors (and later the emperors) would organise a *lustrum*, an expiatory sacrifice on behalf of the entire Roman people. The Romans believed that they could infer the gods' disposition and the outcome of their own undertakings from certain

Figure 15.23 The Roman god Mars
Source: Cologne, Römisch-Germanisches Museum.

omens, or signs, such as the flight of birds, the structure of the liver of a sacrificed animal and oracles (see p. 152). On the eve of an important undertaking, the kings, and later the magistrates with *imperium* (and later still the emperors), would always endeavour to find out what the gods had in store for the Romans. A magistrate with *imperium* (or the emperor) had the right to take auspices (observe the flight of birds for divination purposes). In the imperial age the governors acted in accordance with the prophesies inferred from the emperor's auspices.

In the case of serious incidents and major disasters a special college of priests would consult the Sybilline Books, a collection of oracles named after the Sybil, a prophetess from Rome's legendary past. She was believed to have resided in a cave near Cumae, in the bay of Naples.

The Romans had several colleges of priests. The *pontifices* were responsible for the cult of the principal gods (see p. 160). There were also colleges with specific tasks

Figure 15.24 Reconstruction drawing showing the sanctuary of Lenus-Mars near Trier, one of the most important cities in the Roman Moselle region
Note: As the local deity Lenus showed affinities with Mars, he was identified with that god.
Source: Trier, Rheinisches Landesmuseum.

(for example the inspection of the liver of a sacrificed animal). The priests were Roman notables who performed their priestly tasks alongside their secular tasks.

Like the Greeks, the Romans too believed in life after death. Both peoples thought that the souls of the deceased would enjoy peace in the underworld, providing their bodies had been properly buried. If a deceased had not been buried (or cremated), his shade would roam around miserably, unable to find peace.

The introduction of foreign gods

During the long span of Roman history, the Romans admitted both Greek and Eastern deities into their pantheon. Some Greek gods became very popular in Rome, such as Hercules (a demigod who fought evil in his Twelve Labours and made the world fit for human occupation), Asclepius (a god of healing) and the Dioscuri (Castor and Pollux). Foreign gods were often admitted into the Roman pantheon in

Figure 15.25 Representation of the three gods of the Capitol in Rome: Jupiter (centre), the
principal state god of Rome, Juno and Minerva
Source: Cologne, Römisch-Germanisches Museum

times of misfortune, following the advice of oracles or if the cult of the gods in
question had become widespread among the Roman people. The cult of the fertility
goddess Cybele of Asia Minor, for example, was introduced in Rome during the
difficult Second Punic War and the worship of the Greek god Dionysus (the god
of wine, intoxication and ecstasy), who was called Bacchus in Latin, became very
popular in Rome after this war. Undesirable side-effects of the Bacchus cult, which
included public disorder, were forbidden on the Senate's decree in 186 BC.

In the imperial age a number of Eastern religions spread throughout the Roman
empire. Those religions, which had originally been restricted to a particular city or
people, evolved into world religions. The most important were the cult of the
Egyptian gods Isis and Osiris, the worship of the Persian god Mithras, the Cybele
cult and Christianity.

Like the Greek god Hercules (Greek: Heracles), Mithras was a heroic fighter of
evil. Hercules and Mithras were very popular in the military camps. The cult of
Mithras was confined to men.

Figure 15.26 Bacchus (Dionysus) flanked by two revelling ecstatic creatures
Note: Bacchanalian scenes were very popular all over the Roman world.
Source: Cologne, Römisch-Germanisches Museum.

The cult of Isis and Osiris was a mystery religion. Isis was a fertility goddess who, with the help of her heroic son Horus, managed to recover the body of her husband Osiris, who had been killed by the evil god, and bring him back to life. Osiris then became the god of the underworld. Initiates in Isis' mysteries participated in Osiris' resurrection. Mysteries were a combination of rites, purifications, formulas and theatrical performances with a magical undertone. The Greeks had a mystery cult of their own, which they celebrated at Eleusis, near Athens, in the sanctuary of their fertility goddess Demeter. That explains why Isis was much less popular among the Greeks than among the occupants of Italy, North Africa and Gaul.

The Roman authorities were for a long time suspicious of the Isis cult, which they did not accept until in the second century AD. Usually, however, the Roman authorities were very tolerant towards foreign religions. All that they required was that Roman citizens were prepared to participate in the public ceremonies and to pray to the Roman state gods. They took action only in cases of public disorder (e.g. during the *Bacchanalia*, the celebrations in honour of Bacchus, in 186 BC). It was only with the Jews and the Christians that they came into serious conflict.

The Christians

The Jews and the Christians acknowledged only one god and rejected all the other deities. In this respect they differed from followers of other religions who sometimes devoted extra attention to one god in particular, without however renouncing the other gods (cf. p. 52).

The Jews were an ancient people and they were recognisable as a nation. That is the reason why they, as a people, did not have to conform to the Roman state cult from Caesar's time onwards. The Roman authorities did however take action against the Jews (in particular in Rome) if they made too many converts amongst non-Jews or when tension smouldered in the Jewish communities (see p. 230).

Christianity was a fairly new religion (Jesus died during the reign of the emperor Tiberius, *c.* AD 30), which was not restricted to one people. The Christians' secluded life made them suspect and the Roman authorities came to see the ecclesiastical organisation as a state within the state, which, they feared, might conspire against Rome. Christians started to be persecuted in different places, by governors and local authorities whom the Christians had annoyed, or by mobs searching for scapegoats in times of adversity. The Christians were even persecuted by various emperors.

Nero (54–68) blamed the Christians in Rome for a tremendous fire that reduced half of the city to ashes in 64. He was the first emperor to instigate a major persecution of Christians. On this occasion only the Christians in Rome were persecuted.

Christianity originated as a Jewish sect that was particularly popular amongst non-Jews who felt attracted to the Jewish religion or had converted to Judaism. A dispute regarding an issue of Jewish law was the reason for the separation from Judaism. Most Christians were against enforcing Jewish rules of life on the non-Jews amongst them. Moreover, the Christians did not participate in the major Jewish uprising of 66–70 (see p. 230), which many Jews regarded as betrayal. Around AD 90 the Christians were expelled from the Jewish community.

It was then not long before the Jewish Christians were outnumbered and surpassed in influence by Christians from non-Jewish peoples. The leadership of the Christian communities came to rest with a group of Greek-speaking intellectuals and merchants. They financed the ceremonies, provided the funds for poor relief and furnished the bishops (Greek: *episkopoi* – overseers) and the presbyters (elders) of the Christian communities, which otherwise consisted largely of slaves, freedmen, women and small tradesmen in the cities. In rural areas Christianity found few followers in its early days. The occupants of those areas did not experience the feelings of disorientation associated with migration to a city and continued to adhere to their ancient ancestral rites, which were closely linked with their farming existence.

Slaves and women probably felt attracted to Christianity because in God's eyes they were equal to the other faithful in the Christian communities and they shared equally in the Sacraments. Things were often quite different in other contemporary religions. In the Christian communities even a slave could become a presbyter or a bishop (but a woman could not).

Figure 15.27 Sarcophagus showing Christian scenes

Notes: Left: the snake in Paradise tempts Adam and Eve to eat the forbidden fruit. Centre: the Good Shepherd (this was originally a pastoral rather than a Christian motif; Christian artists Christianised it into the 'Good Shepherd'). Right: the three
young men whom God saved from burning in the furnace.

Source: Trier, Rheinisches Landesmuseum.

The popularity of Christianity among merchants and intellectuals was probably attributable to the latent monotheism inherent in the common popular schools of philosophy. Moreover, the Christians' clear and simple moral code appealed to groups who were tired of the endless conflicts between the various schools of ethical philosophy.

Literate Christians defended their faith in writing against attacks from various directions. In rhetorical written Greek they engaged in polemics with Jewish rabbis, Greek philosophers, the Roman authorities and semi-Christian sects that combined Christian concepts with ancient Near Eastern ideas and Greek philosophy. Around 200 a similar Latin Christian literature emerged in North Africa (the Christian community in Rome continued to use Greek until in the third century; in that city it was mostly Greek-speaking slaves, freedmen and foreigners who were attracted to Christianity). The Christian authors developed a Christian literature that was acceptable to all the literate faithful. They also laid the foundations for a systematic, philosophical–logical doctrine, which was authoritatively preached by the bishops. It was however preached in simple stories and rules which everybody could understand. The Christian elite thus served both the literate and the illiterate. In time, a fair amount of Greek philosophy crept into the Christian doctrine.

The Christians did not hold offices in local or central administration and they did not do military service. Their faith forbade them to take human life and they realised that they would be forced to participate in the worship of the Roman state gods and the emperor cult in the military camps and in administrative functions. The Christians were however prepared to pray for the emperor and the empire and to pay taxes; they were not rebels.

THE CRISIS OF THE THIRD CENTURY AD AND LATE ANTIQUITY

GROWING PRESSURES ON THE NORTHERN AND EASTERN FRONTIERS

The years 161–166 saw a major war between Rome and the Parthians, which was followed by violent invasions of German tribes in the middle Danube region (165–180). In the east, the Roman generals won an overwhelming victory, but the Roman army returning from Mesopotamia brought back a plague, which claimed many victims in the Roman empire. A few years later, in 170, the Germans managed to penetrate into Italy. For the first time since the days of Marius foreign invaders crossed the Alps. It cost the emperor Marcus Aurelius (161–180) great difficulty to expel the Germans and restore Roman control in the frontier region.

But this victory was short-lived, for in the third century over-population and pressure from the hinterland (the Eurasian steppes) were to push the Germans across the Roman frontiers again.

The Germans

The German tribes were in many respects rather like the Celtic tribes (see p. 242). In the first place, they, too, were led by nobles who ruled over kinship groups and serfs and had a personal retinue of warriors. And like the Celts, they had warrior chieftains, elected by warriors' assemblies. The Germans lived in scattered settlements that consisted of a few large farms surrounded by a number of small huts. Agriculture and handicrafts were practised by the free-born poor, dependent farm-hands and women. The male members of the higher classes devoted themselves to warfare and hunting. In terms of material culture, however, the Germans were inferior to most Celtic tribes; they were also less prosperous. Around the beginning of the imperial age extensive trade contacts were established between the Romans and the Germans, via which goods were distributed from the Roman empire into northern Germany and Scandinavia.

During the reigns of Caesar and Augustus the German nobles and their warriors were well trained and heavily armed, but their retainers from the lower classes had little more than a hardened wooden spear and a light shield. Those simple arms were nevertheless quite adequate for guerrilla warfare in the German forests and swamps.

In the course of the imperial age the Germans borrowed much from the Romans' military organisation. They for example borrowed the Romans' method of besieging cities and learned how to keep their armies together for long periods of time.

By AD 69 the rebellious Batavians and their allies from free Germany had learned enough from the Romans to be able to force a Roman military base to surrender (Vetera, near Xanten). The Batavians had been able to observe the Romans' military tactics at close quarters as they had been living inside the Roman frontiers since *c.* 12 BC and had supplied many auxiliaries for the Roman army based along the lower Rhine. Nevertheless, the Romans should have taken the defeat at Vetera as an ominous portent (see p. 230).

We are poorly informed about the Germans' religion and literary tradition in this period because their myths, legends and heroic songs were passed on orally.

Figure 16.1 Marcus Aurelius (ruled AD 161–180), showing mercy on defeated opponents
Notes: Marcus Aurelius did not have a military background – until 161 he was more of an intellectual and a philosopher – but after initial defeats he nevertheless succeeded in halting the German invasions around 180. Later generations admired him for his energy and his self-sacrifice.
Source: Marburg photographic archive.

Figure 16.2 A German farmer ploughing
Source: Cologne, Römisch-Germanisches Museum.

Around 200, major changes took place in Germany. The Goths moved from Scandinavia to the southeast and settled in Wallachia (the Visigoths) and on the Crimean (the Ostrogoths). Around 230 they started to launch attacks on the Roman empire, which evolved into full-fledged wars that devastated the Roman provinces in the Balkans. It took the Romans many years, until 269, to rout the Goths.

Further west new alliances and federations of German tribes emerged, such as the Franks in the middle Rhine area and the Alamanni in the angle between the Rhine and the Danube. A few conflicts broke out along these frontiers in the first half of the third century, but they were only local disputes. Between 253 and 282, however, the Roman empire was confronted with massive invasions in these regions, too. The Roman armies had great difficulty restoring order along these frontiers and vast areas were laid waste in the confrontations with the Germans.

Around 180, Germans started to settle in the northern frontier regions. This marked the beginning of a development which several centuries later was to result in the Germanisation of the areas to the west of the Rhine and to the south of the upper Danube. The Roman emperors did nothing to stop this development; some even encouraged it for the various advantages it implied: ravaged regions would be returned to cultivation and their populations would be able to pay taxes again, the German pressure on the frontiers would decrease and the new occupants of the empire would furnish good recruits for the Roman armies.

The Sasanian empire

In 226 the rebellious Persians defeated their Parthian oppressors and assumed control over the Parthian empire. This new empire, which was ruled by the Sasanians, lasted until about 640.

Parthia had been a fairly loose-knit empire of practically independent provinces, with an upper class of warriors that sponged off the rest of the population. The new Sasanian empire was a centralist, bureaucratic state with high, efficiently collected taxes and – partly thanks to those taxes – a large, strong army. The heavily armed, armoured cavalry was particularly formidable. The stirrup and the type of knight known to us from the Middle Ages were probably introduced in Persia.

The revival of Persian power went hand in hand with an aggressive form of nationalism, both in foreign politics and in religious and cultural life. The Persian kings of the third century aimed to conquer the eastern provinces of the Roman empire, reputedly in order to recover Cyrus's empire. The years between 240 and 283 consequently saw a series of major wars between the Romans and the Persians, in which the Romans had the greatest difficulty holding their own. In 260 the Persians even managed to capture the emperor Valerian (253–260). It was not until under Diocletian (284–305), in the years 296–299, that the Roman armies won victories that caused the Persians to postpone further campaigns.

The Persians regarded their Zoroastrianism (see p. 52) as a superior religion, and despised the religions of the minorities in their empire (e.g. those of the Greeks, the Jews and the Babylonians). The Greek culture that had been introduced here by Alexander the Great and his successors and that had been highly respected by the Parthians gradually declined. The Greek cities and Greek quarters lost their privileges. This heralded the end of the Hellenistic era in these regions.

INTERNAL INSTABILITY IN THE ROMAN EMPIRE

The growing pressures on the frontiers exposed a whole range of weaknesses in the Roman system.

Military problems

The wars against the Germans and the Parthians (and after 226 the Persians) showed that the superiority the Roman armies had enjoyed for so many centuries in the face of most of their enemies was no longer a matter of course. Over the years, those enemies had learned much from the Romans, whereas the military prowess of the

Roman soldiers had suffered a decline. Since the spread of Roman citizenship throughout the frontier regions (see p. 237), from which ever more troops had to be recruited, the number of men who enlisted in order to acquire Roman citizenship had probably decreased considerably. From the works of contemporary Greek and Latin authors we get the impression that only the poorest and men who were not welcome anywhere else now voluntarily enlisted in the armies. Those authors claim that the soldiers did not shrink from terrorising their own people whenever their material position was threatened. The higher officers still came from the senatorial and equestrian orders. Quite a few of those notables lacked the necessary military experience to be able to take effective action in a full-fledged war. In that respect they were surpassed by equestrian officers who had risen from the army's rank and file; they had been promoted to the equestrian order precisely on account of their military capabilities.

In the two centuries that they spent in permanent bases along the frontiers, the armies developed strong regional ties and interests. Most of the soldiers came from the areas in which those armies were stationed (see p. 237). The consequence of this was that when an emperor paid insufficient attention to a threatened frontier, the troops on that frontier would proclaim their own general emperor. In the third century several major wars consequently resulted in usurpations and succession struggles.

Structural defects

After two centuries of peace the Roman empire was no longer capable of coping with a more or less permanent state of war. The higher orders had lost much of their military prowess. The taxation system was too simple and too rigid to furnish the resources required to meet the high extra costs of defence. And there were no longer any extra sources of income in the form of the booty and tributes that had partly financed Rome's conquests in the second and first centuries BC.

All over the empire were countless indefensible unfortified cities. The busy trade was entirely geared to peaceful and reasonably safe conditions. There were very few reserves. Instead of productively investing the profits of their surpluses, the notables had squandered them on ostentatious buildings, popular entertainments and cultural manifestations. And now they were suffering the consequences, for they were having to spend vast amounts on the upkeep of those buildings and on the gymnasia they had instituted and the games and other forms of entertainments they had introduced. They also had to support increasing numbers of poor seasonal labourers in periods when there was no demand for their labour. The lower classes had undoubtedly increased in number in two hundred years of peace and were attracted to cities where public entertainments were provided. We do not know whether the population had suffered a decrease owing to the plague of 166.

In the course of the first and second centuries, wealth became increasingly disproportionately distributed, which ultimately resulted in a concentration of property in the hands of a small number of wealthy citizens. They grew richer and richer through inheritances and the purchase of land, while the numbers of tenants and small landowning farmers who could only just scrape a living increased.

THE SEVERI (193–235)

Septimius Severus (193–211)

In 193 Septimius Severus, a Roman of North African origin, became emperor after the struggle for power that ensued after the murder of Commodus (see Diagram 15.1, p. 232). The army on the Danube won this struggle for him and placed him on the throne.

Septimius Severus realised that now the pressure on the frontiers was increasing he would have to expand and improve his army. He created a number of new legions, greatly raised his soldiers' pay and improved their fringe benefits. From this point onwards soldiers were allowed to marry, they were paid extra allowances in cash and kind and they were granted a plot of land in their own frontier region. Unfortunately, this further strengthened their allegiance to their local communities.

Septimius Severus made it easier for experienced junior officers to rise to higher officer posts and gave the knights more influence in administrative matters. His aims in increasing the soldiers' chances of social advancement were to make military service more attractive and to expand his army. However, his measures created unsolvable financial problems. The cost of defence increased explosively (one of the causes being the substantial raise in the soldiers' pay). These financial problems were to hound all the subsequent Roman emperors.

Septimius Severus and his son Caracalla (ruled 211–217) managed to find money in several ways. They cut the weight and metal content of the coins while attempting to artificially preserve their purchasing power. They instituted legal proceedings designed to result in the confiscation of the property of rich senators whom they did not like or who had sided against them in the struggle of 193. In 199 Septimius Severus moreover acquired a rich booty in a successful campaign against the Parthians. In this war he also annexed a new province ('Mesopotamia' – northern Mesopotamia). The Roman empire then reached its greatest extent.

Figure 16.3 Septimius Severus (AD 193–211)
Source: Rome, Museo Capitolino.

Figure 16.4 Caracalla (ruled AD 211–217)
Source: Rome, Museo Capitolino.

Roman citizenship for all free inhabitants of the empire

In 212 Caracalla granted all free inhabitants of the empire Roman citizenship. It is assumed that this act was motivated by fiscal considerations. In the imperial age, Roman citizenship did not exempt the occupants of the provinces from paying direct taxes. In Italy, the old heartland of the empire, no property taxes had been collected since 167 BC, but in the provinces everybody had to pay direct taxes, except for a small group of citizens and communities to whom one of the emperors had granted special exemption. Exemption from taxation was one of the greatest privileges one could receive from an emperor. There were however also taxes that were imposed specifically on citizens, both in Italy and in the provinces, such as the 5 per cent inheritance tax introduced by Augustus (see p. 225). So on balance, this massive enfranchisement was fiscally advantageous for the state.

In 213 and 215 Caracalla paid barbarian tribes on the northern frontier sums of money to dissuade them from invading the empire; that was cheaper than engaging in warfare. This redemption policy was to remain popular until the end of the imperial age.

The last emperor of the Severan dynasty, Severus Alexander (ruled 222–235), tried to save money by pursuing a consistent peace policy that entailed negotiating with the enemy for as long as possible. He also cut back on incidental grants and donatives.

In spite of all the problems, the Severan era was in most provinces a reasonably prosperous period, in which the cities continued to flourish culturally. It did however sharpen the contrasts between rival social groups. The members of the traditional higher classes and the intellectuals in the imperial services feared the rise of military specialists from the rank and file of the army and despised the soldiers for their greed and lack of discipline. The populace of Rome was not favourably disposed towards the soldiers either. It probably realised that the emperors would not be able to spend as much on the people in Rome if they had to give more to the soldiers; less money would then remain for donatives and games in Rome. These feelings created an unstable political climate.

THE SOLDIER EMPERORS (235–284)

After 235, and in particular after 248, everything went wrong. Wars broke out on all the frontiers (see p. 273) and the individual armies fought one another in constantly recurring struggles for power. After 235 there was no longer an officially recognised dynasty and dozens of emperors and usurpers followed one another in rapid succession for five decades (until 284). These emperors are known as the 'soldier emperors', because their power rested exclusively on their soldiers' might and because they acquired that power through military coups. All that the Senate and the civilian population could do was wait and see which general would emerge victorious from the successive struggles. From time to time the empire's unity even came under threat, when different emperors governed different parts of the empire.

Large parts of the empire were repeatedly devastated by warfare and paid hardly any taxes. The agricultural surpluses decreased and the entire empire was ravaged by famine and pestilence, especially the war-ridden regions. There, and in the adjacent areas, deserters, escaped slaves, bankrupt farmers and other desperate men united in large gangs of robbers. Trade declined owing to the unsafe conditions and the decreasing purchasing power. Numerous cities in the afflicted regions fell into ruin. The municipal councillors got into financial straits, caught between the decreasing profits of their estates and the increasing demands of the armies and tax collectors travelling through their areas. They moreover had to meet the costs of local defence (town walls, emergency militias). The interaction of price increases, the debasement of the coins and extra payments for the soldiers, who revolted against the decrease in their purchasing power, ultimately led to the collapse of the Roman monetary system. The emperors were forced to meet all their soldiers' demands because they owed their position to them and needed the armies in the many wars.

In parts of the empire normal administration was disrupted and arbitrary requisitions exacted by soldiers took the place of regular taxation. In those regions the army effectively assumed administrative control. In many cities the local elite had little money left to finance charity, the construction and upkeep of ostentatious buildings, cultural manifestations and public entertainment. We may suspect that the wealthiest citizens, members of the higher ranking elite, managed to evade the increasing burdens. They were able to buy abandoned land at a low price. Property consequently became more concentrated than ever.

Between 235 and 284 things were not as bad everywhere in the empire. Large areas (Britain, Spain, parts of Asia Minor, Sicily, parts of North Africa and Egypt) were spared the ravages wrought by war. Partly as a consequence of this, the provinces in Africa and Asia became comparatively more important parts of the empire. The Roman empire owed its continued existence in the third century and its slight recovery in the fourth century to the military successes of the soldier emperors who ruled between 260 and 284 and to the reforms that were introduced by those

Figure 16.5 Gate in Aurelian's wall (Aurelian ruled AD 270–275)

emperors and were completed by Diocletian (ruled 284–305). In 260 one of the soldier emperors, Gallienus (ruled 253–268), banned senators from serving as officers. In his opinion those 'gentlemen' lacked the necessary military expertise as they had spent such large parts of their careers engaged in entirely different tasks. He replaced them by experienced soldiers from the equestrian order who had served in the army throughout their professional lives. Gallienus also introduced a system of extra defence behind threatened frontiers. In the years around 255, when he was still ruling together with his father Valerian (ruled 253–260; see p. 274) and was fighting the Franks along the Rhine, he started using mobile forces consisting largely of cavalry, which could move fast from one threatened area to another. Gallienus also created a 'general staff' of equestrian generals experienced in warfare who had risen from the rank and file of the army. Most of the emperors who ruled between 268 and 284 came from this staff.

DIOCLETIAN (ruled 284–305)

Diocletian's reign saw the end of the crisis of the third century. The pressures on the frontiers gradually decreased and Diocletian managed to remain in control for twenty-one years. The incessant succession struggles appeared to have come to an end.

Diocletian tried to prevent a new crisis by introducing a sophisticated and varied programme of reforms. He expanded and reorganised his army and improved the frontier defences. He adopted Gallienus' idea and stationed several mobile field armies behind the fortified frontiers, which would be able to react quickly whenever barbarians crossed the frontiers.

To finance this increased military effort Diocletian introduced a new, more elaborate taxation system that was better adjusted to the taxpayers' ability to pay. From this point onwards a plot of land was taxed according to its extent, its quality and the number of people that worked on it (see p. 221). Allowance was hence made for the land's productivity. Head taxes were introduced in the cities. The existing taxes in kind were increased and the arbitrary requisitions that the troops had been exacting over the past years were regulated into a system of payments and services to the armies and the civil service. In 301 Diocletian also made an attempt to halt the price increases by issuing an edict fixing maximum prices, but that attempt was unsuccessful and so were the monetary reforms with which he tried to put an end to the devaluation of the coins.

To ensure that the land would remain productive, Diocletian bound the farmers to the soil. This was a major step towards the serfdom of the Middle Ages. The craftsmen in the cities he bound to their trades; from now onwards a craftsman's son had to succeed his father. Diocletian's aim was to prevent the craftsmen from giving up their trade so as to avoid paying the heavy taxes.

The municipal councillors (*curiales*) were made financially responsible for levying the taxes in their communities to an even greater extent than before. They were bound to their social class and to their council to prevent them from shirking their responsibilities by enlisting in the army or seeking employment in one of the imperial services.

Further expansion of bureaucracy

The exigencies of the new conditions necessitated changes in the central and provincial administrations. The refined taxation system and the stricter collection of the taxes (in cash and kind) implied more work, also in inspections. Moreover, the central and provincial authorities had to take over ever more of the municipal magistrates' tasks. Those magistrates were no longer capable of meeting the costs involved in maintaining law and order (which was disrupted by robbers and roaming barbarians) and the upkeep of the public works and amenities, while simultaneously paying the (higher) taxes. In the third-century crisis the increasing burdens had brought many *curiales* in the war- and disease-stricken regions into financial difficulties. Their estates were devastated and their cities were ravaged by war and the plague. Nevertheless, they were still required to finance local defence (city walls, emergency militias) and the construction and repair of public works. On top of that they also had to pay the taxes and war requisitions. What's more, the urban magistrates all over the empire had already been heavily taxed at the end of the second century (see p. 275). The local councils had seen their best and wealthiest members depart to the senatorial and equestrian governing elite and to the army and the imperial services, leaving them behind to pay for the upkeep of the urban amenities (games, gymnasia, means of transport, baths, waterworks), which had expanded considerably in two centuries of peace. What had once been prestige-enhancing liberality had by the end of the second century become an expensive obligation, which the local notables tried to offload onto one another. From the late second century onwards it was difficult to find people who were willing to hold the municipal posts that involved expensive liturgies (see p. 103). Whereas wealthy notables had in the past been elected for these posts it now became necessary to assign them to them by turns. Towards the fourth century ever more *curiales* began to aspire to posts in the army or the imperial bureaucracy so as to be able to evade the burdens of local administration.

To ensure that the taxes were efficiently collected and to counterbalance the decline of local administration, Diocletian strengthened the central and provincial administrative machineries. He appointed more officials and split up large provinces into smaller units. This led to the formation of two or even three separate administrative levels in those provinces. Diocletian regrouped the provinces into dioceses. After Diocletian's reign those dioceses were grouped into four large praefectures (see Map 16.1). The extra staff was preferably recruited from the army and to a lesser extent from among students of law and rhetoric and imperial freedmen. The imperial bureaucracy acquired a rather military character. Soldiers who rose from the rank and file of the army to the military and administrative middle cadres had good career prospects. Diocletian tried to keep the *curiales* out of the bureaucracy and the army for the reasons outlined above, but he was not always successful. The expanding army and bureaucracy both needed large numbers of people with organisational experience. Diocletian moreover divided military and civil power. This was a rather revolutionary measure. Since the beginning of Roman history, military tasks, government and the administration of justice had always been united in the powers of the kings, the magistrates with *imperium* and the emperors (and their governors). Now, however, the military tasks were entrusted to separate frontier commanders (*duces* and *comites*, singular *dux* and *comes*) and to the generals who served in the mobile armies.

The Senate and the equestrian order

These high officers and most of his governors Diocletian recruited from the equestrian order. This meant that the senatorial class lost its privileged position in higher administration. The Roman Senate came to be an assembly of fabulously rich landowners who had no say in important administrative matters and had no access to high military functions. But it did retain its influence in Rome's city life. The Senate of the late imperial age (fourth and fifth centuries) has been described as Rome's 'town council'. As the emperors were constantly away on campaigns after 230 and were only rarely to be found in Rome, the Senate took over a large part of their function as benefactors in that city.

From Diocletian's reign onwards the equestrian order grew tremendously and became increasingly heterogeneous, ultimately disintegrating into a number of new classes bound to functions in the army and the bureaucracy.

Emperorship and the emperor's succession

Diocletian appointed one co-emperor and two junior emperors, so that each of the four major armies (those of the Rhine, the upper Danube, the lower Danube and the eastern frontier) could be led by an emperor. The two senior emperors were both

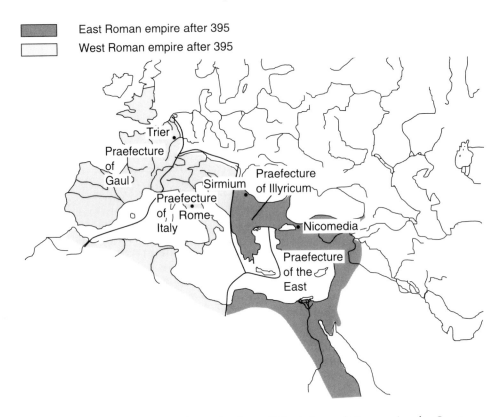

Map 16.1 The Roman empire at the time of Diocletian and Constantine the Great
Notes: The empire has suffered its first losses: Dacia (present-day Rumania) and the angle between the Rhine and the Danube were lost in the years around 270. The empire was divided into four praefectures, each of which was led by an emperor or a junior emperor and a praetorian prefect.

given the title 'Augustus'; the junior emperors were called 'Caesar'. The latter (*Caesares*) were to succeed the former (*Augusti*). This, Diocletian, hoped, would prevent succession struggles (see p. 278). The four emperors did not reside in Rome, but (when they were not away on campaigns with their royal households) in Nicomedia, Milan, Sirmium and Trier (see Map 16.1) – four strategically located centres from where they could quickly reach their frontiers.

Diocletian searched for better ideological foundations for the emperorship, which he hoped would prevent usurpations in the future. He presented himself and his co-ruler Maximian (ruled 286–305) as emperors by the grace of the gods Jupiter and Hercules and he began to surround his court at Nicomedia with the pomp and ceremony of an Oriental absolute despot.

These measures were designed to make the emperor more powerful, but things worked out differently in practice. In the course of the late imperial age the emperors lost direct contact with the local authorities and the local frontier commanders.

Figure 16.6 Diocletian and his co-emperors, represented in close concord
Source: Venice, Marburg photographic archive.

The court and the greater number of administrative levels created an unbridgeable distance between the provincial administrations and the central government.

Diocletian himself abdicated (305), and lived for another eleven years secluded in a large palace at Spalato (present-day Split in former Yugoslavia).

The persecutions of the Christians

The years between 250 and 311 saw a number of systematic persecutions of Christians all over the empire (250, 257–260 and 303–311). These persecutions were inaugurated by the emperors Decius (ruled 249–251) and Valerian (ruled 253–260) because the Christians refused to publicly worship the Roman state gods. They were accused of having brought down the wrath of the gods on the Roman empire. In 260 Gallienus put an end to the persecutions in an attempt to eliminate extra sources of

Figure 16.7 Decius (ruled AD 249–251), one of the soldier emperors
Notes: Decius tried to save the empire by restoring discipline and the old piety towards Rome's state gods. This brought him into conflict with the Christians, who refused to participate in sacrifices to those gods (the consequence was a major general persecution of Christians in 250). In 251 Decius was killed in a battle against the Goths near the mouth of the Danube. The emperors of this period (235–260) had themselves portrayed in the style of the late republic (Fig. 14.6, p. 214), the time of Rome's great military successes.
Source: Rome, Museo Capitolino.

unrest at the low point of the crisis. In the following forty years the number of Christians grew tremendously. Many people turned to the Christian communities for spiritual certainty and material support.

Within the Church arose a separate, hierarchical clergy, which led the Christian communities. Christendom increasingly began to resemble a state within the state. Diocletian watched this development with growing suspicion and when, in 303, he felt things had gone too far he instituted a major persecution. This persecution was to last for another six years after his abdication, until his successor Galerius (305–311) halted it in 311.

CONSTANTINE THE GREAT (ruled 306–337)

Diocletian's attempt to solve the succession problem was not successful. In 306 Constantine, who was not a junior emperor, was acclaimed emperor in Trier. He acquired control over the western half of the empire after a civil war in 312, and in 324 he became sole emperor after defeating his co-emperor Licinius (312–324). Constantine governed the Roman empire from 324 until 337.

Constantine's conversion to Christianity

During the civil war of 312 Constantine came to sympathise with Christianity. He was not baptised until the end of his life, but that was not uncommon among Christians in those days. He may well have already joined the Christian community in 312.

Constantine saw himself as an emperor by the grace of the one universal God of the Christians. He ruled over the civilised Roman empire like God ruled over the cosmos. Almost all of the emperors who succeeded Constantine adhered to the Christian faith.

Constantine soon started to interfere with the internal relations within the Church. When religious struggles broke out concerning the Godhead of Christ, which threatened the unity of Christendom, he himself presided over the council of bishops that was to resolve the dispute. This council was held in 324, in Nicaea in northwest Asia Minor. The confession of faith that was formulated by this council eventually resulted in the Nicene Creed, which was to hold for all Christians for many centuries.

Constantinople

Between 324 and 330 Constantine built a new capital, Constantinople, on the site of the old Greek colony Byzantium in the Bosporus. From that location the emperors could reach the most important frontiers quickly by land and by sea. Constantine and his immediate successors established a pompous court, with a new, complex hierarchy. He also introduced a new Senate, which was to function alongside the Roman Senate. The Senate of Constantinople was filled with local Christian notables and officials, mostly from the eastern half of the empire. The Roman Senate became the bastion of the wealthy conservative landowners all over the empire, east and west, who did not convert to Christianity. The senators who resided in Rome on a permanent basis controlled that city's cultural and social life after the court was permanently moved elsewhere.

Constantine saw to it that the senators regained their influence in central administration. He wanted to make use of their capabilities and hoped that they would place their wealth entirely at the disposal of the state and the community. But he was disappointed. Like many high-ranking officers and officials, the senators started to regard their offices as private vehicles for further enriching themselves and for creating networks of clients within the bureaucracy. Nothing remained of the senators' former devotion to the state, with which they no longer identified themselves. The emperor and his court now embodied the state.

The army

Constantine relied on a well-trained, mobile army which followed him everywhere and consisted largely of cavalry. The frontier troops had now well and truly become garrison troops.

Constantine's mobile army contained a large German element. German mercenaries were good and cheap and the landowners and *curiales* relinquished only the

Figure 16.8a Front and back view of the Aula Palatina, Constantine's immense throne room and audience hall in Trier

Notes: The building is built entirely of brick. The structure's simple shape enhances its overwhelming spatial impression. The aula is 67 m long, 27.5 m wide and 30 m high.

Source: Trier, Rheinisches Landesmuseum.

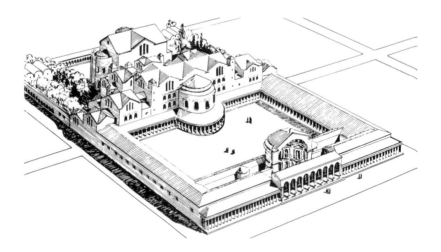

Figure 16.8b The Imperial Baths in Trier, one of the capitals of the Roman empire in the fourth century

Notes: Baths were buildings with large rooms with heated floors and walls that contained swimming pools and basins of hot, tepid and cold water. They were surrounded by dressing rooms, sweating rooms, areas for sunbathing, playing fields and a shop-lined colonnade. In Rome and other large Roman cities the baths were important meeting places. Men and women bathed separately.

Source: Trier, Rheinisches Landesmuseum.

weakest elements from their territories to the armies. They preferred to keep capable, well-trained men at work on their own estates. This they were able to do because Diocletian had bound the farmers to the soil. In 332 Constantine tightened this measure in some provinces where many farmers fled from their land to avoid paying the high taxes. Landowners moreover had the alternative of paying money instead of supplying recruits. That money could be used to hire Germans. The army and the officers who rose from its ranks consequently included progressively more Germans. By around 400, generals of German origin had already acquired decisive influence in the imperial court and administration.

Increased fiscal burdens and the monetary system

Constantine and his immediate successors greatly expanded their bureaucracy and their domestic staff, they commissioned many building projects and raised the military budget even further. Constantine increased the fiscal burdens by introducing new taxes and raising existing ones. Particularly notorious were the taxes he levied on workshops, which impoverished many a craftsman. In some provinces, mostly in the west, Constantine tightened the landowners' grip on their tenants so as to ensure that the workers in rural areas, on whose shoulders rested the greater part of the tax burden, would stay put. This was the second step towards the serfdom of the Middle Ages (Diocletian had already taken the first, see p. 280). In spite of his high expenses, Constantine managed to stabilise the monetary system to some extent. He introduced a new gold coin, the *solidus*, which was to remain the basic currency of the Byzantine empire and Western Europe up to the era of the Crusades.

Figure 16.9 A gold coin showing emperor Constantine the Great (ruled AD 306–337)
Notes: Constantine tried to reorganise the Roman monetary system after the chaos of the third century. The silver and copper money remained poor and unstable, but Constantine did introduce a new stable gold coin, the *solidus*.
Source: Trier, Rheinisches Landesmuseum.

THE ROMAN EMPIRE AFTER CONSTANTINE

The hundred and fifty years following Constantine's reign can be seen as a transitional period, the incubation period of the Middle Ages. The four most important features of this period were the widening of the breach between the eastern and western halves of the empire, the decline of many cities, the continuing Christianisation of the empire and the increasing pressure on the frontiers.

Major wars were fought between the Romans and the Persians between 336 and 364, and the second half of the fourth century saw the beginning of massive German migrations. Population pressure forced the Germans to leave their tribal territories in search of new occupation areas. Around 400 the pressure was further increased by invasions of the Huns, Mongolian horsemen from the hinterland who established an empire in central and eastern Europe extending from Hungary to the Ukraine. They pushed the Germans across the Roman frontiers.

East and West

In the fourth and fifth centuries the two halves of the Roman empire drifted away from one another. After Constantine's death in 337, the western and eastern halves were constantly governed by separate emperors, first from Constantine's own house (until 363) and then from other dynasties (see Appendix 3, p. 302).

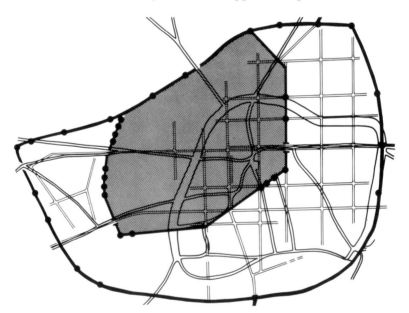

Figure 16.10a The city of Tongeren in Belgium, showing the walled area until AD 275 and the later urban area

Notes: The Roman empire weakened from the third century onwards and was threatened from outside. The towns depopulated as people drifted to the countryside and to the larger cities. Newly built fortifications always enclosed smaller areas than did their predecessors.

Source: H. Rottier, *Stedelijke Structuren*, Coutinho, Muiderberg, 1980, p. 84.

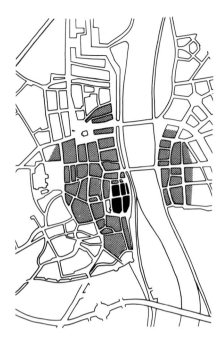

Figure 16.10b Maastricht in its Roman heyday and the fourth-century castellum (dark shading) in which the remaining population lived
Source: H. Rottier, *Stedelijke Structuren*, Coutinho, Muiderberg, 1980, p. 84.

These emperors in effect became increasingly distinct rulers of the western and eastern Roman empires, with separate administrations. After 395 there were no longer any emperors who ruled over the entire empire, although the pretence of a single, unified Roman empire was always maintained.

The western court usually resided in Milan or Ravenna, in Italy. In the east Constantinople was the capital. Constantinople grew rapidly and monopolised the grain surpluses of Egypt and the Crimean. Rome had to make do with the surpluses of North Africa and Sicily, while the capitals in northern Italy were fed by the farmers in the Po valley.

The cities in the eastern half of the empire managed to hold out reasonably well. The old urban elites, the military cadre and the higher personnel of the imperial bureaux evolved into a loyal 'aristocracy of service'. Christianity and the ecclesiastical hierarchy were unifying elements in this part of the empire. In the fifth century, warfare and migrations caused much less devastation in the Asian provinces and Egypt than in the west and the Balkans. In this century the Persians were preoccupied with their enemies along their northeastern frontiers. The Germans did not spread any further than the Balkans; the heavily fortified city of Constantinople cut off their routes to Asia Minor.

Many cities in the west went into decline. The German commanders and the landed elite of high officials and senators began to operate on their own authority, taking progressively less notice of the emperor. With a series of constantly repeated edicts the emperors tried to keep the farmers on their land and the craftsmen in their workshops, but their efforts were in vain. In the fifth century the revenues of the central government in the western empire decreased progressively and it became increasingly difficult to defend the frontiers from the intensifying pressure of the Germans and the Huns.

The *curiales* who governed the cities were under great strain. They had to pay for the upkeep of the public works and the urban amenities out of their own pockets and they were financially responsible for levying the taxes (see p. 280).

The wealthiest and smartest *curiales* managed to find ways of evading the emperors' edicts and escaping to the civil service, the army and the Church (as bishops). More and more farmers, oppressed by the excessively high burden of the taxes imposed by the city magistrates, placed themselves under the patronage of powerful landowners with estates in their neighbourhood, who held high offices in the army or central government. These powerful men took progressively less notice of the *curiales* in the cities. Their *villae* (estates) became 'enclaves' in the city governments' territories, which were governed by the landowners themselves and in which the city magistrates were unable to interfere. These *villae* grew larger and larger and acquired their own workshops and armies and their own financial circuits. They evolved into almost independent economic units. Many farmers and craftsmen settled at these *villae*, seeking refuge against plundering enemies, bandits and the *curiales*' tax collectors. After some time, however, the farmers working at the *villae* were as badly oppressed as the farmers who had remained independent and were squeezed dry by the *curiales*. In the fifth century major farmers' revolts consequently broke out in Gaul, and all over the empire escaped farmers swelled the gangs of robbers.

Many cities suffered a severe decline. Their markets lost important groups of customers from rural areas because the *villae* evolved into almost self-sufficient households with their own workshops and because pauperisation continued unabated in afflicted regions in the fifth century (cf. p. 278). The town councils saw their best and wealthiest members depart, received progressively less tax and were unable to pay for the upkeep of the public amenities in their towns. Sometimes local landowners and/or Christian bishops had to assume responsibility for the remnants of a community and take over its administration.

In the western half of the empire, in particular in Gaul, Britain, the Rhineland and the Danubian regions, this process went much further than in the eastern half, North Africa and parts of Spain and Italy. In the east and North Africa more rich people continued to live in the cities, which more successfully managed to retain their economic functions. Spain and Italy occupied an intermediate position. The large imperial residences (such as Trier and Milan in the west) and the other cities that were important for the government held out reasonably well. With their offices of the central and provincial administrative machineries, law courts and imperial workshops, these cities attracted flocks of people of all classes who were anxious to make a career in the emperor's service.

THE CHRISTIAN EMPIRE

After 312–313 many people converted to Christianity for pragmatic reasons. In the eastern half of the empire and here and there in the west, Christianity became the prevailing religion. Its churches were led by a hierarchical clergy. The Christian communities lost some of their independence and gradually grew into regional groups, led by the bishops of Rome (Italy and the other Western European parts of the empire), Carthage (North Africa), Alexandria (Egypt), Constantinople (the Balkans and Asia Minor), Jerusalem and Antioch (Syria). The Christians in the Persian empire were led by the bishops of Edessa and Seleucia.

In the Persian empire the Christians always remained a despised minority, like the Jews. In the following discussion we will restrict ourselves to Christendom in the Roman empire.

The common people, unlike the clergy, were no longer required to abide by the old strict rules. Now that the empire was led by Christian emperors and was increasingly identified with Christendom, laymen (non-clergy) were allowed to engage in warfare and participate in administration. The bishops became important figures in the cities. Constantine made them responsible for part of the administration of justice.

The financial resources of the church grew rapidly. Many Christians bequeathed estates to the Christian communities and Constantine granted the churches and bishops exemption from various burdensome taxes and services.

But not all Christians identified the empire with Christendom. Some continued to reject the empire as an earthly evil. Others adhered to the old Christian belief that the emperors' wars were less important than the spiritual struggle against the devil and his forces of evil. The fourth century saw the appearance of hermits, ascetics and monks who denied themselves all worldly goods so as to be able to devote themselves entirely to prayer, which they regarded as a weapon in that spiritual struggle. They did not think highly of the heritage of the Classical era (art, literature). Other Christians, on the contrary, borrowed much from Classical philosophy and science and imitated ancient Greek and Latin authors in their works. They created a Christian variant of Classical culture. The fourth and early fifth centuries were the days of the great Church Fathers. Their works have remained authoritative in Christian churches into our times. The best-known Church Father is St Augustine (354–429), the bishop of Hippo in North Africa. To him, the Roman empire was of only relative significance. Far more important was the City of God, the kingdom of heaven, which would one day come on earth. Second in importance was the church militant on earth. The church militant existed in the evil earthly world and foreshadowed and reflected the church triumphant in heaven and in the future world. Here we find Plato's world of forms (see p. 123) combined with the Christian message.

The western half of the empire remained predominantly pagan in late antiquity. In the east and North Africa non-Christian religions lived on only in remote parts of the countryside and among Greek intellectuals and notables in the cities, who cherished the Classical Greek literary culture as an alternative religion. They felt attracted to a new form of Platonism that had originated around the middle of

Figure 16.11 St Vitale at Ravenna, built in the fifth century AD
Notes: The fifth century AD produced several outstanding works of Christian art. Ravenna was the chief
residence of the last west Roman emperors.
Source: Marburg photographic archive.

the third century in the circles of the philosopher Plotinus, who worked in Rome. This neo-Platonism was concerned not with politics, but with personal spiritual experiences. It had a mystical slant (the sudden acquisition, after long study, of knowledge of higher reality, in a moment of 'enlightenment').

The only non-Christian emperor of the time, Julian (361–363), felt attracted to this school of philosophy. He made one last attempt to turn back the clock and undo the victory of Christianity. He also tried to revert to the political regime of the second century AD. But Julian's 'pagan reaction' was short-lived because he ruled for only two years – in 363 he was killed during a major campaign against the Persians. In 380 the emperor Theodosius the Great (ruled 379–395) and his co-emperor Gratian (ruled 375–383, the emperor in the west) made Christianity the state religion. All non-Christian religions were banned.

The end of the west Roman Empire

In 378 the Visigoths (see p. 273) won a major victory over the east Roman emperor Valens at Hadrianople (see Map 16.2). They then forced the Romans to grant them permission to settle inside the frontiers of the Roman empire as a self-governing tribe. They settled in the Balkans, in what is now Bulgaria.

In 406 a large group of western German tribes crossed the Rhine and exacted similar treaties. Like the Visigoths, they promised to supply troops and pay taxes in return.

A few years later a dispute with the Roman authorities over the imposed taxes prompted the Visigoths to migrate again. They crossed the Balkans, invaded Italy and sacked Rome in 410 – an act that shocked the entire Roman world. The Visigoths then settled in southwestern Gaul and northern Spain. Northern Gaul passed into the hands of the Franks, Britain was invaded by Saxons and the Vandals conquered North Africa. The latter put an end to the supply of cheap food from Africa to Rome, which led to serious problems in that city. In the fifth century Rome entered on a long period of decline and depopulation. By the late Middle Ages Rome was no longer a large city. The German tribes in the empire took progressively less notice of the west Roman emperors and established their own, independent kingdoms. After the first years of the fifth century the west Roman emperors governed an empire that had shrunk to Italy and the surrounding islands. The unruly behaviour of Roman commanders in the western provinces may well have contributed to the decline of Roman authority.

The population of the western provinces readily accepted the Germans' control. The new masters demanded less tax than the Roman emperors had done and they took over the political system as they found it. The Germans had moreover been influenced by Roman culture for quite some time. Some German tribes had even converted to a (non-orthodox) form of Christianity already before they settled in the Roman empire. The large landowners started to work together with the German aristocracy and powerful Roman dynasties began to arrange marriages with the German elite, in spite of the fact that the new masters had confiscated and taken over much landed property.

———	Angles, Saxons, Jutes	–·–·–·–	Visigoths – western Goths
– – – –	Vandals	–··–··–	Ostrogoths – eastern Goths
– · – · –	Longobardi (*c.* 600)	———	Burgundians
– – – – –	Huns	············	Franks
· · · · · ·	Goths		

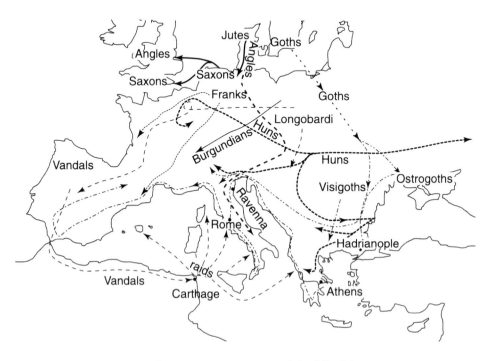

Map 16.2 The German migrations and the fall of the West
Roman empire in the fifth century AD

In Italy, emperorship came to an end in 476, when a German general, Odoacer,
assumed control and had himself proclaimed king of the Germans in Italy. The east
Roman (Byzantine) empire endured throughout the Middle Ages. In the sixth
century the east Roman emperor Justinian (ruled 527–565) managed to reconquer
Italy, North Africa and southern Spain, but between 630 and 650 the conquests of
the Arabs reduced the east Roman empire to Asia Minor, Greece, Sicily and the
coast of southern Italy. In 1453, after further territorial losses in the west (Italy)
and the east (to the Turks, who swept across Asia Minor after 1060), the east
Roman empire ultimately fell to the Turks, who that year captured the capital
Constantinople.

The east Roman empire was a Christian state, with a Greek elite culture, a Roman
law code and a Roman administrative system, and a pompous court characteristic of
late antiquity. It was in the east Roman empire that the Greek Orthodox form of

Christianity came into full bloom. The east Roman empire had a profound cultural influence on late medieval Italy, the Arabian and Turkish states and the Slavic peoples in eastern and southeastern Europe.

PART IV

APPENDICES

1. GREEK AND ROMAN NAMES

The Greeks had a first name and also mentioned their father's name. In the Athenian democracy the father's name was replaced by an indication of the *deme* to which the citizen belonged. But in practice the father's name continued to be used, too.

The Romans had three names: a personal name, a name denoting their *gens* and a surname to distinguish the family within that *gens*. The personal name was often abbreviated in writing: A. = Aulus, M. = Marcus, C. = Gaius, L. = Lucius, P. = Publius, Cn. = Gnaeus, T. = Titus, Tib. = Tiberius, S. = Sextus and Q. = Quintus. Caesar, for example, was officially called C. Julius Caesar. When a man was adopted, he would add his new family's *gens* name and surname to his personal name and add an extra surname to his full new name. This extra surname was derived from his original *gens* name. When C. Octavius was adopted as Caesar's son in the latter's will, he came to be called Gaius Julius Caesar Octavianus. The full names of some of the Romans mentioned in this book are listed below:

P. Cornelius Scipio Africanus (an extra surname based on his victory over the Carthaginians in North Africa in 202 BC)

M. Porcius Cato

Tib. and C. Sempronius Gracchus

C. Marius (his surname is never used)

L. Cornelius Sulla

M. Licinius Crassus

Cn. Pompeius (his father bore the surname Strabo, but that was always omitted in the case of Pompey)

We have sometimes used only one or two of the names, for the sake of brevity (e.g. Caesar, Tib. Gracchus).

In this book we have used the Latin spelling for all Greek and Roman names. This has for a long time been the customary way of writing such names in English-speaking countries.

2. GREEK AND ROMAN MONEY

The following coins were used in Classical Athens:

    1 talent = 6,000 drachmas (silver)
    1 drachma = 6 obols
    100 dr. = 1 *mina*

There were also coins worth four drachmas (silver).

In Pericles' time one drachma was a substantial wage for one day's work. Citizens who attended the meetings of the Council of Five Hundred or a lawsuit at a popular court were paid two obols.

The following coins were used in the early Roman empire:

    1 *aureus* = 25 *denarii* (an *aureus* was a gold coin, *denarii* were of silver)
    1 *denarius* = 4 sesterces
    1 sesterce = 4 *asses* (= 2 *dupondii*) (copper coins)

The talent and the *mina* were units of account.

Around AD 60 an inhabitant of Rome, which was then an expensive city, could live on a monthly allowance of five *modii* (= 45 litres) of grain and five *denariii*. A legionary was in those days paid 225 *denarii* per year. That sum was sufficient to cover his cost of living. Legionaries were not particularly well paid, but they did certainly not belong to the ranks of the minimum wage earners.

3. THE ROMAN EMPERORS

The Julio-Claudian dynasty:

Augustus	27 BC–AD 14
Tiberius	AD 14–37
Caligula	37–41
Claudius	41–54
Nero	54–68

'Julio' refers to the fact that they all descended from C. Julius Caesar Augustus, as he was called after 27 BC. Augustus himself had only one daughter, Julia. Caligula and Nero were her descendants. Augustus' last wife (not Julia's mother) was called Livia. She had previously been married to Tib. Claudius Nero (Claudius was his *gens* name, Nero his surname). Her sons from this previous marriage were Tiberius and Drusus (Tib. Claudius Nero and M. Claudius Nero Drusus. Drusus was the surname of Livia's father, T. Livius Drusus). The emperor Claudius was a descendant of that second son, Drusus.

Diagram A.1 The Julio-Claudian dynasty

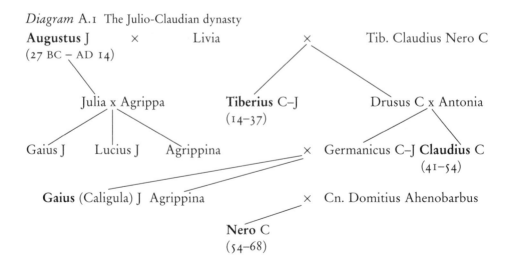

Notes: J = Julii
     C= Claudii

Agrippa: one of Augustus' important generals, who worked together with him from 44 until 13 BC. He died in 12 BC. Augustus adopted his sons Gaius and Lucius, who both died while they were still young, in AD 4 and 2, respectively.

Germanicus: an important general in the wars against the Germans in AD 13–17; Tiberius' adopted son (and hence a Julius) and his appointed successor. He died at an early age in AD 19.

Nero: adopted by Claudius, even though the latter had a son of his own (Britannicus). But Nero was a matrilineal relative of Augustus and could hence claim a more distinguished descent.

Tiberius (14–37) became a Julius by adoption but Claudius remained a member of the Claudian family and therefore we speak of the Julio-Claudian dynasty.

68–69 was the year of the four emperors: Galba
                                       Otho
                                       Vitellius
                                       Vespasian (T. Flavius Vespasianus) 69–79

The Flavian dynasty

The Flavian dynasty began with Vespasian and his two sons ruled after him:

Titus	79–81
Domitian	81–96

After the murder of Domitian, followed a series of emperors who all adopted their successors:

Nerva	96–98
Trajan	98–117
Hadrian	117–138
Antoninus Pius	138–161
Marcus Aurelius	161–180

Marcus Aurelius was succeeded by his son Commodus, 180–192. After the latter's death a struggle for power ensued, which ultimately resulted in a temporary distribution of power in 193. First the empire was governed by Pertinax and Didius Julianus successively, after which Pescennius Niger ruled over Syria, Clodius Albinus over the northwest and Septimius Severus over the rest of the empire. Albinus remained in control alongside Septimius Severus until 197. Then Septimius Severus was sole emperor until 211.

The following emperors reigned from 211 to 235:

Caracalla	211–217
Macrinus	217–218
Elagabalus	218–222
Severus Alexander	222–235

The soldier emperors

The soldier emperors ruled during the crisis of the third century:

Maximinus Thrax	235–238
Gordian I and II	238
Gordian III	238–244
Philippus Arabs	244–249
Decius	249–251
Trebonianus Gallus	251–253
Valerian	253–260

Gallienus ruled as co-emperor with his father Valerian from 253 until 260 and as sole emperor from 260 until 268. Then:

Claudius Gothicus	268–270
Aurelian	270–275
Tacitus	275–276
Probus	276–282
Carus and his two sons	282–284
(Carinus and Numerian)	

The above survey includes only the emperors who may to some extent be regarded as official emperors of the entire empire. The numerous pretenders have been omitted.

The late imperial age

Diocletian and his co-emperor Maximian (Milan) and the junior emperors Galerius (East) and Constantius Chlorus (Trier) ruled from 284 to 305 (Diocletian 284–305; Maximian 286–305; Constantius 293–306 and Galerius 293–311). After 305 Galerius became the most important emperor in the East.

Then the dynasty of Constantius Chlorus came to power:

Constantine the Great	306–337
Constantius II	337–361 (until 350 together with Constans)
Julian	361–363

The emperors who reigned from 363:

Jovian	363–364
Valentinian I (western half)	364–375 and
Valens (east)	364–378

Gratian (the son of Valentinian I; 375–383 in the western half), together with Theodosius I (379–394 in the eastern half; in his last year, 394–395, he was sole emperor of the entire empire). They were succeeded by Arcadius (395–408) and Theodosius II (408–450) in the east and by Honorius (395–423) in the west.

SELECT BIBLIOGRAPHY

WORKS OF GENERAL COVERAGE

Barraclough, G. (ed.), *The Times Atlas of World History*, 4th edn, London, 1993.

Blois, L. and R.J. van der Spek, *Einführung in die alte Welt*, Stuttgart, 1994.

Boardman, J. *et al. The Oxford History of the Classical World*, Oxford, 1986.

Bremen, R. van, *The Limits of Participation. Women and Civic Life in the Greek East in the Hellenistic and Roman Periods*, Amsterdam, 1996.

Bremer, J.M., Th.J.P. van den Hout and R. Peters (eds), *Hidden Futures. Death and Immortality in Ancient Egypt, Anatolia, the Classical, Biblical and Arabic Islamic World*, Amsterdam, 1994.

Burkert, W., *Ancient Mystery Cults*, London, 1987.

Casson, L., *Travel in the Ancient World*, London, 1974.

Crawford, M.H. (ed.), *Sources for Ancient History*, Cambridge, 1983.

Easterling, P.E., *et al.*, *The Cambridge History of Classical Literature I: Greek Literature*, Cambridge, 1985.

Edwards, I.E.S. *et al.*, (eds), *The Cambridge Ancient History*, 3rd/2nd edn, Cambridge, 1961–96.

Fantham, E., *et al.*, *Women in the Classical World. Image and Text*, Oxford, 1994.

Finley, M.I., *The Ancient Economy*, 2nd edn, London, 1985.

——, *Ancient Slavery and Modern Ideology*, London, 1983.

——, *Politics in the Ancient World*, Cambridge, 1983.

——, *Ancient History. Evidence and Models*, London, 1985.

Fornara, C.W., *The Nature of History in Ancient Greece and Rome*, Berkeley, 1983.

Garlan, Y., *War in the Ancient World. A Social History*, London, 1975.

Garnsey, P.D.A., *Non-slave Labour in the Graeco-Roman World*, Cambridge, 1980.

——, *Famine and Food-supply in the Graeco-Roman World*, Cambridge, 1988.

Garnsey, P.D.A. and C.R. Whittaker, *Trade and Famine in Classical Antiquity*, Cambridge, 1983.

Grant, M., *A Guide to the Ancient World: A Dictionary of Classical Names*, New York, 1986.

——, *Greek and Roman Historians. Information and Misinformation*, London/New York, 1995.

Grmek, M.D., *Diseases in the Ancient World*, Baltimore, 1989.

Hanson, V.D., *Hoplites*, London, 1991.

Harris, D.R., *The Origins and Spread of Agriculture and Pastoralism in Eurasia*, London, 1996.

Harris, W.V., *Ancient Literacy*, Cambridge (Mass.), 1989.

Hooff, A.J.L. van, *From Autothanasia to Suicide*, London, 1990.

Howgego, Chr., *Ancient History from Coins*, Oxford/London/New York, 1995.

Kolb, F., *Die Stadt im Altertum*, Munich, 1984.

Meijer, F.J., *Greece, Rome and the Sea*, London, 1986.

Morris, C., *Western Political Thought I: Plato to Augustine*, London, 1967.

Owens, E.J., *The City in the Greek and Roman World*, London, 1991.

Phillips, E.D., *Ancient Medicine*, London, 1972.

Pomeroy, S.B., *Goddesses, Whores, Wives and Slaves: Women in Classical Antiquity*, New York, 1975.

Rankin, H.D., *Celts and the Classical World*, London, 1987.

Reynolds, L.D. and N.G. Wilson, *Scribes and Scholars. A Guide to the Transmission of Greek and Latin Literature*, 3rd edn, Oxford, 1991.

Rich, J. and A. Wallace-Hadrill (eds), *City and Country in the Ancient World*, London, 1991.

Sancisi-Weerdenburg, H., *et al.* (eds), *De agricultura. In memoriam Pieter Willem de Neeve*, Amsterdam, 1993.

Seters, J. van, *In Search of History. Historiography in the Ancient World and the Origins of Biblical History*, Winona Lake, 1996.

Small, D.B. (ed.), *Methods in the Mediterranean. Historical and Archaeological Views on Texts and Archaeology*, Leiden, 1995.

Starr, Ch.G., *A History of the Ancient World*, 2nd edn, Oxford/New York, 1990.

Thomas, N. *Literacy and Orality in Ancient Greece*, Cambridge, 1992.

Versnel, H.S., *Faith, Hope and Worship. Aspects of Religious Mentality in the Ancient World*, Leiden, 1981.

Veyne, P., *Bread and Circuses. Historical Sociology and Political Pluralism*, Harmondsworth, 1990.

Wallace-Hadrill, A., (ed.), *Patronage in Ancient Society*, London, 1988.

White, K.D., *Greek and Roman Technology*, New York, 1984.

Will, E., C. Mossé and P. Goukowsky, *Le monde grec et l' Orient I–II*, Paris, 1975.

Woodford, S., *Cambridge Introduction to the History of Art. Greece and Rome*, Cambridge, 1982.

Woodman, A.J., *Rhetoric in Classical Histiography*, London, 1988.

THE ANCIENT NEAR EAST

Aubet, M.E., *The Phoenicians and the West. Politics, Colonies and Trade*, Cambridge, 1996.

Avi-Yonah, M., *The Jews under Roman and Byzantine Rule: a Political History of Palestine from the Bar Kokhba War to the Arab Conquest*, Jerusalem, 1984.

Bagnall, R.S., *Egypt in Late Antiquity*, Princeton, 1993.

Bagnall, R.S. and B.W. Frier, *The Demography of Roman Egypt*, Cambridge, 1994.

Ben-Tor, A., (ed.) *The Archaeology of Ancient Israel*, New Haven/Jerusalem, 1992.

Bickerman, E.J., *The Jews in the Greek Age*, Cambridge, 1988.

Bowman, A.K., *Egypt After the Pharaohs, 332 BC–AD 642, from Alexander to the Arab Conquest*, London, 1986.

Briant, P., *Histoire de l'empire perse de Cyrus à Alexandre*, Paris, 1996.

Cogan, M., *Imperialism and Religion, Assyria, Judah and Israel in the Eighth and Seventh Century BCE*, Missoula, 1974.

Crawford, H., *Sumer and the Sumerians*, Cambridge, 1991.

Goudriaan, K., *Ethnicity in Ptolemaic Egypt*, Amsterdam, 1988.

Grant, M., *History of Ancient Israel*, London, 1984.

Grimal, P., *A History of Ancient Egypt*, Oxford, 1992.

Gurney, O.R., *The Hittites*, Harmondsworth, 1977.

Harden, D.B., *The Phoenicians*, 2nd edn, Harmondsworth 1980.

Hayes, J.H. and J.M. Miller (eds), *Israelite and Judean History*, London, 1977.

Huß, W., *Karthago*, Darmstadt, 1992.

Jacobsen, T., *The Treasures of Darkness. A History of Mesopotamian Religion*, New Haven, 1976.

James, T.G.H., *An Introduction to Ancient Egypt*, London, 1979.

Kemp, B.J., *Ancient Egypt. Anatomy of a Civilization*, London, 1991.

Knapp, A.B., *The History and Culture of Western Asia and Egypt*, Chicago, 1988.

Kuhrt, A., *The Ancient Near East c. 3000–330 BC*, London, 1996.

Larsen, M.T., *The Conquest of Assyria. Excavations in an Antique Land*, London, 1996.

Lewis, N., *Life in Egypt under Roman Rule*, Oxford, 1983.

——, *Greeks in Ptolemaic Egypt*, Oxford, 1986.

Oates, J., *Babylon*, London, 1979.

Oppenheim, A.L., *Ancient Mesopotamia. Portrait of a Dead Civilization*, 2nd edn, Chicago, 1977.

Postgate, J.N., *Early Mesopotamia. Society and Economy at the Dawn of History*, London, 1992.

Redford, D.B., *Egypt, Canaan and Israel in Ancient Times*, Princeton, 1992.

Russell, D.S., *The Jews from Alexander to Herod*, Oxford, 1967.

Sancisi-Weerdenburg, H., *et al.*, *Achaemenid History I–VIII*, Leiden, 1987–1994.

Schippmann, K., *Grundzüge der parthischen Geschichte*, Darmstadt, 1980.

——, *Grundzüge der Geschichte des Sasanidischen Reiches*, Darmstadt, 1990.

Schürer, E., *The History of the the Jewish People in the Age of Jesus Christ 175 BC–AD 135*, 2nd edn, Edinburgh, 1973.

Silver, M., *Economic Structures of the Ancient Near East*, London, 1986.

Smallwood, E.M., *The Jews under Roman Rule*, Leiden, 1976.

Toorn, K. van der, *Family Religion in Babylonia, Syria and Israel. Continuity and Change in the Forms of Religious Life*, Leiden, 1996.

Trigger, B.G., *et al.*, *Ancient Egypt. A Social History*, Cambridge, 1983.

Wiesehöfer, J., *Das antike Persien von 550 v.Chr.–650 n.Chr.*, Zürich/Munich, 1994.

THE GREEKS

Austin, M.M. & P. Vidal-Naquet, *Economic and Social History of Ancient Greece*, London, 1978.

Bremmer, J.N. (ed.), *Interpretations of Greek Mythology*, London, 1987.

Burkert, W., *Greek Religion*, Cambridge (Mass.), 1985.

Burnet, J., *Greek Philosophy. Thales to Plato*, London, 1968.

Easterling, P.E. and J.V. Muir (eds), *Greek Religion and Society*, Cambridge, 1985.

Finley, M.I., *Ancient Sicily*, 2nd edn, London, 1979.

Garland, R., *The Greek Way of Death*, London, 1985.

——, *The Greek Way of Life from Conception to Old Age*, London, 1990.

Gschnitzer, F., *Griechische Sozialgeschichte*, Stuttgart, 1982.

MacGlew, J.F., *Tyranny and Political Culture in Ancient Greece*, London, 1993.

Mikalson, J.D., *Athenian Popular Religion*, Chapel Hill/London, 1983.

Pritchett, W. Kendrick, *The Greek State at War I–II*, Berkeley, 1974–1991.

Sealey, R., *The Justice of the Greeks*, Ann Arbor, 1994.

Sowerby, R., *The Greeks. An Introduction to their Culture*, London, 1995.

Ste. Croix, G.E.M. de, *The Class-struggle in the Ancient Greek World*, Ithaca/New York/London, 1981.

Tigerstedt, R.A., *The Legend of Sparta in Classical Antiquity*, Stockholm, 1962.

Vernant, J.-P., *Myth and Society in Ancient Greece*, London, 1980.

West, M., *Early Greek Philosophy and the Orient*, Oxford, 1971.

ARCHAIC AND CLASSICAL GREECE

Andrewes, A., *The Greek Tyrants*, London, 1974.

Boardman, J., *The Greeks Overseas. Their Early Colonies and Trade*, 2nd edn, London, 1980.

Borza, E.N., *In the Shadow of Olympus. The Emergence of Macedon*, Princeton, 1990.

Briant, P. and P. Lévècque, *Le monde grec aux temps classiques I: La Ve siècle*, Paris, 1995.

Buck, R.J., *Boiotia and the Boiotian League 432–371 BC*, Edmonton, 1994.

Cartledge, P., *Sparta and Lakonia. A Regional History 1300–362 BC*, London, 1979.

Cartledge, P., P. Millett and S. Todd (eds), *Nomos. Essays in Athenian Law, Politics and Society*, Cambridge, 1991.

Chadwick, J., *The Mycenaean World*, Cambridge, 1976.

Connor, W.R., *The New Politicians of Fifth-century Athens*, Princeton, 1971.

Connor, W.R., et al., *Aspects of Athenian Democracy*, Copenhagen, 1990.

Ellis, W., *Alcibiades*, London, 1989.

Farrar, C., *The Origins of Democratic Thinking. The Invention of Politics in Classical Athens*, Cambridge, 1988.

Fornara, C.W. and L.J. Samons II, *Athens from Clisthenes to Pericles*, Berkeley/Oxford, 1991.

Gardner, R., *Law and Society in Classical Athens*, London, 1987.

Hammond, N.G.L., *Philip of Macedon*, London, 1994.

Hansen, M.H., *Demography and Democracy. The Number of Athenian Citizens in the Fourth Century BC*, Gjellerup, 1986.

——, *The Athenian Democracy in the Age of Demosthenes*, Oxford, 1991.

Hanson, V.D., *The Western Way of War. Infantry Battle in Classical Greece*, London, 1989.

Hopper, R.J., *Trade and Industry in Classical Greece*, London, 1979.

Hornblower, S., *Thucydides*, Baltimore, 1987.

Jones, A.H.M., *The Athenian Democracy*, 2nd edn, Oxford, 1978.

Lintott, A.W., *Violence, Civil Strife and Revolution in the Classical City 750–330 BC*, London, 1982.

Littman, R.J., *The Greek Experiment. Imperialism and Social Conflict 800–400 BC*, London, 1974.

Meiggs, R., *The Athenian Empire*, Oxford, 1972.

Morris, I.M., *Classical Greece. Ancient Histories and Modern Archaeologies*, Cambridge, 1994.

Murray, O., *Early Greece*, Glasgow, 1980.

Murray, O. and S.R.F. Price, *The Greek City from Homer to Alexander*, Oxford, 1990.

Ober, J., *Mass and Élite in Democratic Athens*, Princeton, 1989.

Powell, A., *Athens and Sparta: Constructing Greek Political and Social History from 478 BC*, London, 1988.

Ridgway, D., *The First Western Greeks*, Cambridge, 1992.

Salmon, J.B., *Wealthy Corinth. A History of the City to 338 BC*, Oxford, 1984.

Sanders, L.J., *Dionysius I of Syracuse and Greek Tyranny*, London, 1987.

Sinclair, R.K., *Democracy and Participation in Athens*, Cambridge, 1988.

Snodgrass, A., *Archaic Greece. The Age of Experiment*, London, 1980.

Ste. Croix, G.E.M. de, *The Origins of the Peloponnesian War*, London, 1972.

Stockton, D., *The Classical Athenian Democracy*, Oxford, 1990.

Wees, H. van, *Status Warriors. War, Violence and Society in Homer and History*, Amsterdam, 1992.

Whitley, J., *Style and Society in Dark Age Greece. The Changing Face of a Pre-literate Society 1100–700 BC*, Cambridge, 1991.

THE HELLENISTIC WORLD

Allen, R.E., *The Attalid Kingdom. A Constitutional History*, Oxford, 1981.

Berthold, R.N., *Rhodes in the Hellenistic Age*, Ithaca, 1984.

Bosworth, A.B., *Conquest and Empire. The Reign of Alexander the Great*, Cambridge, 1988.

Cohen, G.M., *The Seleucid Colonies. Studies in Founding Administration and Organization*, Wiesbaden, 1978.

Downey, G., *A History of Antioch in Syria. From Seleucus to the Arab Conquest*, 2nd edn, Princeton, 1974.

Elliger, W., *Ephesos. Geschichte einer antiken Weltstadt*, Stuttgart, 1985.

Ellis, W.M., *Ptolemy of Egypt*, London, 1993.

Fraser, P., *Ptolemaic Alexandria I–III*, Oxford, 1972.

Green, P., *Alexander to Actium. The Historical Evolution of the Hellenistic Age*, Berkeley, 1993.

Gruen, E.S., *The Hellenistic World and the Coming of Rome I–II*, Berkeley, 1984.

Jones, A.H.M., *The Greek City from Alexander to Justinian*, Oxford, 1940.

Koester, H., *History, Culture and Religion of the Hellenistic Age*, Princeton, 1982.

Kuhrt, A. and A.N. Sherwin-White, *From Samarkhand to Sardis. A New Approach to the Seleucid Empire*, Berkeley, 1993.

Kuhrt, A. and A.N. Sherwin-White (eds), *Hellenism in the East*, London, 1987.

Lane Fox, R., *Alexander the Great*, London, 1973.

Momigliano, A., *Alien Wisdom. The Limits of Hellenization*, Cambridge, 1975.

Versnel, H.S., *Ter unus. Isis, Dionysos, Hermes. Three Studies in Henotheism*, Leiden, 1990,

Walbank, F.W., *The Hellenistic World*, Glasgow, 1981.

Will, E., *Histoire politique du monde hellénistique 323–30 av. J.-C. I–II*, Nancy, 1979–1982.

ROME

Alföldy, G., *The Social History of Rome*, Baltimore, 1988.

Aubert, J.J., *Business Managers in Ancient Rome. A Social and Economic Study of Institores, 200 BC–AD 250*, Leiden, 1994.

Balsdon, J.P.V.D., *Romans and Aliens*, London, 1980.

Bonner, S.F., *Education in Ancient Rome*, London, 1977.

Bradley, K.R., *Slavery and Society at Rome*, Cambridge, 1994.

Cornell, T.J. and K. Lomas (eds), *Urban Society in Roman Italy*, London, 1996.

D'Arms, J.H., *Commerce and Social Standing in Ancient Rome*, Cambridge (Mass.), 1981.

Dixon, S., *The Roman Mother*, London, 1988.

Drinkwater, J.F., *Roman Gaul. The Three Provinces, 58 BC–AD 260*, London, 1983.

Duncan-Jones, R., *Structure and Scale in the Roman Economy*, Cambridge, 1990.

Dupont, F., *Daily Life in Ancient Rome*, Oxford, 1992.

Dyson, S.L., *Community and Society in Roman Italy*, Baltimore, 1992.

Gardner, J.F., *Women in Roman Law and Society*, London, 1987.

——, *Being a Roman Citizen*, London, 1993.

Garnsey, P.D.A. and R.P. Saller, *The Roman Empire. Economy, Society and Culture*, London, 1987.

Green, M.P. (ed.), *The Celtic World*, London/New York, 1995.

Griffin, J., *Latin Poets and Roman Life*, 2nd edn, Bristol, 1994.

Jongman, W., *The Economy and Society of Pompeii*, Amsterdam, 1988.

Keay, S.J., *Roman Spain*, London, 1988.

Keppie, L., *The Making of the Roman Army. From Republic to Empire*, London, 1984.

Kostial, M., *Kriegerisches Rom? Zur Frage von Unvermeidbarkeit und Normalität militärischer Konflikte in der römischen Politik*, Stuttgart, 1995.

Ogilvie, R.M., *The Romans and Their Gods*, London, 1979.

Parkin, T.G., *Demography and Roman Society*, Baltimore, 1992.

Rawson, B., *The Family in Ancient Rome*, London, 1985.

——, *Marriage, Divorce and Children in Ancient Rome*, Oxford, 1991.

Rich, J. and G. Shipley, *War and Society in the Roman World*, London, 1995.

Rickman, G., *The Corn-supply of Ancient Rome*, Oxford, 1980.

Richardson, J.S., *The Roman Provincial Administration 227 BC–AD 117*, Basingstoke, 1976.

Robinson, O.F., *Ancient Rome. City Planning and Administration*, London, 1992.

Saller, R.P., *Patriarchy, Property and Death in the Roman Family*, Cambridge, 1994.

Spurr, M.S., *Arable Cultivation in Roman Italy, c. 200 BC–AD 100*, London, 1986.

Stambaugh, J.E., *The Ancient Roman City*, Baltimore, 1988.

Toner, J.P., *Leisure and Ancient Rome*, London, 1995.

Veyne, P., *From Pagan Rome to Byzantium. A History of Private Life*, Cambridge (Mass.), 1987.

Wacher, J., *The Roman World*, London, 1987.

Wallace-Hadrill, A., *To Live as a Roman. Houses and Society in Pompeii and Herculaneum*, Princeton, 1994.

Wallace-Hadrill, J.M., *The Barbarian West*, 4th edn, Oxford, 1985.

Wardman, A., *Rome's Debt to Greece*, London, 1976.

White, K.D., *Roman Farming*, London, 1970.

Wolfram, H., *History of the Goths*, Berkeley, 1987.

EARLY ROME AND THE ROMAN REPUBLIC

Alföldi, A., *Early Rome and the Latins*, Ann Arbor, 1965.

Badian, E., *Roman Imperialism in the Late Republic*, Ithaca/New York, 1971.

Beard, M. and M.H. Crawford, *Rome in the Late Republic*, London, 1985.

Blois, L. de, *The Roman Army and Politics in the First Century BC*, Amsterdam, 1987.

Bradley, K.R., *Slavery and Rebellion in the Roman World 140–70 BC*, London, 1989.

Brunt, P.A., *Social Conflicts in the Roman Republic*, London, 1971.

——, *Italian Manpower*, Oxford, 1971.

Cornell, T.J., *The Beginnings of Rome. Italy and Rome from the Bronze Age to the Punic Wars, c. 1000–264 BC*, London, 1995.

Crawford, M.H., *Coinage and Money under the Roman Republic. Italy and the Mediterranean Economy*, London, 1985.

Evans, R.J., *Caius Marius. A Political Biography*, Pretoria, 1994.

Gabba, E., *Republican Rome. The Army and the Allies*, Oxford, 1976.

Gelzer, M., *Caesar. Der Politiker und Staatsmann*, Munich, 1960.

Gruen, E.S., *The Last Generation of the Roman Republic*, 2nd edn, Berkeley, 1995.

Habicht, Chr., *Cicero the Politician*, Baltimore, 1990.

Harris, W.V., *War and Imperialism in Republican Rome 327–70 BC*, Oxford, 1979.

Hopkins, K., *Conquerors and Slaves*, Cambridge, 1987.

Huzar, E.G., *Mark Antony*, London, 1986.

Keaveney, A., *Sulla, the Last Republican*, London, 1986.

——, *Rome and the Unification of Italy*, London, 1987.

Lazenby, J.F., *Hannibal's War. A Military History of the Second Punic War*, London, 1978.

Lomas, K., *Rome and the Western Greeks. Conquest and Acculturation in Southern Italy*, London, 1993.

MacNamara, E., *The Etruscans*, London, 1990.

Neeve, P.W. de, *Peasants in Peril. Location and Economy in Italy in the Second Century BC*, Amsterdam, 1984.

Nicolet, C., *The World of the Citizen in Republican Rome*, London, 1980.

Ogilvie, R.M., *Early Rome and the Etruscans*, 2nd edn, Glasgow, 1979.

Pallottino, M., *The Etruscans*, Harmondsworth, 1976.

Raaflaub, K.A., *Social Struggles in Archaic Rome: New Perspectives on the Conflict of the Orders*, Berkeley, 1986.

Scullard, H.H., *A History of the Roman World 753–146 BC*, 4th edn, London/New York, 1991.

——, *From the Gracchi to Nero. A History of Rome from 133 BC to AD 68*, 4th edn, London, 1966.

——, *Festivals and Ceremonies of the Roman Republic*, London, 1981.

Stockton, D., *The Gracchi*, Oxford, 1980.

Syme, R., *The Roman Revolution*, Oxford, 1939.

Taylor, L.R., *Roman Voting Assemblies*, 2nd edn, Ann Arbor, 1990.

Vanderbroeck, P.J.J., *Popular Leadership and Collective Behavior in the Late Roman Republic, c. 80–50 BC*, Amsterdam, 1987.

Wiseman, T.P., *New Men in the Roman Senate, 139 BC–AD 14*, Oxford, 1971.

Wood, N., *Cicero's Social and Political Thought*, Berkeley, 1988.

IMPERIAL ROME

Barnes, T.D., *The New Empire of Diocletian and Constantine*, London, 1982.

Barrett, A.A., *Caligula. The Corruption of Power*, London, 1989.

Birley, A.R., *Septimius Severus. The African Emperor*, 2nd edn, London, 1989.

——, *Marcus Aurelius*, 2nd edn, London, 1991.

Blois, L. de, *The Policy of the Emperor Gallienus*, London, 1976.

Bowersock, G.W., *Greek Sophists in the Roman Empire*, Oxford, 1969.

——, *Julian the Apostate*, London, 1980.

——, *Hellenism in Late Antiquity*, Cambridge, 1990.

——, *Fiction as History. Nero to Julian*, Berkeley, 1994.

——, *Martyrdom and Rome*, Cambridge, 1995.

Braund, D., *Ruling Roman Britain. Kings, Queens, Governors and Emperors from Julius Caesar to Agricola*, London, 1996.

Brown, P., *The World of Late Antiquity*, London, 1978.

——, *The Body and Society. Men, Women and Sexual Renunciation in Early Christianity*, New York, 1988.

Cameron, A., *Bread and Circuses. The Roman Emperor and his People*, London, 1973.

——, *The Mediterranean World in Late Antiquity*, London, 1993.

Campbell, J.B., *The Emperor and the Roman Army 31 BC–AD 235*, Oxford, 1984.

Carson, R.A.G., *Coins of the Roman Empire*, London/New York, 1990.

Chadwick, H., *The Early Church*, 10th edn, Harmondsworth, 1980.

Demandt, A., *Die Spätantike. Römische Geschichte von Diocletian bis Justinian 284–565 n.Chr.*, Munich, 1989.

Duncan-Jones, R., *Money and Government in the Roman Empire*, Cambridge, 1994.

Evans, J.A.S., *The Age of Justinian. The Circumstances of Imperial Power*, London, 1996.

Flinterman, J.J., *Power, Paideia and Pythagoreanism. Greek Identity, Conceptions of the Relationship between Philosophers and Monarchs and Political Ideas in Philostratus' Life of Apollonius*, Amsterdam, 1995.

Frend, W.H.C., *Martyrdom and Persecution in the Early Church*, London, 1965.

——, *The Rise of Christianity. The Early Christians in the First Six Centuries*, London, 1984.

Grant, M., *The Antonines. The Roman Empire in Transition*, London/New York, 1994.

Griffin, M.T., *Nero. The End of a Dynasty*, London, 1984.

Hahn, J., *Der Philosoph in der Gesellschaft*, Stuttgart, 1989.

Halfmann, H., *Itinera principum. Geschichte und Typologie der Kaiserreisen im römischen Reich*, Stuttgart, 1986.

Issac, B., *The Limits of Empire. The Roman Army in the East*, Oxford, 1992.

Jones, A.H.M., *The Later Roman Empire, 284–602. A Social, Economic and Administrative Survey I–II*, Oxford, 1964.

——, *Augustus*, 2nd edn, London, 1977.

——, *The Decline of the Ancient World*, 3rd edn, London/New York, 1975.

Jones, B.W., *The Emperor Titus*, London, 1984.

Jones, C.P., *Plutarch and Rome*, Oxford, 1972.

——, *Culture and Society in Lucian*, Cambridge (Mass.), 1986.

King, A. & M. Henig, *The Roman West in the Third Century*, Oxford, 1981 (B.A.R. International Series 109.1).

Lane Fox, R., *Pagans and Christians in the Mediterranean World from the Second Century AD to the Conversion of Constantine*, Harmondsworth, 1986.

Levick, B., *Claudius*, London, 1990.

Lewit, T., *Agricultural Production in the Roman Economy AD 200–400*, London, 1991.

Liebeschuetz, J.H.G.W. *From Diocletian to the Arab Conquest: Change in the Late Roman Empire*, Aldershot, 1990.

Ligt, L. de, *Fairs and Markets in the Roman Empire*, Amsterdam, 1993.

Lintott, A.W., *Imperium Romanum. Politics and Administration*, London, 1993.

MacMullen, R., *Enemies of the Roman Order. Treason, Unrest and Alienation in the Empire*, Cambridge (Mass.), 1966.

——, *Roman Social Relations, 50 BC to AD 284*, New Haven, 1974.

——, *Paganism in the Roman Empire*, New Haven, 1981.

——, *Christianizing the Roman Empire AD 100–400*, New Haven, 1984.

——, *Constantine*, London, 1987.

Meeks, W.A., *The First Urban Christians. The Social World of the Apostle Paul*, New Haven, 1983.

——, *The Origins of Christian Morality. The First Two Centuries*, New Haven, 1994.

Millar, F.G.B., *The Emperor in the Roman World*, 2nd edn, Oxford, 1991.

——, *The Roman Near East*, Oxford, 1993.

Price, S.R.F., *Rituals and Power. The Roman Imperial Cult in Asia Minor*, Cambridge, 1984.

Raaflaub, K. and M. Toher, *Between Republic and Empire. Interpretations of Augustus and his Principate*, Berkeley, 1990.

Rich, J. (ed.), *The City in Late Antiquity*, London, 1996.

Robert, L., Une vision de Perpétue martyre à Carthage en *203*, in *Opera minora selecta V*, Amsterdam, 1989.

Russell, D.A., *Antonine Literature*, Oxford, 1990.

Saller, R.P., *Personal Patronage under the Early Empire*, Cambridge, 1982.

Seager, R., *Tiberius*, London, 1972.

Shotter, D., *Augustus Caesar*, London, 1991.

Swain, S.R., *Hellenism and Empire. Language, Classicism and Power in the Greek World* AD *50–250*, Oxford, 1996.

Starr, Ch.G., *The Roman Empire 27* BC–AD *476. A Study in Survival*, Oxford, 1982.

Talbert, R.J.A., *The Senate of Imperial Rome*, Princeton, 1984.

Whittaker, C.R., *Frontiers of the Roman Empire*, Baltimore, 1994.

Wiedemann, Th.E.J., *Adults and Children in the Roman Empire*, London, 1989.

——, *Emperors and Gladiators*, London, 1992.

Yavetz, Z., *Plebs and Princeps*, London, 1969.

Zanker, P., *The Power of Images in the Age of Agustus*, Ann Arbor, 1988.

INDEX

f following a page number indicates a caption to a map or illustration
(d) = divinity